K.

Arun Gandhi was born in 1934 in South Africa. At ten he was sent to India to stay with his grandfather, the Mahatma, for eighteen months, and witnessed Gandhi's national campaign of nonviolence first-hand. In 1957 Arun returned to India to work as a journalist for the *Times of India*. With his wife Sunanda he founded the Centre for Social Unity and in 1991 they opened the MK Gandhi Institute for Nonviolence in Tennessee.

BY THE SAME AUTHOR

*A Patch of White*
*Kasturba—Wife of Gandhi*
*Morarji Papers: The Rise and Fall of the Janata Party Government*
*World Without Violence: Can Gandhi's Dream Become Reality?*
*Testament to Truth*
*Voices of Poverty* (with Sunanda Gandhi and Sten Berg)

# Kasturba

## A LIFE

ARUN GANDHI

*Foreword by Lord Richard Attenborough*

PENGUIN BOOKS

Penguin Books India (P) Ltd., 11 Community Centre, Panchsheel Park, New Delhi 110 017, India
Penguin Books Ltd., 27 Wrights Lane, London W8 5TZ, UK
Penguin Putnam Inc., 375 Hudson Street, New York, NY 10014, USA
Penguin Books Australia Ltd., Ringwood, Victoria, Australia
Penguin Books Canada Ltd., 10 Alcorn Avenue, Suite 300, Toronto, Ontario, M4V 3B2, Canada
Penguin Books (NZ) Ltd., Cnr Rosedale and Airborne Roads, Albany, Auckland, New Zealand

First published in Great Britain by Blake Publishing Ltd 1998
First published in India by Penguin Books India 2000

Copyright © Arun Gandhi 2000

10 9 8 7 6 5 4 3 2 1

Printed at Chaman Offset Printers, New Delhi

*This book commemorates the 50th anniversary of the assassination of Mahatma Gandhi on 30 January 1948.*

*I must acknowledge with heartfelt gratitude*
*Carol Lynn Yellin's help in editing this manuscript,*
*for her suggestions and for her advice.*
*I am eternally grateful to her.*

*This book is dedicated to my wife, Sunanda, whose help in researching the life of my grandmother, Kasturba, was tremendous, and to all the unknown women around the world whose selfless sacrifice enables their husbands to attain positions of prominence.*

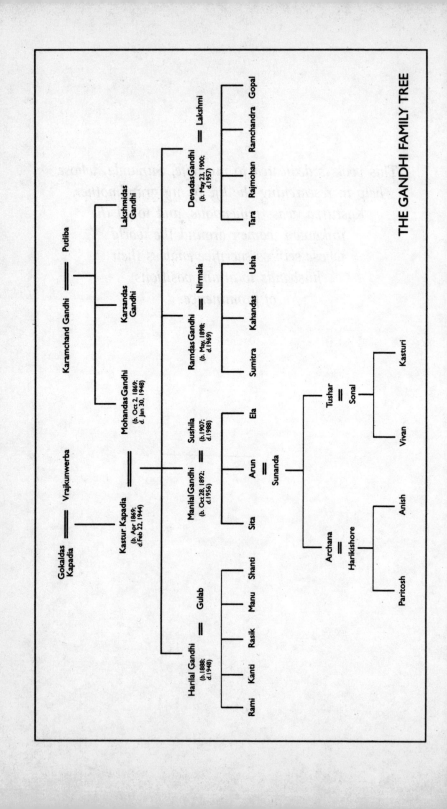

THE GANDHI FAMILY TREE

# Foreword

When I began in-depth research for the film *Gandhi*, one of the most endearing revelations was the importance of the role played by the Mahatma's wife, Kastur.

'Ba', as she was known, was an extraordinary woman: forgiving, courageous and incredibly loyal. As Gandhiji's most devoted disciple, she was also his severest and most influential critic. The marriage was not one of their own choosing, yet it developed into a true love match, largely through Ba's willingness to share every aspect of the spartan lifestyle her husband imposed on himself and his closest followers.

Ba was portrayed in the film by a remarkable actress called Rohini Hattangady. She, I sincerely believe, captured the essence of a woman who was no mere footnote in history but the Mahatma's partner in every sense of the word.

And now, through the words of her grandson, Arun, Ba's story is at last set down for posterity. A labour of love that is welcome indeed.

Lord Attenborough CBE

# Contents

# Chronology

| | |
|---|---|
| 1857 | Sepoy Mutiny |
| 1869 | Completion of the Suez Canal |
| | Birth of Kastur Kapadia (April) |
| | Birth of Mohandas Karamchand Gandhi (2 October) |
| 1870 | Indian census |
| 1876 | Preliminary agreement reached for the betrothal of Mohandas and Kastur |
| 1882 | Mohandas and Kastur are married |
| 1885 | Death of Karamchand Gandhi (16 November) |
| | Birth of Mohandas' and Kastur's first child (20 November) which died four days later |
| 1888 | Birth of Harilal Gandhi |
| | Mohandas starts at Samaldas University (January) |
| | Mohandas leaves Rajkot for England (10 August) |
| 1891 | Mohandas returns to India (summer) |
| 1892 | Birth of Manilal Gandhi (28 October) |
| 1893 | Mohandas leaves India for South Africa (April) |
| 1896 | Mohandas returns to Rajkot (summer) |
| 1897 | Mohandas returns with his family to South Africa (13 January) |
| 1898 | Birth of Ramdas Gandhi (May) |
| 1899 | Indian famine |
| | Boers declare war on Britain (October) |
| 1900 | Birth of Devadas Gandhi (23 May) |
| 1901 | Gandhi family return to India |
| 1902 | Mohandas returns to South Africa (November) |
| 1904 | Kastur and the children travel back to South Africa |
| 1906 | Zulu uprising |
| | Gandhi family move to Phoenix Settlement |

| 1907 | Passing of the Asiatic Registration Act (21 March) |
|------|---------------------------------------------------|
| 1909 | Union of South Africa Act passed by the British Government (October) |
| 1914 | Passing of the Indian Relief Bill (June) |
| 1915 | Gandhi family return to India (9 January) |
| 1918 | Worldwide Spanish 'flu epidemic leaves a heavy toll on the Indian population |
| 1919 | Passing of the Rowlatt Act (18 March) |
|      | Hartal against the Rowlatt Act |
| 1922 | Mohandas sentenced to six years in Yeravda Prison (18 March) |
| 1930 | The Salt March leaves Sabarmati ashram (12 March) |
| 1932 | Mohandas begins his 'epic fast' (20 September) |
| 1942 | Mohandas and Kastur interned in the Aga Khan Palace |
| 1944 | Death of Kasturba Gandhi (22 February) |
| 1948 | Assassination of Mohandas Gandhi (30 January) |

# Introduction

An unknown Eastern philosopher once said: "Nothing can ever grow under a banyan tree." This is as true of individuals. Mohandas Karamchand Gandhi's stature was by far more enormous than a banyan tree — it dwarfed everyone else. My grandmother, Kastur, and my father, Manilal, were two who submerged their identities and blended themselves into his image and philosophy.

For those brought up in a modern western society such acts of self-sacrifice in the interest of a person, a programme or a philosophy are difficult to understand and accept. In the eastern society it is the family and legacy that supercedes every other consideration.

Western scholars have, understandably, blamed Mohandas Gandhi for not giving others a chance to flourish or blossom. However, my grandfather had a vision; a world view that transcended the self. Consequently, neither Kastur nor my father ever thought about their personal achievements or accomplishments and preferred to merge their lives into that of my grandfather. The vision, the quest, the world was more important to them than their personal image.

For everyone who knew her, Kastur was always Ba or "Great Mother", Grandmother. My greatest regret will always be that I did not get the opportunity to know her better. The last time I met my grandmother I was just five years old. This was in 1939. My father, Manilal, her second son, had chosen to live in South Africa to work for nonviolent social and political change, a movement that my grandfather had started in 1893.

Since my father was the only one of the four Gandhi sons to adopt voluntary poverty and devote his life to nonviolence, our family reunions in India had to be judiciously spaced out, on an average of once in three or four years.

For most of us who have grown up in eastern culture the daily affirmation of love, as in western families, is unheard of. Our parents or grandparents never told us that they loved us. They did not have to because their actions and concerns for us conveyed their love more eloquently than words could express. I just knew that the whole family loved me.

Apart from my love for Ba what compelled me to research the life of Grandmother was the fact that the few existing references, or memoirs of those who lived with her, depicted her as an ever-bumbling fool who had no idea what her husband was trying to achieve.

I refused to believe this could be true. It was not my or my parents' experience. She may not have gone to school and could not read or write much but received from her parents, her parents-in-law and the family, the best upbringing one can hope for. I did not want history to record a negative image of my grandmother. Our painstaking research confirmed that she played a significant role in the struggle for India's freedom and in the 'making of the Mahatma'.

Without her unstinted cooperation, my grandfather could not have achieved the spiritual heights that he did. Many a wife has left her husband for much less than what Grandmother was asked to give up. She made the sacrifice not simply because Grandfather wanted her to but because she was convinced it was the right way.

Imagine for a moment the all-too-familiar scenario where a wife refuses to cooperate with her husband in whatever he is trying to achieve. It would, most certainly, lead to domestic disharmony and even a breakup of the alliance. Grandmother never followed anyone slavishly. She followed with conviction just as my father, Manilal, did.

In his autobiography *The Story of My Experiments with Truth*, my grandfather confesses that he learned the rudiments of nonviolence from my grandmother. She was never passive, nor aggressive, but always stood up for what she was convinced was right and just. When Grandfather was in the wrong she did not argue with him but quietly, nonviolently, led him to the realisation of the truth. That, Grandfather said, is the true essence of the philosophy of nonviolence.

Researching my grandmother's life was not easy. She wrote very little herself. Her family records, as well as the government records of births and deaths, were washed away in floods that ravaged Porbandar at the turn of the century.

Her parents and her brother died young leaving no written record of family history except for the references in Grandfather's writings to the Makanji family and Ba.

In our research my wife, Sunanda, and I had to depend on oral history, which was often clouded by the awe-inspiring memories of my grandfather. It was sometimes an exercise in patience and perseverance to keep the interviewee focused on Grandmother. Since 1960 we have recorded interviews with scores of people from all walks of life who knew Ba and had lived and worked with her.

Grandmother's life story is unusual and inspiring. I hope you enjoy this labour of love.

Arun Gandhi, 1998

# 1

There is no record of the exact day of Kastur Kapadia's birth. In ancient India, official birth records were never properly kept. We know Grandmother was born in 1869, the same year as grandfather, Mohandas Karamchand Gandhi. They were also born in the same town: the coastal city of Porbandar, on India's Kathiawar peninsula. Kathiawar is in the present-day state of Gujarat. Some have surmised that the difference in their ages was only a few months. Years later, long after Kastur had become Kasturba*, it is said they would sometimes playfully disagree about which one was the older. However, since Grandfather's birth was October 2, 1869, and Ba's birthday was in April, she must have had the better of any such arguments.

With two brothers — one older and one younger — little Kastur grew up as the only daughter and the middle child of wealthy and indulgent parents — Gokaldas and Vrajkunwerba Kapadia. Many Gandhi biographers have used Makanji rather than Kapadia as my grandmother's family name, a confusion arising from the common Indian custom identifying sons by the names of their fathers. Kastur's grandfather was Makanji Kapadia, so her father, Gokaldas, as the son of Makanji, was often addressed as Gokaldas Makanji rather than Gokaldas Kapadia. A leading citizen and one-time mayor of Porbandar, Gokaldas had inherited the trading house dealing in cloth, grain, and cotton shipments to markets in Africa and what was then known as Arabia. Prospering as a merchant, he had opened branches in Bombay and

---

* The suffix "-ba" was added after she became a mother, and her husband was universally known as Mahatma Gandhi.

Calcutta, and added extensive real estate holdings in both those cities as well as in Porbandar, to the family fortune.

Porbandar was a city-state, a strip of coastal land no more than 24 miles wide at any point. It had a population of 72,000 according to the 1870 census. It was one of India's many miniature principalities ruled by local Hindu and Muslim princes. It was known as "The White City" because its high walls and sturdy houses built of creamy-white limestone were visible for miles.

This limestone, somewhat clayish in quality, joins together more firmly after each rainfall, hardening to a marble-like texture and beauty. Porbandar still has the distinction of being the only place in India where a house can be built without cement. All one has to do is pile up the limestone blocks as desired and wait for the rains to come. Generations earlier the Kapadia and Gandhi homes, like others in old Porbandar, had been built that way.

By the late 1860s, Porbandar's once-impenetrable walls were gone — destroyed by order of the British, the most recent foreign rulers to claim dominion over India. Through the agency of the British East India Company, a commercial enterprise chartered by Queen Elizabeth I on the last day of the 16th century — December 31, 1599— to engage in the spice trade, the British had gradually seized control of the subcontinent from a fragmented Mogul Empire. They had made their governance official in the mid-19th century, after putting down the hard-fought Sepoy Rebellion of 1857 (called Sepoy "Mutiny" by the British), and had declared India a Crown Colony of the British Empire under Queen Victoria. The British hold on India became tighter following the completion of the Suez Canal, which was opened in 1869, the very year that my grandparents were born.

Porbandar remained as originally built — a cluster of crowded homes and narrow lanes. The Indian tradition of large joint families, in which several generations and various branches of one family share living quarters and expenses, has created a sense of claustrophobia.

Here, in one such small room, in the bungalow-style house her parents shared with other family members, Kastur was born. Despite their wealth, the Kapadias did not live ostentatiously. Their home, though well appointed and handsomely furnished, had no garden or outdoor courtyard where children could play. A few houses down the lane was the Gandhi family home which had a small, private courtyard. Since the two families were friends and neighbours, it seems likely that the Kapadia children and the Gandhi children would have both played in the open courtyard.

They would not have been playmates for long, however. Girls and boys growing up in Hindu families lived in separate worlds, even as small children.

Mohandas was given free run of the entire neighbourhood, usually under the watchful eye of his older sister or the family nurse, Rambha. They had trouble keeping up with Mohan, who was full of curiosity. He would slip away to the courtyard of the nearby temple where there were trees to climb; or wander out into the streets to follow some ceremonial parade. He loved to tease his mother, scribbling all over the floor with chalk long before he learned to write, and once, as a very small child, he removed the statue of a god from its niche in the family prayer room so that he could sit there himself. His energies became more channelled when, at about the age of six, he began attending school in Porbandar. He struggled with alphabets and arithmetic but, as he reported in his autobiography many years later: "I recollect nothing more of those days than having learned, in company with other boys, to call our teacher all kinds of names."

Kastur, meanwhile, was learning too — not arithmetic, and not in a schoolroom — but in the home of her parents. She was learning the art of being a good wife, mother and housekeeper. And since girls in India were married at a very early age, they had to start learning their marital responsibilities at an age when small girls today would be entering kindergarten.

She was learning the oft-told stories about the mythical heroines of India's glorious past, all of whom were model wives. She learned of Anasuya, who proved faithful to her husband, a learned and holy man, when her chastity was tested by the gods; of Savitri, who outwitted the god of death to bring her husband back to life and win a kingdom for their children; of Taramati, the good wife of a virtuous king, who found a way to help her husband keep his vow of truthfulness when he was tested by the gods; of Sita, the beloved wife of the great Lord Rama.

There have been countless interpretations of child marriage as set forth in the Sutras, the ancient scriptures of the Hindus. Justification of the practice revolved around the need to preserve the virginity of young girls often threatened with rape and kidnapping by invading armies. Child marriages, it was said, protected girls living in large Indian households from the taint of becoming objects of untoward sexual advances. Even more importantly, child marriages saved young girls from becoming wayward themselves.

My grandfather, in his untiring battle against child marriage, would one day deal with such arguments: "Why this morbid anxiety about female purity? Why should men appropriate to themselves the right to regulate female purity? Have women any say in the matter of male purity?"

On a more practical level, child marriages were defended by some who believed that if a girl had to spend all her life in the home of her husband, it was best she learn to adjust from childhood. Whatever the origin or justification of the custom, for the Hindus living in Porbandar in the 1870s, the betrothal and marriage of girl children was an accepted and essential practice. Such a marriage was a union of families and not just of individuals.

Sometime in the year 1876, when Kastur Kapadia and Mohandas Gandhi were both seven years old, their fathers reached a preliminary agreement for their betrothal. Karamchand Gandhi, the father of Mohan was, like his father before him, the dewan or Prime Minister to the Rana of Porbandar, the local ruler. It was natural, therefore, for Gokaldas and Vrajkunwerba Kapadia to want to unite their family with that of their neighbours, the Gandhis, about whose history, probity, and suitability there could be no doubt.

For the Gandhis, too, the union of the two families would be timely and propitious. Little Mohan was the fourth and last child of Karamchand Gandhi and his much younger fourth wife Putliba. Karamchand was eager to get the boy settled before something happened to him. Mohan had been betrothed successively to two other little girls, both of whom had died (infant mortality was high in India). And now, to make matters more urgent, Karamchand was appointed dewan of the princely state of Rajkot, the regional headquarters for the British colonial administrative officials. Karamchand moved his family to Rajkot.

On the day chosen by the temple astrologers as auspicious for the formal betrothal ceremony, a group of men, led by Karamchand Gandhi, called at the home of Gokaldas Kapadia. In the presence of all assembled, Karamchand made the offer which was accepted by Gokaldas. A priest brought forward a large brass plate filled with fruits, flowers, and gold ornaments, and members of the Gandhi family touched the plate to bless it. The small bride-to-be, beautifully attired for the occasion, was led forth from the women's rooms. The plate was placed on her head, and the priest blessed her. The betrothal was arranged.

At seven years of age, Kastur was unaware of the significance of what was taking place, but she received some splendid presents, which made her happy.

Young Mohan was not present and did not know of the ceremony. Only much later would he be told of his betrothal, his third.

Because the story of Kasturba Gandhi's life has for so long been enmeshed in, or overshadowed by, the story of Mahatma Gandhi, it is difficult to establish many facts about her early years. The history and genealogy of my grandfather's family has been thoroughly researched and documented, but no scholars have ever delved into Ba's family background. And when I went searching for official records which might give more than a hint of who the Kapadias were and how they lived, I discovered that disastrous local floods during the 1930s and 1940s had destroyed all such documents, including those kept by the family priest. Nevertheless, a review of what happened to Kastur in this period of young life and a consideration of the setting in which those events occurred, can lead to certain assumptions.

Perhaps more significant is the fact that the actual wedding did not take place until 1882 — six years after the betrothal. That Gokaldas and Vrajkunwerba Kapadia would allow their only daughter to remain unmarried until the age of 13 suggests they were more concerned for her welfare than for the opinion of the orthodox community of Porbandar. Most girls were married by the age of eight.

According to family recollections, two other Kapadia daughters, whom Kastur never knew, had died several years before she was born. And it is said that her family cherished her; she grew up with all the security and self esteem that loving parental acceptance and protection can bestow. By all accounts, Kastur was an enchanting youngster: intelligent, independent (some say self-willed), fearless and unusually pretty.

Further evidence of familial concern for Kastur's best interests and future well-being can be found in her parents' considered choice of young Mohan Gandhi as her bridegroom. They knew that, as dewan, his father Karamchand, and his grandfather Uttamchand before him, had proved to be just, courageous, loyal, and incorruptible. Both men, when matters of principle were involved, had risked incurring the wrath of the rulers they served, as well as the displeasure of the British colonial government officials who guided those rulers.

Uttamchand Gandhi had once been forced to flee and take refuge in a neighbouring state for giving sanctuary in his own home to a man unjustly accused of wrongdoing by the temporary ruler of Porbandar, a tyrannical queen-mother serving as regent for her young son. After the queen died, the Gandhi family returned to Porbandar and in due course, Uttamchand's son Karamchand became dewan. One day, when he overheard a petty British official speaking in insulting terms about his employer, the Rana of Porbandar, he demanded that the officer apologise then and there. For his effrontery, Karamchand was arrested, tied to a tree like a common criminal, and left on public display for several hours before being released. These stories of the righteousness of the Gandhis had become almost legendary. Gokaldas Kapadia was certain that young Mohan, growing up with such a heritage, would become a man of principle, a just and responsible husband.

Then there was Mohan's mother, Putliba Gandhi, who, as a mother-in-law, would become one of the most important people in Kastur's life, supervising all of her everyday activities. Vrajkunwerba Kapadia knew Putliba Gandhi well as a friend and neighbour and felt certain this gentle, intensely religious woman would do no harm to her only daughter. An oft-repeated story in Porbandar was of how Putliba, warned that a deadly scorpion was crawling over her bare feet, simply scooped it up with her hand and dropped it out of the window.

# 2

It promised to be the biggest wedding in Porbandar — or at least the most festive one anybody could remember.

Karamchand Gandhi had proposed the plan in a letter written some time in the summer of 1882, to his only surviving brother, Tulsidas, now the head of the Gandhi household in Porbandar. The time had come, Karamchand decided — the long-awaited marriages of Mohandas, 13, and Karsandas, his brother, 16, were to take place that autumn. What Karamchand had in mind, however, was a triple marriage ceremony.

His brother Tulsidas' 17-year-old son Motilal was the only other unwed young man in the entire Gandhi family, and Karamchand, in his letter to Tulsidas asked, "Why not have a triple wedding?"

Some Gandhi biographers have suggested that Karamchand proposed having a triple wedding to save money. This may be so, but any savings would have been mainly for the benefit of the brides' parents. Weddings can be ruinously expensive. By tradition most of the costs were borne by the bride's family. But decisions as to how many wedding guests to invite, what kind of food to serve, what entertainment to provide, were not left to the discretion of the families involved. The community council of their caste or subcaste decided these matters — in this case, the Modh Vania caste committee in Porbandar — which set minimum standards based on the position, wealth, and prestige of the bridal couple's parents. No excuses. Families wishing to protect their social, financial and religious position had to celebrate a wedding in a suitable and expected manner. They often went deeply into debt to do so.

7

The idea of letting three bridal families share the burden of these huge outlays of cash must have been vastly appealing to a man like Karamchand, as noted for his thoughtfulness as for his common sense.

But there were other considerations as well. Karamchand was now past 60, an advanced age for Indians at that time, and travel was becoming difficult for him. In those days before railroads came to the Kathiawar peninsula, it took five days by ox-cart to cover the 125 miles between Rajkot and Porbandar.

His brother Tulsidas was only two years younger, and both men wanted all the young Gandhis in their charge to be married while they could still take their rightful places in the ceremonies and celebrations. Besides, at such a big wedding they themselves could no doubt have the last huge celebration of their lives.

Karamchand did not disclose the wedding plans to his sons until all arrangements had been made. Sixteen-year-old Karsandas took an immediate interest in the prospect, wondering aloud what his bride-to-be, a girl named Ganga, would be like. But young Mohandas reacted with indifference. A first-year student at the local Rajkot high school now, he was still shy and self-absorbed. Though vaguely aware that he was betrothed he had given little thought to marriage, and, unlike Kastur, he had received no instruction about the subject whatsoever. But once Mohandas grew accustomed to the idea — to a 13-year-old, getting married meant acquiring a new friend, a sort of permanent playmate — he too became intrigued. Karamchand arranged for the boys to miss school, and the whole family made plans to travel to Porbandar together for several days of wedding festivities.

For Kastur and the other prospective brides in Porbandar — Ganga, who was to marry Karsandas, and Harkunwar, betrothed to Motilal Gandhi — the activities had begun months earlier. Though no one had told Kastur what all the secret messages and whispered conversations were about, she sensed that something momentous was taking place.

Weddings usually took place at the bride's home, but this time since three couples were to be wed, a hall had to be hired. Menus for the wedding feast had to be drawn up, decorations, flowers, cooking utensils and serving pieces acquired. Extra servants would be needed; drummers, flautists, singers must be engaged. Carriages must be rented and mares for the bridegrooms to ride had to be found. Trousseaus had to be bought, new clothes for the families must be made, and a hundred other things attended to.

Before inviting a single guest Gokaldas Kapadia wrote out an invitation in red ink and, with his wife Vrajkunwerba, went to the temple and laid it at the feet of their family god. Only after the Lord was invited were friends and relatives given their invitations. In ancient India invitations had to be personally delivered, not mailed.

Kastur was excited. It was the event for which she had been preparing for so long. But now that the time had come, it was confusing and overwhelming. She was happy but keenly aware that she would soon be leaving her parents, her brothers, the familiar surroundings of Porbandar and her childhood behind. For a 13-year-old girl, it was more than a bit scary.

Such doubts were fleeting — her confidence in the future was strong. In her room in Porbandar, ready for the long trip to Rajkot, was her ornate cedar wood chest filled with new clothes. Another carved teakwood box held her wedding jewellery: gold bracelets, necklaces, bangles; gold rings and studs for her ears and her nose.

In Rajkot, as the wedding date approached, plans had changed. Karamchand Gandhi was delayed by urgent official duties. The Thakore of Rajkot, the local prince whom he served as prime minister, considered him indispensable. To make sure the rest of the family arrived in time for the festivities, Karamchand sent them off on the five-day ox-cart journey; he would follow soon. The prince had offered Karamchand the use of his own fast horses, the royal buggy, and an experienced driver. Karamchand promised Putliba and his sons he would be there for the ceremony on time.

For the entire week preceding the wedding the Kapadia house was filled with relatives, friends, neighbours, helping cook sumptuous delicacies for the wedding feast. As they worked they sang wedding songs for Kastur. Some were humorous to tease or amuse the bride and help relieve her nervousness; others were instructive to convey advice and information for newlyweds.

The day before the wedding, Kastur was given a special beauty treatment with pithi, a fragrant mixture of turmeric, almond and sandalwood mixed in fresh cream. This was a ritual performed for all prospective Hindu brides. Kastur's mother, aunts, female cousins and friends took turns daubing this ointment on her young body. A similar ritual was performed for each of the young bridegrooms by their male relatives.

On the day of the wedding, Kastur's married female friends and relatives gave her a ceremonial bath with water made fragrant by herbs and perfumes. She was groomed and then, using a paste made from henna leaves, the women painted intricate designs on Kastur's hands and feet. She was then ready to be dressed in her beautiful new sari.

Smiling now, Vrajkunwerba touched her daughter's forehead lightly with her finger, placing there a dot of red powder on wax, the familiar vermillion kumkum mark, a sign of being blessed. Finally, the traditional red sari, a cobweb of filmy silk, was arranged over her head and shoulders as the wedding veil. Kastur was ready.

But mixed with joy there was consternation at the Gandhi home. Karamchand had not yet arrived from Rajkot. It would be sad if the children he loved had to be married without him. Postponement was unthinkable; the exact moment of the wedding is chosen with great care. To ensure the union takes place at a propitious moment a blade of grass is placed between their palms, to be withdrawn at the exact instant when the position of the stars and planets is right.

At last Karamchand's buggy arrived, much to the relief of the family. But Karamchand was bandaged and bruised and limping, and had much to explain.

To arrive on time the horses sped over the rough, dirt roads, he said, and the light buggy bounced and bumped so that every bone in his body was shaken. Early this morning, fearing he was going to miss the weddings, he began egging the driver on.

"Can't you get the horses to move faster?" Karamchand groused.

"We're going as fast as we can, sir," the poor man would reply.

Then it happened. The right wheels of the buggy hit a loose boulder on the road. The buggy tilted crazily to the left and then overturned. Karamchand and the driver were both badly shaken. Then he realized that he also had cuts and bruises all over his body.

With the help of some farmers, they set the buggy on its wheels. It seemed to be intact. While they rested the horses, Karamchand tore up a white dhoti, or loincloth and used it to bandage his wounds. They had resumed the journey and somehow got to Porbandar — in time. The ceremonies, Karamchand announced triumphantly, could take place exactly as planned.

He brushed aside the concern of the family; he maintained he was not seriously hurt As soon as he cleaned up, he would be as good as new.

The three brides, hidden inside curtained carriages, their faces veiled, were brought by their parents to the wedding hall. Inside, three canopies had been set up where the actual ceremonies would take place. Decorative poles, festooned with flowers, marked the four corners of each canopy, and at each corner were piled brass pots in the form of a pyramid. The brides waited.

Meanwhile, a stately procession led by a band of musicians was making its way through the lanes of Porbandar. The grooms, in all their finery, mounted the rented mares (also decorated and garlanded with flowers) and began their journey to the hall. On foot were their mothers and other female relatives, singing special wedding songs. Then came everyone else — relatives, friends, wedding guests, even some curious bystanders. This time, all agreed — it was the biggest wedding celebration Porbandar had ever seen.

Mohandas was brought to the decorated booth and seated on a low wooden stool facing east. Only after Mohandas had been seated was Kastur brought to the booth by her maternal uncle and seated on another stool, which faced to the west. Through her veil, she got only a peek at the boy who was waiting for her. Almost immediately, a white curtain was drawn between them. She was glad to see her parents, Gokaldas and Vrajkunwerba, seated next to her facing to the north.

For many minutes, Kastur sat listening as the priest recited the marriage vows in Sanskrit. At last, her father Gokaldas rose and holding several blades of grass in his hand announced the cycle, the age, the year, the season, the position of the planets, the day, the continent, the country, the province, the town, and the place where the ceremony was being held. After these precise directions were conveyed to a listening god, Gokaldas declared that he was handing over his healthy daughter Kastur to the bridegroom Mohandas, and he relinquished all claims on her. He then took Kastur's hand and placed it in Mohandas' right hand with a blade of grass separating the two palms.

But the ceremony was not over. The newlyweds were then seated next to each other while the priest said a few more verses, and then it was time to perform the final ritual, the Saptapadi, or Seven Steps. Mohan and Kastur stood up, side by side, looking very serious.

Together, they took the first of seven steps as husband and wife, repeating with each step the verses they had memorised. Seven small heaps of rice had been arranged to mark the steps, and Kastur had been instructed to trample one heap of rice with the big toe of her right foot, with each step forward (the significance of trampling the rice-heaps is not known). Here is what they said that day, Mohandas speaking first, Kastur responding.

Take one step, that we may have strength of will.
*In every worthy wish of yours, I shall be your helpmate.*
Take the second step, that we may be filled with vigour.
*In every worthy wish of yours, I shall be your helpmate.*
Take the third step, that we may live in ever-increasing prosperity.
*Your joys and sorrows I will share.*

**11**

Take the fourth step, that we may be ever full of joy.
*I will ever live devoted to you, speaking words of love and praying for your happiness.*
Take the fifth step, that we may serve the people.
*I will follow close behind you always, and help you to keep your vow of serving the people.*
Take the sixth step, that we may follow our religious vows in life.
*I will follow you in observing our religious vows and duties.*
Take the seventh step, that we may ever live as friends.
*It is the fruit of my good deeds that I have you as my husband.*
*You are my best friend, my highest guru,*
*and my sovereign lord.*

The words of the Saptapadi were traditional. They probably had no more special meaning to the young bride and groom than did any of the other strange and solemn words that had been spoken. But some of those vows my grandparents recited on their wedding day would take on an extraordinary significance for them in their 62 years of married life.

"And oh! That first night. Two innocent children all unwittingly hurled themselves into the ocean of life."

With those words, written almost half a century later, my grandfather began the account of his wedding night that appears in his autobiography *The Story of My Experiments with Truth*. "We were too nervous to face each other," he reported. "And we were certainly too shy. How was I to talk to her and what was I to say?"

Mohandas was 13 and, by his own confession, knew very little about sex beyond a few whispered hints he had recently received from his considerate sister-in-law Nandkunwarben, the wife of his older brother Lakshimidas (there is reason to wonder, given the strict taboo in sexual matters between men and women in Indian families, just how explicit his sister-in-law could have been).

"The coaching couldn't carry me far," he wrote, adding that he never knew and never inquired whether or not Kastur had been given any helpful information or instruction. "But no coaching really is necessary on such matters. We gradually began to know each other and to speak freely," writes Grandfather.

There will always be much that is unknown about the intimate relationship of Kasturba and Mohandas Gandhi. My grandmother left no written records and, in later life she never confided her innermost feelings or personal reminiscences to anyone. But we can, by conjecture, arrive at some understanding of what Ba's experiences may have been.

My grandmother belonged to a generation of Indian women who were schooled to be patient and passive. But at that moment, with the silence between them growing ever more oppressive, young Kastur must have suspected that Mohan knew even less than she did about what was supposed to happen next. She waited, wondering what she should do — if anything.

And then, as was his habit in moments of crisis, Mohan smiled. It was a smile that in future years would delight his comrades, confound his critics and disarm his enemies. On this night, it dispelled all his bride's uncertainties.

A good Hindu wife follows her husband's lead in all things. Kastur smiled at Mohan. They began to speak. Together, they embarked on the adventure of marriage.

# 3

Kastur took little notice of the weather on the cool sunny morning she set out for Rajkot with her new family. In all of her 13 years, Kastur had never been beyond the borders of Porbandar. Going to Rajkot was like going to another universe. Kastur found the idea exciting. She had always been fearless, undaunted by the usual terrors of childhood: insects, serpents, wild animals, or the dark of night. Why should she find a strange city intimidating?

Hindu men and women usually travelled separately. Thus, the bride-grooms, Mohandas and Karsandas, rode in one carriage with their older brother Lakshimidas and their father Karamchand, still on the mend from his injuries, while the brides, Kastur and Ganga, travelled in another coach with the older sister-in-law Nandkunwarben and their new mother-in-law Putliba. It was a good opportunity for all these Gandhi women to become acquainted.

When the carriages pulled up in front of the Gandhi home in Rajkot, the travellers found Mohan's sister, Raliatben, waiting. There were two final Hindu marriage customs to be observed. Before the newlyweds were allowed to enter, Raliatben stopped them with the traditional request — each of her brothers had to present her with a suitable gift to gain entry. Mohandas and Karsandas complied.

Then came the mother-in-law's traditional greeting to new daughters-in-law, somewhat akin to the Western custom of carrying the bride across the threshold of her new house for good luck.

Putliba put down a measure of rice at the front door and then invited the older couple, Ganga and Karsandas, to come in first, as was their due. Ganga was actually a few months younger than Kastur, but she had married the older brother making her higher in status. As they entered, Ganga tilted the measure with her toe, spilling the rice out onto the floor and stepping on it — this, it was said, would bring prosperity to the newlyweds. Now, it was the younger couple's turn; Putliba set out another measure of rice. Mohandas and Kastur entered, and Kastur, repeating the ritual, was welcomed to her new home.

A new home, a new life, even a new name: Kasturbai Gandhi. The suffix "-bai" would usually be added to her name Kastur now that she was an adult married woman. And it all took some getting used to. In the days that followed, Kasturbai was often homesick for her old home in Porbandar. Her life as youngest daughter-in-law in the busy Gandhi household was very different from her former life as favourite daughter in the ease and comfort of the Kapadia house.

A regional version of secluding females — what my grandfather called Kathiawar's "own peculiar, useless and barbarous purdah", decreed that young husbands and wives must ignore each other during daylight hours. Any show of affection, even the exchange of a few casual words, was considered indecent. Young married women were not to be seen by older men in the family or visiting strangers.

Though Hindu women were not required to hide their bodies with the tent-like chador worn by Muslim women, they were expected to cover their heads and faces with their saris in the presence of elders of either sex.

Mohandas had returned to high school so that their only time together was late at night, in their own small bedroom just above the main gate of the house.

Kasturbai was not idle during the day. As the youngest daughter-in-law in a joint family, it was her duty to perform without a murmur of protest whatever tasks the older women might assign to her. This was another accepted fact of life. Kasturbai knew that by right, all her in-laws, not just her mother-in-law Putliba, but also Nandkunwarba, even Ganga, could order her around. But she was lucky. Unlike many young brides, she was never treated like a chattel in her new home. Putliba was kind, discerning, wise — not at all the tyrannical mother-in-law of stories. In assigning daily tasks to the younger women, Putliba played no favourites and she liked to instruct by example rather than command. She was usually the last person to go to bed at night and the last to take her meals. What kept all of them busy was the amount of work that had to be done in the bustling Gandhi household.

As the dewan of Rajkot, Karamchand Gandhi had a daily stream of visitors who had to be properly entertained: tea, snacks, or full meals, depending on what time they came to visit. Karamchand had never been one to worry about money, and had never accumulated enough resources for his family to live lavishly. As a result, the Gandhis did not have the army of servants and cooks that one might have expected to find in the home of a minister of state; not even the usual staff of servants found in the homes of successful merchants (men like Gokaldas Kapadia).

In the Gandhi household, everyone was expected to participate in household chores. The dewan himself, it was said, had sometimes been seen sitting under a tree in the courtyard, peeling vegetables for his wife while receiving official visitors.

Kasturbai's mother-in-law was a cheerfully devout woman who took little interest in fine clothes and jewellery, and faithfully observed all vows and fasts prescribed for self-discipline and self-purification, even adding special vows of her own invention. Her daily rituals of purification had become the regimen for her whole household. Putliba wouldn't eat without first saying her prayers, and wouldn't pray without first having her bath, and wouldn't bathe without first visiting the latrine. Ritual safeguards against spiritual pollution were not new to Kasturbai — her parents, too, were religious.

Not long after she settled into her new home, Kasturbai noticed a change in the quiet, likeable boy she had married. In an attempt to play the typical role of a dominant Indian husband, Mohandas was becoming very possessive and jealous.

It all started when he bought several little pamphlets at the bazaar, the sort of thing written in those days to educate young husbands about their conjugal rights and responsibilities. Aware that he had much to learn, Mohandas read the booklets from cover to cover. What impressed him was not the practical advice given, but the commendable exhortation that a husband must always be faithful to his wife. He found that idea compelling. And not just because it appealed to what he later described as his "innate passion for truth". Mohandas was in the throes of first love. He was "passionately fond" of Kasturbai; he could think of nothing else all day long. To be false to her was unthinkable.

To him it was obvious that a wife, too, should pledge faithfulness; however his adolescent strategy for ensuring mutual fidelity was both unsophisticated and unenlightened. He concluded that it was the duty of the faithful husband to exert his authority over his wife and to make sure that she kept her pledge.

One night Mohandas announced to Kasturbai that from now on he wanted to be kept fully informed about where she went and when, and about whom she met and why. In fact, he declared, she should not go out of the house without his consent.

However, the notion of having to request permission from Mohandas for her every move sounded like oppression to Kastur. With her many household duties, she seldom had time to gallivant. She only accompanied other Gandhi women to call on friends or neighbours, or go with Putliba to the nearby temple for prayers. Nandkunwarba and Ganga never went in search of their husbands to tell them they were going out, so why should she? Besides, it was embarrassing and humiliating.

My grandmother's spirit was always proud and free. Those who remembered her have testified that Ba would never allow anyone to dictate to her — not even her husband. Yet her manner was naturally accommodating; never challenging. And her instincts were essentially conservative. She had no inborn desire to flout tradition. At this point in her young life, she was not ready to rebel openly against accepted practices or established authority (this would change in the years to come).

On the night of their first confrontation, Kasturbai assured Mohandas she would always be a faithful wife. For her, any other course was unthinkable. She raised no objections to the restrictions he proposed. But she made no promise to observe them.

The next day, without consulting Mohandas, Kasturbai arranged to go with Putliba to the temple for prayers. How could Mohandas object? She was following the example of his own mother, the most virtuous of women. She went to the temple again the following day and the next. The day after that Kasturbai went with her sisters-in-law to call on friends. By actions, not words, she was making it clear to Mohandas how much she objected to his high-handedness.

Mohandas reacted vigorously and attempted to impose even more restraints. They had their first quarrel.

"Are you suggesting that I should obey you and not your mother?" Kasturbai asked.

The new husband had no answer.

"When she or other elders in the house ask me to go out with them, am I to tell them I cannot stir out without my husband's permission?"

Finally, Mohandas acknowledged that Kasturbai was not the girl to brook such restraints. The orders were rescinded and normal life resumed.

The young husband was learning a hard truth about his wife: she obeyed as she chose. Unless he could convince her of the correctness of his decisions, she was prepared quietly to ignore them and go her own way (that would not change in the years to come).

Mohandas still remained troubled and preoccupied. He was neglecting his studies.

Word came from Porbandar that Kasturbai's family wanted her to come for an extended visit. It is customary for Indian parents to arrange frequent and lengthy separation of young married couples. During the months she spent in Porbandar, Kasturbai happily settled back into the comfortable, undemanding routine of life in the Kapadia household. She seemed to be discovering anew the everyday enjoyments of calling on relatives and friends, chatting and singing: she loved to sing. In visits to the Gandhi house, where the newlyweds Motilal and Harkunwar lived, she exchanged confidences with another recent bride.

In such conversations, Kasturbai undoubtedly shared some of her confused feelings about her husband and her marriage: how she thought about Mohandas all day long — it made the cooking and the chores go faster. How eager she was, they both were, to be alone together in their room at night. How playful he could be: mischievous in fact, but agreeably so. He had his strange little ways. He always kept a small lamp lit in their room, something she wasn't used to. But she never objected; she truly wanted to please him in all things.

Why, then, in the first few months of her marriage, had she defied her husband and gone against his wishes? Not just once, but repeatedly. She tried to explain to her friend and to herself.

It was because Mohandas had changed. He had become another person: disagreeable and unreasonable. But was that any reason for defying him — something no good wife should ever do? How could she make him understand that she had her own life to live, her own duties to perform? She wanted to be a good wife, but she also had to be true to herself.

Kastur loved to listen to the stories women told. Tales of the great heroines of ancient India. One of the stories Kastur often asked for was the true story of the brave queen Rani Laxmibai of Jhansi. In 1857, only a few years before Kastur herself was born, Rani had died on the battlefield. She was leading Indian troops against their colonial overlords. The British called this brief rebellion the Sepoy Mutiny.

Kastur's mother was pleased to tell her daughter the story of a woman's selfless patriotism, hoping, perhaps, that her daughter would grow up to emulate the courage of Rani Laxmibai. Vrajkunwerba had no illusions that Kastur would ever lead troops into battle, of course, but there were many different ways a woman could be courageous.

In Kasturbai's absence Mohandas had studied hard, making up for time missed from school during the weeks of endless wedding celebrations. He wrestled with geography, and lost marks for his bad handwriting, but his marks in English and geometry were much improved. He was passed to a higher grade. This was better than the other recent Gandhi bridegrooms had done. Marriage marked the end of schooling for my grandfather's older brother Karsandas, and his cousin Motilal in Porbandar.

All the while Mohandas was devoting himself to his studies, his inmost thoughts had been centred on his wife. Desperately lonely for Kasturbai, fervently yearning for her return, he had devised an experiment for them to carry out, a new project to bring them closer together: he was going to teach his illiterate wife to read and write. His ambition, as explained in his autobiography, was "to make my wife an ideal wife. ... [T]o make her live a pure life, learn what I learned, and identify her life and thought with mine."

He revealed the plan to Kasturbai as soon as she returned to Rajkot, keeping her awake late into the night outlining his course of instruction starting with the alphabet, and expecting her enthusiastic acceptance of the project. Instead, she seemed wary, unresponsive.

In truth, Kasturbai was surprised and shocked. How could her husband be so unpredictable, so inconsistent? First, he had wanted her to become the most subservient wife. Now he was suggesting she should become the most emancipated and do something totally unconventional, something that went against all tradition. He wanted her to learn to read and write! Her misgivings were almost instinctual. But with her usual protective reticence, she said nothing.

The experiment got underway. Each night in their room, the young couple would spread out the books Mohandas had selected, take up the slates he had provided, and go to work. But each night, just as regularly, they would abandon the effort almost as soon as it began, and go to bed. The trouble, according to Gandhi's later recollections, was that Kasturbai, the reluctant student, "was not impatient of her ignorance." He, the zealous instructor, found his fervour to teach his wife overwhelmed by his passion to make love to her.

From Kasturbai's point of view, there were larger problems. First was the matter of simple exhaustion. Her day was long and strenuous, but her studies with Mohandas could not begin until after nightfall. By that time she had neither the stamina nor the inclination to sit through the lessons he had prepared.

More than that, Kasturbai had every reason to fear the effect her studies might have on her relationship with the other women in the Gandhi family, the women with whom she would be spending the rest of her days. Of the three daughters-in-law sharing the household, Kasturbai had come from the most prominent and most prosperous family. Her father had been mayor of Porbandar. She had grown up in an affluent home, wanting for nothing. Until now, their differences had been of no consequence, and Kasturbai had been careful to keep it that way. By word and deed, Vrajkunwerba and Putliba taught her that to prevent small misunderstandings from becoming lifelong feuds, the habitual practice of courtesy and consideration was essential in the crowded world of homebound women in an Indian joint family.

What would happen now if she learned to read and write — became educated? Would her sisters-in-law feel she was trying to prove she was better than they were? Would she be subjected to their resentment, ridicule and condemnation? What would Putliba think of her? And what would she think of herself? Would her own attitude towards life change if education were forced upon her? Did she want to be changed? My grandmother had an indomitable spirit, but she was not yet inclined to pioneer a revolution. And a hundred years ago the idea of education for Indian women was revolutionary indeed.

Kasturbai's illiteracy was not unusual; quite the reverse. Except for a tiny number of wealthy princesses sent abroad for study, almost all Indian women in those days were illiterate. Not one woman in Kasturbai's family — her mother, her mother-in-law, her sisters-in-law, Mohandas' sister Raliatben — was able to read or write. Education outside the family home was unheard of. There were few schools of any kind and virtually none for girls.

Mohandas' ill-fated tutoring experiment continued sporadically for many weeks, being abandoned, then resumed several times before he was forced to admit that his attempts to educate his wife were failing. It was a failure my grandfather would lament repeatedly in later years, ascribing it to his own shortcomings — his "lustful love".

But it seems to me that Bapu's assessment of this failure in no way took into account Ba's point of view.

And what was significant is this: she never protested or openly opposed her husband's wishes. She simply chose not to master her lessons. A pattern was being set.

Obsessed for so many months by the complexities of his new role as husband, Mohandas had made few close friends in school. Now, in his second year of high school, he and a Muslim schoolmate called Sheik

Mehtab had struck up a friendship. A tall, handsome athletic youth, Mehtab lived across the street from the Gandhis. He was two or three years older than Mohandas and had originally been a friend and classmate of Mohandas' older brother Karsandas. Unlike Karsandas, Mehtab was still attending the Rajkot high school where Mohandas saw him every day.

Their friendship distressed Kasturbai. A perceptive judge of character, she suspected his intentions from the beginning. She soon learned that Mehtab was known in the neighbourhood as something of a wastrel who was lazy and boastful. Then she was told that neither Putliba nor Lakshimidas, Mohandas' level-headed oldest brother, had ever considered Mehtab fit company for Karsandas.

It should be noted that their objections were to Mehtab himself not his religion. The Kathiawar peninsula, somewhat cut off from the rest of India and therefore a frequent sanctuary for those fleeing persecution elsewhere, was remarkably free of the religious hatreds that beset other regions. For centuries, Buddhists, Muslims, Jains, Parsis, Christians, as well as adherents of all the varying sects of Hinduism (somewhat analogous to the various denominations of Protestantism) had found refuge there, living and working side by side. My grandfather later said it was in Rajkot and Porbandar that he got "an early grounding in toleration for all branches of Hinduism and its sister religions" — an attitude he tried to pass on to his followers.

At one point Kasturbai took it upon herself to warn Mohandas against spending too much time with Sheik Mehtab. Mohandas, disregarding (and possibly resenting) her advice, persisted in the friendship. That is where matters stood when the time came for Kasturbai to make another lengthy visit to Porbandar. With his wife away, Mohandas soon became Mehtab's inseparable companion, and Mehtab became a guiding influence in his life.

One day Mohandas confessed to his new friend that he was plagued by unreasonable fears of the dark and of creatures that came out at night. This embarrassed him, he said, because his wife had none of these fears. Kasturbai would go out in darkness where Mohandas feared to tread; she could sleep soundly, while he, lying awake, was in terror of snakes, thieves, and ghosts.

Mehtab had an answer: eat meat. He attributed Mohandas' timidity to vegetarianism that was a basic tenet of Vaishnava-sect followers of Vishnu. Mehtab boasted he could hold live serpents in his hand, and could defy thieves. He stated that he did not believe in ghosts — all because he, as a Muslim, could eat meat. His size, strength, and athletic prowess (he was the high school's star runner) were all due to meat eating. This was also why the English were able to dominate Indians. Mehtab quoted the Gujarati doggerel gaining popularity among young Indians:

Behold the mighty Englishman
He rules the Indian small
Because, being a meat-eater,
He is five cubits tall.

Mehtab informed Mohandas that many of his Hindu high school teachers were now secretly eating meat. So was his own brother, Karsandas.

Mohandas had long since begun to question the validity of certain Hindu practices, starting with the rigidities of the caste system. As a little boy he had seen Uka clean the bucket latrines at the Gandhi house and once asked his mother why Uka was considered Untouchable. Why was it believed that their very shadows could contaminate, and anyone who so much as brushed against them had to be purified by an immediate bath?

Putliba had, momentarily, eased her son's mind by explaining that it wasn't always necessary to perform ablutions after coming into contact with an Untouchable; if one touched someone from another religion, a Muslim perhaps, the pollution could be harmlessly transferred. Later on, in a spirit of pre-adolescent rebellion, Mohandas and one of his young cousins had challenged a lesser prohibition of the Vaishnava faith. Secretly retrieving cigarette butts discarded by a transgressing uncle, they had briefly (and unhappily) tried smoking.

More recently, Mohandas had stopped going to temple — the ostentatious glitter and pomp had never appealed to him. What did such outward displays of excessive wealth have to do with inner spiritual values? He had grown increasingly skeptical about all religiously prescribed dogma, and was secretly beginning to regard himself as an atheist.

After due consideration of his friend Mehtab's urging, Mohandas decided that, for him, meat eating posed no moral problems except for the deception involved. His parents, of course, could never know. If meat eating would make him strong and daring, it was an experiment worth trying. And as part of a reform that could help free India, it was a patriotic duty to be performed.

His first taste of meat — a feast of goat's meat and baker's bread (another first) which was supplied by Mehtab and eaten in privacy on a secluded riverbank on the outskirts of town made Mohandas sick. He had nightmares that night. But remorse soon faded when he reminded himself of his duty to grow stronger. More secret feasts followed, even a few visits to restaurants where meat dishes were served. By the time Kasturbai returned to Rajkot, Mohandas had actually acquired a taste for meat dishes. The experiment had become an established habit.

Kasturbai soon realised that her husband, once again, had changed. His attempts to teach her to read and write were forgotten. They seldom talked, even at night. Upon reaching their room, they went straight to bed — in the dark. Mohandas made it a point now to turn off the nightlight. He left for school early, arrived home late, and ate little for dinner, complaining of "digestive" problems. His parents accepted the explanation. But it did not ring true to Kasturbai.

Only gradually, and with horror, did she allow herself to suspect the most likely reason for this latest transformation in her husband. Mohandas had become a meat eater!

Kasturbai had been born and bred a Vaishnava Hindu, and abhorrence of meat eating was stronger among the Vaishnavas. Most Vaishnava Hindus had absorbed many of the basic teachings of Jainism. To them, therefore, the eating of meat was tantamount to eating human flesh.

If Mohandas had now become a meat-eater, she was certain that Sheik Mehtab was the most likely instigator of such wickedness. Living in close proximity with him, Kasturbai became more convinced that this was the horrifying truth. But what could she do about it? She could not now confront Mohandas with her new suspicions. She certainly could not discuss the matter with Putliba, and it would be improper to speak of it with her sisters-in-law. If Mohandas wanted to eat meat, Kasturbai could not stop him. All she could do was keep her silence and pray.

Somehow, her prayers were answered.

Mohandas' experiment with meat eating stretched out over a full year. To his disappointment, it added not a single cubit to his size but added immensely to his guilt. My grandfather was no doubt beginning to realise that my grandmother knew and understood him better than anyone else. In the end, his guilt overcame his enthusiasm for "food reform". He could not live with the deception and decided to confess his guilt to his ailing father. It took him a while to muster the courage. He wrote a letter and one day, when his father was lying in bed alone, handed it over to him.

On reading his son's confession his father cried and so did

Mohandas. They embraced, his father forgave him and Mohandas kept his vow to shun meat for ever.

Mohandas' friendship with Mehtab had meanwhile cast another shadow over his relationship with his wife. Though Kasturbai was unaware of it, Mohandas sometimes discussed with Mehtab his uncertainties about their intimate marital relations. His own feelings of desire for his young wife were constant and intense. Though she seemed to return his love with a tender affection, he sometimes expected her to be more demonstrative.

One day, talking to Mehtab, Mohandas wondered aloud whether Kasturbai was more or less responsive in lovemaking than other women were. With his own lack of experience, he had no way of knowing. Mehtab, a self-proclaimed "expert" in these matters, had an answer — as usual. It was more unnerving than helpful.

"Don't worry," he said. "Women are often very timid about such things; or, perhaps, she has someone else she likes better than you."

That night Kasturbai had to face a flood of angry questions and accusations about her fidelity — she could hardly believe what Mohandas was saying. The nights that followed were the same. It was a period of lonely emotional torment for her. She knew who was behind this mischief, but was helpless to defend herself. And there was no one to whom she could turn for help or counsel.

There was worse to come.

Mehtab's next suggestion was that Mohandas would probably find it interesting to visit a brothel where he could learn about other women. Mehtab knew just the place. He offered to make all the arrangements, even pay the bill in advance. Mohandas allowed himself to be persuaded, but the outcome was disastrous. The ardent but jealous husband, once in the presence of a woman other than the wife to whom he had sworn eternal fidelity, was unable to perform.

"I was almost struck blind and dumb," Gandhi wrote in his autobiography. "I sat next to the woman on her bed, but I was tongue-tied. She naturally lost patience with me, and showed me the door with abuses and insults. I felt as though my manhood had been injured, and wished to sink into the ground for shame."

Once outside on the street, however, he felt an enormous sense of relief. He had not broken his vows to be true to Kasturbai.

Sometime later — we do not know just when — Mohandas confessed all of this to Kasturbai. He went to her half expecting to be met with anger, recriminations, and retribution. After his own recent accusations, such reactions on Kasturbai's part would surely have been justified, which could very well have led to further indiscretions on Mohandas' part. What he needed was understanding, solace, sympathy — and these he got in good measure. It was the first real test of their marriage and Kasturbai met this crisis with generosity and trust, and a maturity that was scarcely to be expected from a 15-year-old girl.

Sometime in the summer of the year of 1885, Kasturbai had joyous news for her husband and her family: she was expecting their first child.

# 4

Kasturbai's glad tidings were overshadowed by another matter of much graver concern. Her father-in-law Karamchand Gandhi had never fully recovered from the injuries suffered in his accident on the way to the wedding in Porbandar. Now he suffered complications. He had continued as dewan in Rajkot. An English surgeon in Bombay had recommended an operation, but this was overruled by the family physician because of Karamchand's age and weakness. The family watched helplessly as his health got progressively worse.

Finally, Karamchand was confined to his bed. The nursing duties fell on the family. For Mohan, nursing his father was an opportunity to demonstrate his devotion to both his parents. Also, nursing came naturally to him. My grandfather, from earliest childhood, always showed compassion for anything that was injured or suffering. His older sister Raliatben recalled how young Mohan once climbed a neighbour's guava tree and, with strips of torn cloth, tried to bandage the broken skin on fruit pecked at by birds.

For weeks, Mohandas spent his leisure time at his father's side. He came home directly from school, bathed and fed Karamchand, dressed his wound, and compounded his drugs and medicines that had to be prepared at home. During his illness, Karamchand became preoccupied with religion, and Mohan would sit quietly in the evenings and listen to the many priests and holy men (Vaishnava, Jain, Muslim, Parsi) who came to his father's bedside to discuss religion, sing hymns, and read scriptures. One night Mohan heard for the first time a Gujarati translation of the Ramayana, the story of Lord Rama who was regarded as an incarnation of the Supreme God Vishnu.

Its central message, that "Truth is the foundation of all merit and virtue," made such a favourable impression on Mohan that he gained a new insight into religion in general and Hinduism in particular. Finally, after all the callers had departed, Mohan would bathe his father's feet, then knead and massage his legs until the old dewan was relaxed and ready for sleep.

This dawn-to-midnight schedule left Mohan with little time for study and no time at all to spend with Sheik Mehtab — for which Kasturbai was duly thankful. Despite the unsatisfactory "food reform" experiment and other more devastating misadventures initiated by Mehtab, Mohan had never quite broken off their friendship. He explained that, since the association could no longer lead him astray, he now intended to "reform" his friend — a dubious prospect at best, in Kasturbai's view. With a baby on the way, she believed more firmly than ever that Mehtab was not a proper companion for her husband. She was relieved to see the friendship languish.

Kasturbai herself could think of little else. She was only 15 and marvelled at the month-by-month transformation wrought by pregnancy, feeling the first movement of life she carried within herself. She delighted in the pregnancy and all the attention she got from everyone. From time to time she thought about the ordeal and wondered how she would withstand it — many women died in childbirth — but she resolved not to dwell on the unknown.

The beginning of a new life within her banished any thought of the ending of another. She found little time to worry about her father-in-law's illness. Such was not the case for Mohan. His constant anxiety about his sick father was superceded only by his unceasing desire for his young wife. Each evening at Karamchand's bedside, ministering to his needs, Mohan let his mind wander to the little room above the main gate where Kasturbai would be waiting for him and he waited with growing impatience for his father's customary words of dismissal: "That will do for today, son. You may go to bed."

Members of the family who realised Karamchand's health was failing rapidly began to call on the family. One day Karamchand's cousin was visiting. That night he said to Mohan: "Don't worry about your father. I will sit by his side." Thus relieved of his nightly duties shortly after ten o'clock on November 16, 1885, Mohan rushed into his bedroom and woke up Kasturbai. She usually waited up for her husband, but this night she had dropped off to sleep early, exhausted from the day's activities.

Mohandas slipped into bed beside her. Five minutes later, there was a knock on the door. The voice of the servant called Mohan urgently. "Come quickly! Your father is dying!" Mohan leaped out of bed, flung on his clothes and raced back to his father's room. He was too late. Karamchand lay still and lifeless.

A great wave of grief swept over Mohan. He would have to live with the shameful knowledge that during the moment of his father's death he lay wrapped in the embrace of his pregnant wife.

On November 20, four days after the death of Karamchand Gandhi, Kasturbai delivered a child prematurely. In a few days the child died.

"The poor mite that was born to my wife scarcely breathed for more than three or four days," so my grandfather wrote years later in his autobiography. Then passing his own moral judgment, he added, "Nothing else could be expected."

Mohan was convinced that the death of his and Kasturbai's firstborn child, the baby son they had longed for, was a punishment for his reckless self-indulgence. He blamed only himself — never Kasturbai. In his words Kasturbai "never played the temptress." The memory of circumstances surrounding these successive family tragedies of death, birth and death would haunt my grandfather for as long as he lived, altering his thoughts and actions in unforeseen ways.

Life was forever changed for Kasturbai, too, in ways we can only imagine. No bells were rung, no songs were sung, no gifts arrived for the tiny infant she knew so briefly. But as far as I can discover, she never discussed the matter with anyone. I believe even after she became the mother of four sons, Ba carried in her heart a burden of silent sorrow for her lost firstborn son.

In the late spring, Kasturbai returned to Porbandar for another of her periodic visits. Her parents were concerned about their daughter's health after the experience of a premature birth. This was to be the longest separation since their marriage. Kasturbai needed a change.

There had been another subtle alteration in their relationship. Mohan was now concentrating on his studies with a disconcerting new urgency she did not yet understand.

In Porbandar, Kasturbai quickly recovered her old optimism and self-confidence. She visited the Gandhi home in Porbandar and played with the children of Mohan's brothers and cousins. This helped her heal the wounds of her own loss.

In Rajkot, meanwhile, decisions were being made that would affect the future course of Kasturbai's life. The Gandhi family's fortunes were in decline following the death of Karamchand. The dewan had set aside no money for his family's future, and the small pension he had been receiving from the ruler of Rajkot no longer arrived; the household was now wholly dependent on the earnings of Mohandas' older brothers. As sons of a Prime Minister, they would have been candidates for appointment to the post held by their father. But times had changed. With the British dictating all such appointments neither 26-year-old Lakshimidas Gandhi nor 19-year-old Karsandas Gandhi had the knowledge or the proficiency in English which the post now required.

Lakshimidas, who by virtue of seniority was the new head of the household, held a minor job as a law clerk. Karsandas was a sub-inspector of the royal Rajkot police. Neither position commanded a large income or much prestige. All the family's expectations for the future were now concentrated on Mohan. His mother Putliba, especially, was determined that her youngest son should eventually become a dewan in the family tradition. That meant he must not only finish high school with good marks, but must also become the first in his family to go to college and obtain a degree.

Mohan adopted these ambitions as his own. By the time Kasturbai returned to Rajkot at the end of the year his scholastic ranking was so improved that his small scholarship of four rupees [about 21p today], had been increased to ten rupees which he dutifully turned over to Lakshimidas, the head of the family. In his final year of high school, he was doing even better. He spent much of his time preparing for the college matriculation examinations, tests which required a solid command of written and spoken English which Mohandas lacked since he had learned his high school English from Indian teachers. These teachers, themselves, were markedly deficient in the subject.

None of this mattered to Kasturbai. The kind of learning her husband was acquiring was far less important to her than the kind of man he was becoming. Mohan seemed increasingly sure of himself. His gawky awkwardness was giving way to an alert self-awareness; his quickness of movement appeared to be fuelled by some inexhaustible store of energy. His shyness remained, but now he seemed rooted more in deliberation than in diffidence. Mohan, in short, was growing up. That pleased her. One other thing was clear: he was still in love with her, still eager for her embraces. But Kasturbai, perceptive as always, sensed that she was no longer the be-all and end-all of her husband's thoughts and endeavours. For reasons she could not explain, that pleased her, too.

In November, 1887, shortly after his 18th birthday, Mohandas confidently travelled alone by bullock-cart to Ahmadabad, the largest city in the Kathiawar region, to take the matriculation examinations. He managed to pass, without much distinction, but still doing better than most: 2,200 of the 3,000 students who took the examinations failed. He applied for admission to Samaldas College in the princely state of Bhavnagar, some 90 miles southeast of Rajkot. Samaldas was a small, new college chosen by the family in preference to Bombay University because it was closer to home and less costly. Admitted for the term beginning in January of 1888, Mohan set off for a new life; this time travelling part way by camel-cart and part way by train. In Bhavnagar, in rented lodgings, he lived alone for the first time in his life.

Before leaving for college, Mohan learned that Kasturbai was pregnant again. During her second pregnancy, Kasturbai tried to keep her hopes and fears in balance. She accompanied her mother-in-law to the temple almost daily to pray for the birth of a healthy child — if possible, a son. She missed Mohan, thought of him every day, but she was not lonely. Her oldest sister-in-law Nandkunwarba was pregnant also, and the two developed a closeness they had not known previously. That spring Nandkunwarba and Lakshimidas became parents of their first child, a daughter. The family celebrated with restraint — they were all still awaiting the arrival of a Gandhi son and heir.

The months passed but not quickly enough for Mohan. He had realised almost from the day of his arrival at Samaldas College that he was floundering. He understood little that was said in classes. Lessons were conducted in English; his marks were abominable; he was fighting loneliness, frustration, and an oppressive awareness that he was soon to assume the responsibilities of parenthood. When his first term ended in May, he quit college and went home to Kasturbai determined never to return to Samaldas College.

With the baby due soon Kasturbai was pleased to have him home again. This time there had been no talk of her going to her parents' home in Porbandar for the birth — perhaps fearing the journey would be too difficult. In any case, Kasturbai was thankful. The thought of having Mohan on hand to greet their newborn and join in all the celebrations took away the last of her foreboding.

But his return to Rajkot had plunged the rest of the family into crisis. Their plans for the future were now in jeopardy. The family consulted Mavji Dave, an old friend of Karamchand who, since the dewan's death, had become the family's most trusted adviser. A learned Brahmin, in tune with the times, Mavji Dave made a startling suggestion: Mohan must go to England to study law.

Such an idea would never have occurred to anyone in the Gandhi family. Sending Mohan to Bhavnagar, barely 100 miles away, had been a financial strain. How could they even think of England? Apart from the expense involved, a member of an orthodox Hindu family could not dream of crossing the ocean and being polluted by an alien society and its strange culture. But Mavji Dave, a pragmatist, reminded the family of their lofty aspirations for the youngest Gandhi brother, and assured them that the study of English law was the surest route to high office in British-ruled India.

"Think of that barrister, who has just come back from England," he said. "He could have the dewan's post for the asking." Mavji Dave spoke of his own son, recently returned from three years of study at the Inns of Court in London where all students seeking admittance to the English bar were trained. He said Indian students were finding the course there not too difficult. His son could give Mohan advice and notes of introduction.

Mohan wondered if he could ever live up to his family's expectations. He found the prospect of law studies in England instantly irresistible, an answer to all his problems. The rest of the family acknowledged the value of English education, but they reacted cautiously. Lakshimidas and Karsandas wondered where they would ever find the four or five thousand rupees needed, according to Mavji Dave, for three years of study in England. Putliba, who had heard that young Indians in London were tempted to drink wine, eat meat, smoke cigars, and consort with strange women, worried about the religious risks involved in allowing a young man to go abroad alone. To Kasturbai, who had no notion of just where England was, the entire idea was incomprehensible. Besides, her mind was elsewhere.

The debates about Mohan's future were still unresolved on the day Kasturbai went into labour. The family waited anxiously for the delivery. This time all went well. When Kasturbai gave birth to a healthy baby boy, the entire household rejoiced. Relatives and friends were notified, feasts were prepared, gifts presented, sweets distributed. Six days after the baby's birth, after performing the prescribed purification rites, Kasturbai emerged from the birthing room for the observance of a solemn religious ritual. According to Hindu belief, the Lord writes down a child's destiny on the sixth day of life. A name given to the infant on that day helps the Lord identify the child.

The son born to Kasturbai and Mohandas was given the name of Harilal which means "the Son of God".

Important as these events were to Kasturbai, they provided only a momentary diversion from worry for the rest of the family — and particularly for Mohandas. In the weeks following Harilal's birth, his mother struggled with her religious misgivings about sending a son to England, Mohandas and his brothers feverishly sought to raise funds for the trip. His mood alternated between elation and depression.

Mohan could persuade his mother Putliba to consent, but would he be able to convince Mr. Frederick Lely, the British political agent and advisor to the Rana of Porbandar, to grant him a scholarship?

Mr. Lely was aware of the Gandhi family's estimable record of civic service to the state of Porbandar, and might reasonably be expected to grant a state scholarship to Mohan. It was surely within his power to do so. In each of British India's more than six hundred princely states the Hindu or Muslim rulers were entitled to retain their wealth and their thrones, only if they accepted the "advice" of a British political agent or resident — officials such as Frederick Lely in Porbandar. Actually, the British political agents were the *de facto* rulers of the princely states.

With high hopes, Mohan went by appointment to Mr. Lely's residence to present his cause. It was his first personal encounter with British officialdom. Upon approaching Mr. Lely, he bowed politely as Indians would to an elder, palms together. But, even before he could explain the reason for his visit he was curtly interrupted. "No help can be given to you now," Mr. Lely declared, murmuring something about financial aid for study in England being available only to those who had already earned a college degree.

With that, Mr. Lely turned his attention to weightier matters, unaware, as the British historian Geoffrey Ashe put it, "that he had just stood face to face with the ruin of the Empire."

This ignominious dismissal left Mohan more determined than ever to go to England. On his return to Rajkot, he and his brothers redoubled their efforts to find 5,000 rupees somewhere, anywhere. Mohan wrote to distant cousins requesting money. One or two indicated they might help, but reneged on their promises when caste leaders objected. Lakshimidas went to local officials asking for assistance on his brother's behalf. The British political agent in Rajkot, a Colonel Watson, offered nothing more than a letter of introduction to someone in England. The local ruling prince, the Thakore of Rajkot, presented Mohan with a signed photograph of himself. Even Sheik Mehtab, as friend and former schoolmate of both Karsandas and Mohan, was recruited into the fund-raising campaign; he wrote a letter to one of his own cousins asking for a loan for Mohan — to no avail.

There remained one other possibility. Mohan suggested the family mortgage Kasturbai's jewellery. A woman's jewels were her property.

Kasturbai was pained by the suggestion not so much because she was attached to her jewels but because secretly she dreaded the separation. She feared that she would lose her husband to western culture. She also knew going to England was something he considered very important. She resolved to bear whatever came without complaint.

Putliba relented only after consulting a Jain monk Becharji Swami, another trusted family friend and now Putliba's main spiritual adviser. He suggested that Mohan make a solemn vow to his mother in his presence that he would not touch wine, women, or meat while he was away. Putliba believed in vows, and she believed in her son. He could go now, with her blessings.

On August 10, 1888, friends and relatives gathered at the Gandhi home in Rajkot to honour Mohandas as he set out for Bombay. He was accompanied by his brother Lakshimidas who was safeguarding the passage money. Several years later, writing for an obscure English journal, *The Vegetarian*, Mohandas depicted this emotion-filled occasion:

"My mother was hiding her eyes, full of tears, in her hands, but her sobbing was clearly heard. I was among a circle of some fifty friends. If I wept, they would think me too weak; perhaps they would not allow me to go to England. Therefore I did not weep, even though my heart was breaking. Last, but not least, came the leave-taking with my wife, it would be contrary to custom for me to see or talk to her in the presence of friends. So I had to see her in a separate room. She, of course, had begun sobbing long before I went to her and stood like a dumb statue for a moment. I kissed her, and she said, 'Don't go.' What followed I need not describe."

Lakshimidas had planned to book passage for Mohan on a voyage leaving for England in August, but on arriving in Bombay, where they stayed in the home of their sister Raliatben and her husband, they heard that a ship had recently gone down in stormy seas. Already uneasy about ocean travel, Lakshimidas accepted the advice of knowledgeable travellers that Mohan's departure should be delayed a few weeks until the rough monsoon seas had calmed. Since he could not remain away from his work that long, Lakshimidas left Mohan in Bombay with Raliatben and her husband Vrandavandas, to whom he also entrusted the passage money.

No sooner had Lakshimidas departed than word came from the Modh Vania caste elders in Bombay that the council, headed by a distant relative of the Gandhis, disapproved of Mohan's trip. No Modh Vania member had ever crossed the "black waters" to England, and none could go there without compromising their religion. Summoned to appear before the council, Mohan somehow mustered the courage to object. "I have already promised my mother to abstain from the things you fear most. I am sure my vows will keep me safe."

The council was unconvinced. But Mohan, in one of the first of his many eventual refusals to submit to the irrational exercise of authority, held firm. He would not agree to cancel his plans.

The head of the council then pronounced judgment: "This boy shall be treated as an outcast from today. Whoever helps him or goes to see him off at the dock shall be punished."

Mohan was excommunicated! The edict would affect his entire family, but the most immediate effect was on his brother-in-law Vrandavandas. For fear that he too would lose caste, Raliatben's husband refused to turn over the passage money to Mohan — even after receiving a letter from the faithful Lakshimidas authorising him to do so. Mohan himself resolved this final impasse. He borrowed passage money from a friend who could later be repaid by Vrandavandas. In that way, Vrandavandas could truthfully claim not to have helped his brother-in-law.

On September 4, 1888, Mohandas Gandhi boarded the S.S. *Clyde* in Bombay and sailed for England. Westward across the Arabian Sea, up through the Red Sea, the Suez Canal into the Mediterranean Sea, then to the straits of Gibraltar, and northward on the Atlantic Ocean to the English Channel — the voyage would take seven weeks.

In Rajkot, Kasturbai Gandhi began a long and lonely vigil that would last for three years.

# 5

Her husband's expulsion from his Modh Vania caste brought wrenching changes to Kasturbai's life. As Mohan's immediate family, she and Harilal were included in his excommunication ban. It was as if she had suddenly been set adrift in an ocean.

To help fill the void created by Mohan's absence, and make the long months pass more quickly, Kasturbai had counted on taking her little son to Porbandar for regular visits with his maternal grandparents. But since the Kapadia family was also Modh Vania, she and Harilal were, in effect, disobeying caste injunctions whenever they visited her parents in Porbandar.

Her nights were long and lonely. Thanks to little Harilal, her days were full and sweet.

From today's perspective, when I examine the Hindu culture of that time, I cannot help but note how many facets of that culture were reflected in their later endeavours in reshaping the world in which they lived. Bapu and Ba boldly challenged certain accepted beliefs and outworn customs of their Hindu heritage. But they also found creative new uses and powerful new meanings for many other ancient practices of Hinduism. That, I believe, may be the ultimate measure of their success and effectiveness as reformers. How natural was Bapu's lifelong concern about the minutest details of day-to-day living: food, clothing, cleanliness, health care? How inevitable was his concern for diet as political testimony? How inescapable his dedication to fasting as a moral enterprise? How valid was his emphasis on the self-reliance achieved through such household activities as spinning and weaving, and how ingenious was his transformation of these everyday tasks into declarations of independence?

Above all, how crucial was Ba's alliance with him in these matters? Her active participation in her husband's experiments came gradually, but it grew steadily. It was always an authentic expression of her own beliefs and experiences, her own sensibilities.

In the end Ba was able to translate his teachings as no one else could; into a simple, sometimes silent, always straightforward message that reached the minds and touched the souls of untold millions of women. Through Ba, women in the remotest villages of India learned that they too could be an integral part of their nation's struggle for self-determination.

Putliba Gandhi, however, was no ordinary widow, and her family was no ordinary family. By her very presence she still commanded love and respect. Her position in the household had remained unchanged, even after her oldest son Lakshimidas succeeded her husband as head of the joint family. Putliba participated with her sons in all family decisions. Her daughters-in-law still looked to her for guidance in housekeeping duties.

Kasturbai found particular comfort in her relationship with Putliba; there was an empathy between them. Though not a widow, as such, Kasturbai was without a husband. She also was aware of a great void in her life during the years Mohan was away. She knew that her mother-in-law missed Mohan too. Putliba often remarked on how the lively, mischievous little boy, Harilal, reminded her of Mohan at the same age. There was so much to learn about being a mother, and so much she had to teach Harilal.

As the months passed, Kasturbai became ever more conscious of substantial changes in the Gandhi family's financial circumstances. When Karamchand was Prime Minister, he had kept the house filled with visitors. After his death, the entertaining had stopped. Kasturbai's brothers-in-law found it difficult to earn the money needed to maintain the household in accustomed comfort. Now there were still more mouths to feed. During the years Mohandas was in London, a second daughter was born to Nandkunwar and Lakshimidas, and Ganga and Karsandas became the parents of a baby girl. Mohandas' expenses were higher than expected. In the end, his three years in London would cost more than twice the original estimates, sending the family further into debt.

Kasturbai was acutely aware that she and Harilal were as dependent on her brothers-in-law as were their own wives and children. Before long, she found herself trying to make whatever small savings she could.

She had to forget the ways of her comfortable girlhood. New clothes were out of the question. She could borrow a sari from her sisters-in-law if she wanted to give some variety to older clothes. In any case, without her wedding jewels, she could not dress as elegantly as she once had. Kasturbai also tried to cut down on her intake of food, following the example of Putliba who had always insisted on being the last in the family to take food. Sometimes when there were unexpected guests, she ate just cooked rice and milk. Kasturbai decided as long as there was plenty for Harilal to eat, she could do with less.

Her only indulgence was making sweets to send to Mohan in London. Made with wheat flour, molasses and clarified butter, golpapadi was one of the few confections that could survive the long ocean voyage to England. Mohan had a special fondness for golpapadi.

To Kasturbai, England remained a mysterious unknown territory — a land of myth and fantasy. It was difficult for her to place Mohan in that landscape and to picture in her mind what he was doing, where he was living, and whom he was seeing. Mail in India of that period was never private. In this case it could not be since Ba could not read. This hardship was, we are sure, the hardest for her to bear. It is surely the most difficult for us to fathom.

Mohan's letters were mostly addressed to his brother Lakshimidas. The only news of Mohan that filtered down to Kasturbai was conveyed to her by her sister-in-law, titbits of information Nandkunwar gleaned from Lakshimidas.

Sometime during Mohan's second year away from home, he sent his family a photograph of himself. When Putliba showed the portrait to Kasturbai, she was amazed and bewildered. Could that be her Indian husband, pictured in half-profile, unturbaned, wearing the dark European-style suit, the white shirt with stiff wing collar, the bow tie, slightly askew? Could that strange, grave-faced young man with the deep-set eyes, the full sensuous lips, and the sleek black hair so meticulously combed and parted, be Mohan the father of little Harilal? It was as if she had never seen him before. Then she noticed the familiar protruding right ear and was oddly comforted. Yes, it was her Mohan. But from then on, each time she looked at the photograph, she thought about a day to come when she and her husband would meet again. Would she know him then?

The shy, eager student named Mohandas Gandhi, 19 years of age, disembarked at Southampton in the autumn of 1888. He was dressed in Bombay's best which had been chosen for the occasion. Like a true innocent abroad, he soon discovered, to his mortification, that he was possibly the only man in England on that chilly autumn day who was wearing a white flannel suit. It was the first of many shocks he would suffer in his encounters with an exotic new culture.

The knowledgeable, stylishly attired barrister named Mohandas Gandhi who sailed for home three years later nearly 22 years of age in the summer of 1891, was a man of many parts. An accomplished scholar, he had mastered Latin and French, and earned a college degree. A professional man, he had completed law studies, been called to the bar, and was enrolled in the High Court. A man of the world, he was a reasonably competent bridge player, and had received instruction in social dancing, violin playing, and public speaking. A seasoned traveller, he had visited the Great Exhibition in Paris where he had passed judgement on its greatest wonder, the Eiffel Tower. "I do not know what purpose it serves," he wrote. "It was the toy of the Exhibition."

Kasturbai's husband obviously underwent some remarkable changes during his three years overseas. That the outer Mohan changed more than the inner Mohan was not so immediately apparent. But what we find most significant when we review the record of my grandfather's years in London is that the transformations were, for the most part, wrought by his own will, through his own initiative, and with an outpouring of effort, energy, and perseverance that was truly extraordinary.

The first changes were superficial — alterations of style, appearance, and deportment made during his early months abroad. On his first day in London, Mohan was greeted by Dr. P. J. Mehta, a family acquaintance from Bombay and an experienced expatriate. Dr. Mehta smiled at the sight of the white flannels, but he frowned when a curious Mohan reached out to stroke the smooth glossy fur of the top hat he was wearing. The good doctor proceeded to outline some of the strange rules of European etiquette that every self-respecting young Indian in London had to learn.

"Do not touch other people's things," Dr. Mehta said. "Do not ask questions as we do in India on first acquaintance. Do not talk loudly. Never address people as 'Sir' while speaking to them, as we do in India; only servants and subordinates address their masters that way."

Once settled in suitable lodgings in West Kensington, and enrolled for his law studies at the Inner Temple — of the four Inns of Court it was the one favoured by most Indian students — the ever-inquiring Mohan was keen to learn more about the social graces. He undertook what he later described as "the all-too-impossible task of becoming an English gentleman." At considerable expense, he bought new clothes, including a top hat, an evening suit made in Bond Street, a morning coat, a double-breasted waistcoat and dark striped trousers, silk shirts and ties, patent leather shoes with spats, leather gloves, and a silver-mounted walking stick. He spent hours before a mirror, combing and parting his unruly hair, and teaching himself to tie a cravat. He even wrote home and asked his "good and noble-hearted brother" to send him a double gold watch-chain. Lakshimidas obliged.

Then came private instruction in ballroom dancing, violin lessons and tutoring in elocution to fit into English society.

Within a few months, however, came the sobering realisation that he was rapidly depleting funds earmarked for his legal (not his social) education. Remembering his family responsibilities, Mohan asked himself (as in the case of the Eiffel Tower) just what purpose was being served. What use would these accomplishments be back home in India? Retrenchment began. He cancelled the lessons and sold the violin he had bought; but he was too practical-minded to discard his new clothes.

He left the boarding house and moved into less costly rented rooms where he prepared his own economical meals which featured large quantities of oatmeal porridge and hot cocoa. To save money, he began walking about London. Thus began my grandfather's enthusiasm for walking very fast — a habit which would persist for a lifetime. I still recall how I had to scurry to keep up with him when I visited India as a boy. As a self-imposed curb against any further splurging, he kept scrupulous accounts. He took time each night to list every farthing spent during the day, even minuscule expenditures for postage stamps, shoelaces, and the like. Meticulous bookkeeping also became habitual. In later years my grandfather handled public funds with such accuracy and economy that accounts of the movements he led often showed a surplus balance. Finally, he turned his full attention to serious education.

In Mohan's case, such education continued to include a good deal more than what he was learning in his law studies at the Inner Temple. To improve his English, he spent an hour each day reading the *Times* and the *Daily Telegraph*. Still mindful of his dismissal by Mr. Lely, the British resident in Porbandar, for lack of a college diploma, Mohan enrolled in private tutorial classes where he learned French and Latin and gained enough knowledge of the sciences to earn his bachelor's degree by passing the difficult London Matriculation Examination (on his second try) in June of 1890. All the while, he was keeping up with the regular curriculum of study at the Inner Temple, where he used his newly-acquired skills in languages to read the entire book on Roman Law in Latin. Few students were so conscientious. Most relied entirely on "cramming" notes to prepare for final examinations, a practice Mohan considered fraudulent. Besides, he had invested good money in the textbook.

As if all this were not enough, Mohandas was also getting what may have been, for him, the most consequential kind of education England then had to offer. It was an education both religious and political in nature, one that allowed him to measure values of his own ancient Eastern culture against the most socially-advanced Western thought.

It began serendipitously four or five months after he arrived in England, when he was struggling hard to keep his sworn vow to avoid meat. One day, while walking along Farringdon Street not far from the Inner Temple, a somewhat homesick and very hungry Mohandas stumbled upon one of the few vegetarian restaurants then in existence in central London, and certainly the first he had seen. There he enjoyed his first satisfying meal since leaving India. And there he made his first contact with members of the Vegetarian Society, a small band of English freethinkers bent on re-evaluating all the settled norms of Victorian society — like the Jains or Vaishnavas of India, these men and women were opposed to the killing of animals for food. As opposed, indeed, as Putliba or Kasturbai.

That restaurant, The Central, soon became Mohandas' regular eating place — his club, his bookstore. The people he met there were a part of the worldwide group of reformers who extolled the economic as well as the health benefits of vegetarianism, and declared it to be the only humane and morally defensible diet for all of humankind. He became a true convert; or, as he later described it, a "vegetarian by choice." He attended their conferences, wrote for their publications (an article about India appearing in *The Vegetarian* was his first published writing), and was elected to their executive committee, even though he still became nervous and tongue-tied whenever he rose to speak in meetings.

The Theosophists* in their assessment of the world's religions, were especially drawn to Hinduism. Two theosophist vegetarians, surprised at Mohandas' admission that he had never read the *Bhagavad Gita* either in the original Sanskrit or in a Gujarati translation, asked him to join them in studying *The Song Celestial*, an English translation of the classic Hindu epic by Sir Edwin Arnold who was already known to Mohandas as a distinguished fellow member of the Vegetarian Society. This introduction to one of the great sacred scriptures of his own religion moved Mohandas deeply.

---

* A group founded in 1875, derived from the beliefs of Brahmanism and Buddhism, but which denied the existence of personal gods.

His religious curiosity aroused, Mohandas read further. He learned about the life of the Prophet Mohammed, spiritual hero to millions of his Muslim countrymen. What impressed Mohandas, even more than the stories of the Prophet's bravery, were the accounts of his simplicity, his austerity — how Prophet Mohammed fasted, mended his own shoes, patched his own cloak. During this same period, at the urging of a Christian vegetarian, Mohandas was reading the Bible for the first time. He plodded through the Old Testament, disliking especially the Book of Numbers. But the New Testament made a lasting impression on him — especially the "Sermon on the Mount" in which he heard an echo of the Hindu teaching on the virtues of renunciation. Its message of turning the other cheek, not resisting evil, also called to mind some familiar lines of Gujarati poetry he had memorised as a child, an oft-quoted poem which concluded:

...the truly noble know all men as one,
And return with gladness good for evil done.

Mohandas Gandhi, a young man in pursuit of his destiny, seemed to be rediscovering India in England.

India, of course, and those who were waiting for him there, had never been far from his thoughts. Awareness of his family was a constant burden. Mohandas wondered if he would be able to fulfill all their expectations when he returned home.

# 6

E arlier that year, in Rajkot, the Gandhi family had faced a tragedy and made a decision.

Suddenly, unexpectedly, in the spring of 1891, Putliba Gandhi became ill. Within days, she was dead. The question arose: *should Mohandas be told?* Mohandas was devoted to Putliba, closer to her than any of her other children. Would any good be served by notifying him of her death while he was in the midst of preparing for his final law examinations? It seemed best to wait. Time enough to give Mohandas the painful news after he returned to India.

Kasturbai agreed with the decision made by the family. She had been longing for the moment she would see her husband again, dreaming of the day little Harilal could be with the father he had never had a chance to know. But now, remembering how stricken Mohandas had been at the time of his father's death, she worried about his reaction to his mother's death and to receiving the news so abruptly at the moment of his homecoming.

Kasturbai herself knew how irreplaceable Putliba's love and guidance was. Under her mother-in-law's wing she had felt secure and protected, confident and capable. Without Putliba she was bereft, overwhelmed by sorrow and uncertainty. Wouldn't Mohandas feel the same? Everyone was expecting so much of him. But would he be able, after so sad a homecoming, to take hold and take charge of a family that was rapidly crumbling?

All Kasturbai could do was to wait patiently for his return. Wait and hope, and prepare to welcome him back into the household in Rajkot.

The family was aware that highly educated young men returning from England with Western mannerisms and dress usually wanted to make changes in the ancient Indian atmosphere of their own households. Anticipating this, Lakshimidas had instructed his wife Nandkunwarben to prepare for Mohandas' return by purchasing English crockery and fine chinaware to replace the brass *thalis* (plates) and *vadkas* (bowls), on which the family meals were customarily served. He also bought chairs so they could all eat at a table, instead of sitting on floors, Indian fashion.

When the S.S. *Assam* steamed into Bombay's magnificent deepwater harbour in mid-August, Lakshimidas was waiting on the dock at Ballard Pier. He had travelled alone from Rajkot to meet Mohandas, but as he watched the disembarking passengers, he almost failed to recognise his young, westernised brother in his English outfit. His joy at seeing Mohandas, his pride in his brother's newly acquired prestige as a barrister was tinged with a slight apprehension.

"Will he ever be able to fit into our eastern way of life?" Lakshimidas asked himself as he moved forward to greet Mohandas.

"How is Mother?" Mohandas inquired at once. But Lakshimidas parried the question, and explained that their friend, Dr. P. J. Mehta, who had been the first to welcome Mohandas to London, was now back in Bombay and had invited them to stay with him for a few days before returning to Rajkot.

That evening Mohandas pursued the question again: "How is Mother?" Lakshimidas knew that he could not ignore the question any longer and broke the sad news as gently as he could.

Writing in his autobiography years later, my grandfather still had difficulty describing the "severe shock" of that moment. "I must not dwell upon it," he wrote. After acknowledging that his sorrow was even greater than at the time of his father's death, he added: "But I did not give myself up to any wild expression of grief. ... I took to life just as though nothing had happened."

Lakshimidas suggested that they delay their return to Rajkot — it had been Putliba's last wish that Mohandas seek readmission into the Modh Vania caste, Lakshimidas said. For three years they had lived with the ban without complaint, but the problem had taken on new import, new reality at the time of Putliba's death. Her funeral ceremony had been curtailed, certain rituals were omitted, some old friends did not attend — much to the dismay of all who loved her. If that could happen to one so faultless as Putliba, what hope was there for the rest of them? The family also worried that Mohandas' continued excommunication could cloud his future as a lawyer. Lakshimidas had recently gone to the caste elders in Rajkot for advice, and he now described to his younger brother the procedures he must follow to gain expiation for his forbidden foreign sojourn. Mohandas agreed to comply with the elders' recommendations, even though caste restrictions were no longer a matter of personal concern for him, and never would be again. He would seek readmission for the sake of his family and to honour his mother, not because of any desire to redeem himself.

Leaving Bombay, Lakshimidas and Mohandas set out on a penitential pilgrimage to Nasik, a holy place about a hundred miles to the north-east. There, before invited witnesses, Mohandas dutifully immersed himself in the sacred waters of the Godavari River for a propitiatory bath. From Nasik, they travelled on to Rajkot for the next step in his rehabilitation, a ceremonial dinner arranged by Lakshimidas and Karsandas. Acting on behalf of their younger brother, they had reserved a hall, ordered food prepared, and invited all Rajkot caste elders to attend. Most had accepted. As a further act of penance, Mohandas himself stripped to the waist and served the dinner to the guests. Though this seemed like nonsense to him, Mohandas was coaxed by his brothers to carry out his part in the ceremony. When the Rajkot elders accepted food from him, it signalled the end of his excommunication.

Kasturbai had counted the hours, waiting anxiously for her first glimpse of her husband. But their reunion, when at last it came, was initially awkward and restrained.

She and Mohandas were both 22; they had not seen each other for almost three years. Much had happened in that period. She needed time to become reacquainted with this stranger of a husband. He looked, dressed, even spoke, so differently from the Mohandas she remembered. He had changed in ways she could not comprehend.

Kasturbai had matured into a beautiful woman. Mohandas realised that at once. He was captivated by his wife's beauty — as he had always been. Perhaps, after three long years of vigilant self-restraint, three years of monitoring all his sexual desires, even his thoughts, he was more attracted to her than ever before.

How could he have forgotten how lovely Kasturbai was? How enchanting she was to behold! Her smooth skin, her large eyes framed by thick lashes, her tiny figure, shapely and supple as ever under the soft folds of her bright-coloured sari! How beguiling it was to watch her comb her long, gleaming black hair; to study the simple grace of her movements; to hear, at her every step, the musical tinkle of the tiny

**47**

silver bells that encircled her slender bare ankles. Any man would envy him, enjoying the loving devotion of this proud and beautiful creature. After the austere and lonely years abroad, he deserved a season of self-indulgence at home before facing up to the responsibilities awaiting him. In his wife's embrace Mohandas could forget all else.

For Kasturbai, too, the years of yearning were over — years of going to bed alone night after night. Only now that Mohandas was home again did she realise how great her loneliness had been. It was reassuring to know that England had not changed him, at least in one respect. He still found her desirable. She was delighted, too, at the pleasure Mohandas took in their son: playing and joking with Harilal, effortlessly winning the little boy's devotion as well as other children in the household.

For the next few weeks the whole family seemed joyful and carefree — relieved of pent-up tensions. But after a time, Mohandas began to grow restive. He had welcomed the Western touches the family had provided but now declared this was not enough. He bought English cocoa and oatmeal and asked that porridge be served for breakfast. He told Kasturbai that he had decided their son Harilal would henceforth be brought up like an English child: hardy and tough — as all the Gandhi children should be. He bought shoes for the boys and insisted that they no longer go barefoot. He took the children on long walks into the countryside. He made up a schedule of exercises, and conducted calisthenics classes for them every morning.

Kasturbai said nothing. If he wanted it that way there was no reason for her to protest. In fact, she and her sisters-in-law, Nandkunwarben and Gangaben, were happy to have him take the children off their hands for part of the time each day.

But Mohandas' zeal for giving instruction grew, and it soon extended to Kasturbai. So once again, to Kasturbai's dismay, the nightly reading lessons began. But once again, to Mohandas' dismay, his wife displayed absolutely no interest in the project. Worse still, she seemed to have no understanding of why he considered it so important. Kasturbai's failure to comprehend the dignity of his profession rankled even more than her failure to appreciate his magnanimous aspirations for her.

Mohandas persisted. Kasturbai resisted. And the days passed. Then other familiar and distressing patterns began to emerge. Mohandas' unfounded jealousies, unfair suspicions, unjust accusations. Kasturbai's repeated and unequivocal denials.

Kasturbai was alarmed. Mohandas had not changed at all. They seemed to be picking up the threads of life where they left off years ago, when he was a mere schoolboy. But now he was a barrister. Surely a barrister had better ways to spend his time than teaching his wife to read and write, or keeping track of her every move, or accusing her of indiscreet acts she had neither the desire nor the opportunity to commit.

The whole family was concerned about Mohandas. Kasturbai could tell from her talks with her sisters-in-law. Lakshimidas and Karsandas had planned to support Mohandas financially only as long as he was a student. Now that he had brought his costly English education back to India, they expected him to use it, and assume responsibility for a major part of the family expenses. This had become a matter of increasing urgency because Lakshimidas, the family's principal breadwinner, had suffered a setback in his own career.

While Mohandas was in London, Lakshimidas had been appointed, through the influence of his Uncle Tulsidas, to an undemanding but remunerative position as secretary to the crown prince of Porbandar. Lakshimidas' duties had required only occasional trips to Porbandar. His wages had greatly enhanced the family income, and an even more important post seemed to be in prospect when the young prince became the Rana. As it turned out, the heir to Porbandar's throne was a profligate who, unbeknown to Lakshimidas, had made off with some of the crown jewels from the state treasury. There were questions about this by the new British political agent who had recently arrived in Porbandar. It was a British resident's duty to prevent local royalty from converting state moneys into private wealth. The young crown prince claimed he had acted on the advice of his secretary. As a result, Lakshimidas had lost the job, the income, and the promise of a better position to come.

Kasturbai knew all about these worries. Yet Mohandas seemed totally oblivious and unaware of any household problems and seemed unconcerned about his obligations to his brothers. He had made no move to seek a suitable appointment, or find a well-paying position or earn any money whatsoever. All his attention was focused on her: Kasturbai. Kasturbai knew the strength of the attraction Mohandas felt for her, but she now wondered if she didn't also serve as a distraction for her husband. Was he seeking diversion by both their quarrels and lovemaking and ignoring matters of far greater consequence? She realised that the time had come for her to speak up.

One night, in the privacy of their own bedroom, she confronted Mohandas. She reminded him of his debt to his brothers and spoke about the on-going household expenditures. These costs, she pointed out, had increased with their Western innovations, and the changes he had insisted upon. What Lakshimidas needed now was help from him.

Kasturbai had never expressed her opinions so openly before. By the time she finished, Mohandas was indignant — indignant and shaken.

The next day, without explanation, Mohandas sent Kasturbai off on the train with Harilal to visit her parents in Porbandar.

"Perhaps only a Hindu wife would tolerate such hardships," my grandfather wrote many years later, in discussing his relationship with my grandmother during the early decades of their marriage. "And that is why I have regarded women as an incarnation of tolerance. A servant wrongly suspected may throw up his job, a son in the case may leave his father's roof, and a friend may put an end to the friendship. The wife, if she suspects her husband, will keep quiet. If the husband suspects her, she is ruined. Where is she to go? And I can never forget or forgive myself for having driven my wife to that desperation."

I also admire my grandfather's forthright (and oft-repeated) admissions of his own offences as a jealous and domineering husband. But I believe his portrayal of my grandmother's reactions to this jealousy and domination may have been distorted by his urgency to condemn his own shortcomings. Indeed, we find that Bapu has done Ba a disservice in his autobiographical writings by his frequent depictions of her as ever meek and submissive. Such characterisations of Ba have been widely accepted and repeated by Gandhi biographers. But in my view she was never as spineless and long-suffering, as tolerant of abuse, as altogether helpless and desperate, as Bapu (and his biographers) would have us believe. That she may sometimes have appeared to be so was due more to the circumstances of her life than to the nature of her temperament.

I base this conclusion on my own memories and on the recollections of others who knew her well and on my grandfather's correspondence with the family. Speaking apparently from experience, he sometimes cautions against incurring Ba's displeasure. In a long letter written to my father from a South African prison in 1909, for example, Bapu advises 16-year-old Manilal, who was temporarily in charge of farm and family matters at Phoenix Settlement, on everything from household finances, to diet tips, to recommended readings, and counsels him to "cheerfully bear Ba's ill temper".

In truth, it was Kasturbai, not Mohandas, who had learned how to bear a spouse's ill temper, and to do so cheerfully. Certainly this must have been the case in that autumn of 1891 when she was "banished" to Porbandar shortly after Mohandas' return from England. To Kasturbai, the trip would have seemed like a holiday. She was eager to see her parents again and have them see their grandson. Visits had been difficult during the years of Mohandas' absence, but now, with the excommunication ban lifted there were no household complications. Travel between Rajkot and Porbandar was simpler now, too, since the railroad had come to Kathiawar. She had sensed that Mohandas' main problem was with himself, not her. A short vacation, a separation, would give him breathing space — time to think about his future, perhaps do something about it, and to get over his displeasure with her. She was confident he would insist on her early return, and all would be well.

Kasturbai was not surprised, therefore, when Mohandas sent for her within a month after her departure. (Or, as Mohandas reported in his autobiography, "I consented to receive her back only after I had made her thoroughly miserable.")

She and Harilal returned happily to Rajkot where she found, to her satisfaction that things had changed for the better. No more lessons, no more suspicions, no more quarrels, and only a new seriousness between them. And a new tenderness on Kasturbai's part, as she learned more of her husband's true worries and insecurities.

Mohandas confided his fears to Kasturbai one night, not long after her return from Porbandar. She listened attentively, though his explanations seemed addressed as much to himself as to her. He had now turned his full attention to getting started in his career, something he admitted he had been avoiding. He had explored the idea of starting a practice in Rajkot, but he felt he would be inviting ridicule if he did, and for good reason — in spite of his three years of study in England, he felt unqualified to practice law in India.

"Who will be fool enough to employ a person like me," Mohandas asked. "One who doesn't even have the knowledge of a law clerk?"

Although he was well versed in the Common Law, well read in Roman Law, he knew nothing whatsoever about Hindu and Muslim Law. A home-trained vakil, or law clerk, such as his brother Lakshimidas, was far more familiar with Indian law, yet he, as an English-educated barrister, would normally be expected to charge fees ten times as high as a vakil. That, he declared, would only add the sins of arrogance and fraud to his offence of ignorance.

Kasturbai consoled him as best she could and beseeched him to tell his brothers of his misgivings and seek their advice. He had done just that, he said. And then he disclosed his plan. He and Lakshimidas had agreed that he should go to Bombay for a time. There were already too many lawyers and not enough cases in small provincial towns like Rajkot and Porbandar. But in the city of Bombay there would be many opportunities. There he could study, become acquainted with Indian law, gain some much-needed court experience, even earn some fees. He would set up a household there, he said, but to save on expenses, Kasturbai and Harilal would have to stay in Rajkot for the time being. They might perhaps join him later.

Again, they were to be separated. But now Kasturbai fully understood why this was necessary. In Bombay, Mohandas could fulfill the family's dream and become a successful advocate.

A few weeks later, when she sent her husband off to the city to seek his fortune, Kasturbai gave him her good wishes. But she did not give him her news. Only when he was more settled, and when she was absolutely certain it was true, would she let him know that she was pregnant again.

For Mohandas, he was still feeling uprooted after the years in London, still unsure of his own abilities, still grief-stricken because of his mother's death, (and still guilt-ridden, it would seem) by a memory of the circumstances of his father's death. This was coupled with his inability to free himself from what he called the "shackles of lust" — the next six months of his life were bleaker than any he had ever known. In Bombay he found only discouragement and disenchantment.

He rented rooms and hired a cook — a man so incompetent that Mohandas ended up doing most of the cooking himself. He bought some law books, he studied the Civil Procedure Code and the Evidence Act, and every day he walked the several miles to and from the High Court where he observed the great and famous Bombay lawyers at work. But the court proceedings were so dull that he often fell asleep.

Meanwhile, his brothers were still paying all his expenses, his debts were mounting each month, and a letter from Lakshimidas had brought unexpected news. Kasturbai was expecting another child, my father, Manilal.

This was cause for rejoicing, of course, but it also increased Mohandas' crushing sense of responsibility. One more child, one more soul to look after. Now, more than ever, he must earn money. But the weeks passed, and Mohandas remained a briefless barrister. As a stopgap measure he applied for a part-time position teaching English at a boys' high school. The salary listed was only 75 rupees a month, but that was better than nothing. He did not get the job. The school, he was told, hired only graduates of Indian universities. His London Matriculation degree with Latin as his second language did not qualify him for a teaching post.

Then, at last, a petty court case came his way — and without his paying a commission to a tout. Mohandas proudly donned his barrister's wig and gown for the first time, and appeared for the defendant in a simple case in the Small Claims Court. But when he rose to cross-examine the plaintiff's witnesses, his old fear of public speaking overcame him. He could not think of a single question, could not utter a single word. A ripple of laughter ran through the courtroom. Humiliated, Mohandas sank into his chair. He advised his poor client to hire another lawyer, refunded the fee of 30 rupees paid in advance, and fled from court, resolving then and there to take no more cases until he had courage enough to conduct them (not until he found himself in South Africa would he find that courage).

Finally, the word came from Rajkot. Lakshimidas could no longer afford to pay Mohandas' expenses. He urged Mohandas to leave Bombay, return home, and try his luck in Kathiawar, even if it meant doing clerical work. Lakshimidas, himself a petty pleader, could give him some applications and memorials to write, to get him started.

With defeat looming large, Mohandas boarded the train, left the city, and returned to Rajkot to face a joyfully expectant Kasturbai.

The second son of Kasturbai and Mohandas Gandhi, was born in Rajkot on October 28, 1892 — an event I find noteworthy because this child (named Manilal), would grow up to become my father. Manilal's birth was celebrated with the customary religious festivities. Sweets were distributed; ceremonies performed; gifts received.

Kasturbai visited the temple to give thanks. The arrival of another healthy son was a good omen — a harbinger of better times.

All her concerns for her husband, all the anxieties she had felt over the past many months, were forgotten. Their life seemed to be settling into a comfortable pattern. Mohandas was home in Rajkot, he had opened his own office and was writing enough petitions and memorials for Lakshimidas and his vakil friends, drafting enough briefs for other barristers, to earn the 300-rupees-a-month income that had evaded him in Bombay. For Kasturbai this was success enough. She was no longer beholden to her in-laws. Harilal was lively as ever, Manilal was a calm and lovable baby, and she was content, happier than she had been for years.

But what was contentment for Kasturbai soon became frustration and disillusionment for Mohandas. An embarrassing altercation in the early spring of 1892 left him at odds with his brother, affronted by British officialdom, and chagrined to realise how ignorant he was of the ways of the colonists.

The incident occurred when Lakshimidas, still out of favour with the new British resident in Porbandar because of the crown prince's misdeeds, persuaded Mohandas to undertake a delicate mission.

Lakshimidas learned that Mohandas and this officer, a Mr. Charles Ollivant, had met socially in London once or twice under friendly and agreeable circumstances. As a British administrator on furlough from service to the Empire and about to take up new duties in Kathiawar, Mr. Ollivant had enjoyed conversing with a student from Rajkot. Now Lakshimidas, hoping to regain a place of influence in Porbandar, asked his younger brother to use his influence with his English friend.

Mohandas was reluctant. "It was a trifling friendship," he told Lakshimidas. "It should not be used for such purposes.

Lakshimidas disagreed. 'You do not know Kathiawar. Only influence counts here. It is not proper for you, a brother, to shirk your duty when you can clearly put in a good word about me to an officer you know."

This was his older brother's first request for help of any kind, and Mohandas did not have the heart to decline. Mohandas made the trip from Rajkot to Porbandar and presented himself once again as a supplicant at the door of the British resident.

Predictably, Mr. Ollivant was rude. When Mohandas, after mentioning their meeting in London, began to explain the purpose of his visit, the political agent interrupted him. "Surely you have not come here to abuse our acquaintance," he said.

Mohandas tried to continue, but Mr. Ollivant interrupted again. "Your brother is an intriguer," he barked out. "He can expect no more work from Porbandar. If he has anything to say to me let him apply through proper channels." He asked his caller to leave. "Please hear me out," Mohandas tried to protest But Mr. Ollivant called a servant and ordered him thrown out — bodily.

Shamed and outraged, Mohandas immediately wrote out a demand for an apology, threatening legal action if it were not forthcoming.

Ollivant's reply was curt and final. "You are at liberty to proceed as you wish." But in British India, as Mohandas well knew, the only court of appeals in a princely state such as Porbandar was, of course, the British resident.

Mohandas returned to Rajkot and told his older brother of this latest fiasco. Lakshimidas was grieved. But Mohandas remained aggrieved. He had been physically assaulted! English law should not permit such arrogant abuse of authority! He consulted other lawyers, wondering if he had any recourse. They advised him not to pursue the matter, to do so would mean his ruin. They said he was still fresh from England, still hot-blooded. He did not understand life in his own country. Such incidents were common, they told him. To get along in India, he must learn to pocket the insults of the British officers.

My grandmother knew of Grandfather's many disappointments and disillusionments. What was there to say? There clearly was no place for him in the petty politics of Kathiawar. He would never follow in his father's footsteps and become the dewan of Rajkot or Porbandar. Such a dream was no longer attainable, nor was it worth seeking. Even a ministership or a judgeship seemed unlikely for one as inept as he was at playing the local games of intrigue. And his Bombay experience had put his future as a barrister in question.

To Grandmother, to the family, to Mohandas himself, his career appeared to be ending before it began. His failure seemed complete.

# 7

The letter, unheralded and unsolicited, arrived in Rajkot in mid-March of 1893. It offered Mohandas instant escape from the professional doldrums, and prospective rescue from a financial quagmire. It brought Kasturbai new hopes — and new uncertainties.

The letter came from a longtime friend of the family, a prosperous Muslim merchant of Porbandar whose shipping and trading firm, Dada Abdullah & Company, flourished in South Africa where there was a sizeable population of Indians. They had heard of Mohandas and his qualifications, and felt the young Indian barrister could be useful to their firm, assisting their South African lawyers in a big case involving a claim of £40,000 against another Indian merchant in South Africa. The whole matter would take about a year for which Mohandas would receive a fee of £105. The firm would pay all his living expenses and provide a first-class, round-trip ticket to Durban, the chief port of the British Crown Colony of Natal.

Seasoned traveller that he had become, Mohandas was immediately intrigued by this chance to get away, to see a new part of the world, have new experiences. Of course, he knew even less about South African law than he did about Indian law. Also it was unclear whether Dada Abdullah & Company wanted to engage him as a qualified advocate or as a glorified clerk, and the fee was a modest one, even in those days. But this offer, coming when his morale was at the lowest ebb, seemed providential. He could not reject it.

Mohandas found it difficult to contemplate another parting with Kasturbai. He loved her dearly. The thought of leaving her once again to seek an uncertain future in an unfamiliar country gave him pause, and he said so. But, by way of consolation to them both, he added, "We are bound to meet again in a year."

To Mohandas' surprise, Kasturbai (more attuned to his aspirations and disappointments than he knew) was quickly convinced he should go, especially after he explained about his fee. With all his own expenses paid, the entire sum could go to Lakshimidas — £105, more than enough to cover all household expenses for her and their sons while he was away.

Kasturbai found comfort and reassurance in the thought of such financial security — even for just one year. It pained her that her husband, the most qualified of the Gandhi brothers, the one on whom the whole family had pinned its faith, had not yet made good in life, and she had lately begun to wonder if he ever would. Proud and self-reliant by nature, she had lived for too many years with a daily awareness of her dependence on her brothers-in-law, ever conscious of the hard times the family was facing, and of the fact that the debt Lakshimidas had incurred to send Mohandas to London was still unpaid. But Kasturbai was also optimistic by nature. She told herself that, given this new chance in this new and faraway place, Mohandas would at last succeed.

Kasturbai, with her two small sons, saw Mohandas off on the train to Bombay in mid-April of 1893, to set forth once again on the "black waters". This time he sailed southward, across the Indian Ocean to Natal. All her hopes went with him.

She kept her fears to herself.

When his ship arrived at the quay in Durban after a month at sea, Mohandas was on deck, standing at the rail. He inhaled the brisk autumn air, basked in the bright sunshine, and admired the city's wide, clean beaches, and its tree-lined boulevards. This was his first close-up view of the land where he would spend, all told, some 22 years. But his indelible first impression of South Africa on that day in May in 1893 had nothing to do with the fine climate and splendid scenery. What gripped Mohandas' attention, what brought him up short, was his instant awareness of the country's pervasive colour prejudice — a prejudice so blatantly visible that he could discern it from the deck of his ship before he even disembarked.

As he stood watching a crowd of Durban townspeople hurry up the gangway to greet arriving friends, Mohandas could not help but observe what he later described with admirable restraint as the "snobbishness" of white Europeans toward the darker-skinned people among them. Nothing Mohandas had experienced in India or in England had prepared him for the kind of gratuitous insults he was seeing and hearing.

At that moment, a tall, distinguished-looking Muslim stepped forward. It was Dada Abdullah himself, the firm's principal partner and most influential trader, come to welcome his new employee. But even as they exchanged greetings, Mohandas was stung to realise that Abdullah was one of the very Indians who had just been treated with such obvious contempt by the white South Africans. Never one to put up with indignities, however meek and docile he might appear, Mohandas fully expected his new employer to take offence, demand apologies then and there. Dada Abdullah hadn't even noticed the scorn or the taunts. He was obviously used to them. That disturbed Mohandas most of all.

In the weeks that followed, Mohandas learned more about the peculiarities of South Africa. His European-style attire set him apart from other Indians. An educated Indian barrister was regarded with curiosity by whites and non-whites alike. The lawsuit Mohandas was hired to work on would be conducted some 400 miles away in Pretoria, the capital of Transvaal.

Shortly after Mohandas' arrival in Durban, the firm's lawyer in Pretoria sent word that he needed Dada Abdullah's help in preparing the long-delayed lawsuit. Abdullah, busy with other affairs, dispatched his newly-hired barrister to represent him.

Mohandas boarded the train in Durban just before it left for the overnight trip to the Transvaal border where, since the South African railway system was still under construction, he would have to transfer to a stagecoach for the rest of the journey. A first-class ticket had been booked for him, and he was shown to his compartment. He settled into his seat, shuttered the windows, and brought out a book to read. It was cold and the night would be long.

When the train made its first stop at Pietermaritzburg, only some 50 miles from Durban, a white South African entered the compartment. At the sight of Mohandas he recoiled.

"You!" he barked. "What are you doing in here?"

Perplexed, Mohandas stuttered a reply, "Travelling to Pretoria."

"Don't you know you are not allowed in here? You must go to the van compartment reserved for blacks."

"But I have a first-class ticket," Mohandas said, pulling it out of his pocket to prove the point.

This seemed to enrage the white passenger. He stormed out of the coach, hut returned shortly with a railway official who also ordered Mohandas to move to the third-class van compartment.

Mohandas argued that he had been permitted aboard the first-class compartment in Durban, and he had every right to be there.

"I refuse to get out voluntarily."

Infuriated at such impertinence from a presumptuous "coolie", the two men summoned a constable, and together they pushed Mohandas out onto the train platform. They threw his luggage out after him, and the train steamed away into the night.

It was 9.00pm; no other trains were due until morning. There was nothing for Mohandas to do but follow along as his luggage was carted into Pietermartizburg's dark, unheated railway station.

During the long hours that followed, sitting huddled in that cold, unlit waiting room thousands of miles from home, too humiliated to confront the stationmaster and reclaim his luggage (which contained his overcoat), and more miserable than he had ever been before, Mohandas asked himself some fateful questions.

Should he abandon his mission, take the earliest train back to Durban and the next ship back to India? No. He could not give up — not again. A panoramic view of his past life became starkly visible — all the times he had failed, times he had disappointed his family. He thought of Kasturbai, bearing the brunt of those disappointments, but never turning her ire on him, always encouraging him when a new opportunity arose. He must now seize this opportunity — he was, after all, a man of action. He must stay in South Africa and fight prejudice.

It took Mohandas three more days to reach Pretoria. Along the way, his new resolve was tested time and again — and not found wanting. The iron had entered his soul.

In Pretoria, the firm's English lawyer, Mr. A. W. Baker, received Mohandas cordially and helped him find living quarters. Then he put him to work reviewing the complexities of Dada Abdullah's lawsuit and translating the correspondence, much of which was in Gujarati. Besides being an attorney, Mr. Baker was a devout Christian and lay preacher. In the succeeding months, he would spend many hours trying to convert Mohandas to Christianity. Although glad to meet and talk with others interested in religion, Mohandas would reach the same conclusion he had in England: he should not think of embracing another religion before he more fully understood his own.

Soon after arriving in Pretoria, Mohandas invited the city's entire Indian population to come together to discuss their problems. A large crowd showed up. Overcoming the shyness that had always left him tongue-tied, Mohandas gave what he later described as his first public speech.

His goal was to inform Indians of their rights, and inspire them to give voice to their grievances. He urged them to be honest and truthful in the business dealings; to be clean in their habits and sanitary in their living conditions; to forget their differences of religion, caste, class, and region; and to learn to speak English. Only after delivering this little homily on responsibilities did he turn to the question of rights. He suggested that they form a permanent association to document discrimination against Indians and present grievances to the Transvaal authorities.

However, his first order of business was Dada Abdullah's lawsuit. The defendant in the case, Tyeb Sheth, was not only Abdullah's cousin, but also his counterpart — he was the wealthiest and most influential Indian merchant in Pretoria and was one of the first to support Mohandas' efforts to organise and unite Pretoria's Indian population. The case, involving promissory notes, bookkeeping practices, and several fine points of law had remained unsettled for months. Even before leaving Durban, Mohandas had startled Abdullah by suggesting that an out-of-court settlement of his claim for damages might be a good solution for both plaintiff and defendant. Now, having met and talked with Tyeb Sheth, and conferred with the other attorneys, he saw that the facts favoured Abdullah. But he also realised that if the case dragged on, it could prove ruinous to both litigants. Only the lawyers would make money.

It took months of negotiations and reams of correspondence to convince both Dada Abdullah and Tyeb Sheth to go to arbitration. When they did, the decision favoured Abdullah — he was awarded £37,000, almost the full amount of his claim. But Mohandas took the process one step further. He saved Tyeb Sheth from bankruptcy (and certain ignominy in the Muslim community) by persuading Abdullah to accept payment in installments rather than the usual lump sum. This happy outcome restored goodwill between the relatives, and convinced Mohandas that a lawyer's true function was "to unite parties driven asunder."

With the lawsuit settled and his contract fulfilled, Mohandas returned to Durban in May of 1894, full of self-confidence and eager to book passage on the next ship home to India. Of late, he had been thinking of Kasturbai constantly. His vow of lifelong fidelity remained unbroken. He was longing to see her and his sons. But, again, fate took a hand.

On the day before he was to sail, Dada Abdullah honoured him with a large farewell party. Leading members of Natal's Indian community came to meet the young barrister who had done such good work in Pretoria. While waiting for lunch to be served, Mohandas picked up that morning's edition of the *Natal Mercury*, and his eye fell on a small news item buried at the bottom of an inside page under the caption "Indian Franchise". A bill had been introduced into the Natal Legislative Assembly to deprive Indians of their right to vote. What had happened in the Boer republics was now happening in Natal.

"Hello, what is this? Have you seen this news item?" he asked the friends who had gathered. He read the paragraph aloud.

Dada Abdullah, speaking for the group, said it made little sense to them. "We are businessmen," he explained. "We have little education. We buy the newspapers only to read the market rates." As for politics, "Our European attorneys are our eyes and ears."

But for several moments, he said nothing further. Tomorrow, he would be leaving. He was going home to India to make a living; to get ahead in his profession. He was going home to Kasturbai, to his sons, to his family. If he uttered a single word, he feared he would find himself more deeply involved than he wished to be in problems that were not his concern. Then he remembered the humiliations he had suffered simply because of his colour. He knew the Indian franchise matter was his concern. He could not remain silent.

"If this bill passes, it will be the first nail in our coffin," he said. "We will not be able to live here with self-respect."

"Well, then; what is your advice?" Dada Abdullah asked.

Before Mohandas could reply, someone from the back of the crowd shouted: "Cancel your departure and stay here, and we promise to fight under your direction." Another voice suggested that if he did, the community should pay his fees. Mohandas was moved.

"There can be no fees for public work," he protested, saying that if he was to stay, he would earn his living as a lawyer and help them without fee. But they would need considerable money, he said, and a great deal of manpower if they wanted to fight the government.

"The money and the manpower will be available," said Dada Abdullah. "Just lead us on."

With that, Mohandas' farewell party turned into a working committee to plan the first petition in the Indian franchise campaign.

For weeks, Kasturbai had been telling her sons that their father would soon be home. But when Mohandas' letter arrived announcing he would stay in South Africa for a while to help the Indian community oppose the unjust laws, she felt a mixture of relief and apprehension. Relief that, at last, her husband had found something he would do well.

She did not fully comprehend what all the trouble was about in South Africa, but she was glad the Indians in that strange land held Mohandas in high regard and looked to him for guidance — and that he would still be able to send money home. Apprehension because their separation would continue for — how long?

Kasturbai was more troubled by his absence than she cared to admit. Her misgivings were not for herself; she had long since grown accustomed to their constant partings and reunions. Though they had been married for some 11 years now, they had lived together a total of only about four years of that time. She could accept this ongoing separation from her husband, like all the others, as a way to help him prosper. But what of her sons? How were Harilal and Manilal being affected by Mohandas' frequent and lengthy disappearances from their lives? Were they to grow up thinking of him as a visitor to the Gandhi household?

Harilal remembered the games, the walks, and the songs this stranger had shared with him. But Harilal had spent less than two of his now six years of life with Mohandas. By emotional attachment no less than physical proximity, he was much closer to his ever-present uncles, particularly his Uncle Lakshimidas, than to his own father. And little Manilal, just six months old when Mohandas left, had no memory at all of his real father. Manilal was now in his second year; walking, talking, learning so fast, changing so much each day that Mohandas would not even recognise his son. Not now, nor on whatever future day he came back home.

Could time lost ever be found again; could missed opportunities ever be reclaimed? Would there still be a place in her sons' lives for Mohandas when he returned?

These were questions Kasturbai asked herself as she went about her timeless tasks on each unchanging day, dreaming of a time when she might be with Mohandas again. Perhaps they would have their own house; a home of her own. And she was too tired some nights to remember to say a silent prayer for her husband's safe return from a distant place called South Africa.

# 8

For two more years Kasturbai waited. For two more years she lived apart from her husband, virtually incommunicado, her only knowledge of him coming from the businesslike letters he sent to his brothers, again only trickles of information filtered down to her through their wives. She was told that Mohandas had opened a law office in Durban. Soon after that she learned that he was regularly sending money to Lakshimidas, sums ample enough to pay off the debts incurred. She also gathered that he had made no mention of any plans to return to India, issued no call for his wife and sons to join him in South Africa.

The months passed, the children took up more and more of Kasturbai's time, but it was Mohandas who occupied her thoughts. He was so unpredictable, so impetuous, so open and trusting — too trusting, sometimes. Though she had complete faith in him and in God, she worried about how he was living, who his companions were, who was caring for him, who was protecting him from further disappointments in that distant land. Then she heard (not without a pang) that in order to live in a style considered suitable for a successful barrister, Mohandas had moved out of his cramped bachelor quarters and taken a large, well-furnished house in one of the more elegant sections of the city of Durban. Since there was no one but himself to live in it, Mohandas wrote, he had hired a cook and invited several of the clerks who worked for him in his office to move in with him. Knowing his penchant for noble deeds, Kasturbai was not surprised at this, but she reflected, somewhat ruefully, that while she was the one who secretly longed to have a house of her own, it was Mohandas who kept setting up homes for himself — first in Bhavangar, then in London, next in Bombay, and now in South Africa. He seemed always to be creating his own life, and she was beginning to wonder if she would ever become a permanent part of it.

My grandmother must have sensed, once again, that her husband was changing, becoming a new kind of person. But the degree to which he was being transformed was in no way revealed in the second-hand reports she was receiving.

Perhaps my grandfather himself did not understand, could not convey, the significance of what was happening to him during those early years in South Africa. It is only in retrospect, I believe, that we can see that this was when and where the transformation began.

Day by day and step by step, the future Mahatma was discovering truths, inventing strategies, setting patterns, which would guide his own future actions, and inspire future generations of human rights crusaders. The wordless orator, the failed advocate, the self-doubting young barrister who had fled in shame from a Bombay courtroom had vanished. In Durban during these years, another Mohandas was emerging. A Mohandas who was a tireless foe of oppression, and a resourceful servant of the people. He was becoming a sometimes cajoling, sometimes commanding leader of men.

Improvising as he went, he took others with him. His refusal to accept fees for public service (his established rule for all public work thereafter) was announced quite casually on the day he agreed to stay in South Africa and lead the franchise campaign. To ease his way, a number of Durban's Indian businessmen immediately offered Mohandas generous retainers for legal advice and counsel.

His law practice was soon so remunerative he could pay for his own household expenses in Durban, support his family in Rajkot, and have a surplus left over to spend on his public service endeavours.

This assumption of decency on the part of his adversaries, this belief that they could be reached by appeals to mortality, would become another abiding precept of Gandhian philosophy. Meanwhile, the Gandhi name became synonymous with calls for reform. In the summer of 1894, he organised an association he called the Natal Indian Congress and became its first executive secretary.

Although Mohandas' attention seemed centred on political activities and social causes, his preoccupation throughout this period was religion. "I had gone to South Africa for travel, for escape from intrigues, for my own livelihood," he wrote in his autobiography. "But I found myself in search of God ..." He asked friends in India to send him books about Hinduism and Buddhism. He studied the Theosophical Society's English translation of the classic Hindu *Upanishads*. He learned more about Zoroastrianism in a book called *The Sayings of Zarathustra*. He read Washington Irving's biography of the Prophet Mohammed. And he began to glimpse what he later called "the infinite possibilities of universal love."

Mohandas announced to friends and co-workers that he was taking a six-month leave, beginning in June of 1896. He wanted to travel to India to publicise their cause, he explained; he wanted to make the Indian people aware of the problems their brethren faced in South Africa, and ask Indian leaders to back the campaign for reforms. And — oh, yes — while he was in India, he would also collect his wife and sons and bring them back to live with him in Beach Grove Villa.

Living apart from her husband had been difficult, but living with him was more confusing. Kasturbai reached this conclusion within days after Mohandas arrived in Rajkot in the summer of 1896, ending an absence of more than three years. Not that his homecoming was not sweet, nor that their time together (when they had any time together) was less than blissful.

But her happiness had to be contained, smothered. A wife did not show such emotions in public, not even in her own family, not even before her own children. To express her joy, she cooked all of Mohandas' favourite foods, but she couldn't come out of the kitchen to serve him the dishes she so lovingly prepared, let alone sit and eat with him. The honour of serving food to the men of the house was for her eldest sister-in-law Nandkunwarben, who, since the death of Putliba, had been the acknowledged head of the Gandhi women's household.

They had so much stored up to talk about — what had happened during the past three years to their sons, to the family, to their friends, and to them. Mohandas told her about South Africa and spoke of his plans to take her there. She wasn't sure at first whether she was excited or frightened by this idea. Then he described the house he had waiting for her and she knew it was a dream in the making. Kasturbai always longed to hear more, but Mohandas was working so long and hard — writing, talking to people, answering the many letters that arrived from South Africa — that he often fell asleep in the midst of their nocturnal conversations. She never had the heart to wake him up just to ask more questions. She would lie there by his side, thinking about this man who was her husband.

She had known him in many guises — as a timid schoolboy, as a passionate and unbearably possessive young bridegroom, as an earnest but uninspired college student, as a bereaved son mourning the loss of beloved parents, as a muddled and lost young husband trying vainly to use his English education to support his family in an ancient Indian culture. But she had never seen him as he was now — a self-assured young lawyer whose advice was respected even by elders: a leader.

This South African experience had made him more thoughtful, more mature, more forceful, and — what was it? — more like himself. As if he were coming into his own. Everyone had noticed the changes in Mohandas, she was sure of that. Her brothers and sisters-in-law treated him with unaccustomed deference now. And Kasturbai could see that Mohandas accepted all this as his due. Or was it simply that he was thinking of his work, and he expected everyone to know and accept the fact that his work came first, before anything else?

Sometimes she felt unsettled, overwhelmed almost, by all these changes. This new kind of husband who had some consuming mission he could not ignore and she did not yet understand. The new respect everyone showed now that he was prosperous and successful, the new urgency of his demands upon himself — all this was puzzling.

And here, amidst it all, her unchanging self — trying to picture the new life waiting for her and her sons in South Africa, wondering what would happen to them in that strange land.

Mohandas had made the house in Rajkot his headquarters for conducting business at home and abroad, and his first order of business was writing, publishing, and distributing a pamphlet entitled *The Grievances of the British Indians in South Africa*. In this brief discourse, Mohandas detailed soberly and without exaggeration how colour prejudice affected the lives of Indians in South Africa, and discussed what could be done to combat it; he stated, in summary, his basic political tenet: "Our method in South Africa is to conquer this hatred by love."

"You could ask the boys to help you with all this work," she said. Kasturbai had been trying for days to devise some way for her sons to spend more time with their busy father. Here it was.

"Harilal's handwriting is very neat now, and Manilal can help paste the stamps. I'm sure the other children would like to help, too."

Mohandas thought it was a fine idea. Next day he not only enlisted his own sons and the other Gandhi children in the pamphlet-mailing project, but also asked all the schoolchildren in the neighbourhood to join in. Working together for several hours daily, these young volunteers finished the job in a few days. Ever the pragmatist, Mohandas rewarded them with used foreign postage stamps from his voluminous South African correspondence and, always the instructor, urged them to start stamp collections.

No sooner was the mailing dispatched than Mohandas' energies were diverted to another community service. News came that bubonic plague had gripped Bombay. Precautions had to be taken in Rajkot.

Mohandas volunteered to work with a local sanitation committee which toured the city, inspecting the homes (and latrines) of rich and poor alike, pointing out disease-breeding conditions. Other committee members disdained to visit the dwellings of the Untouchables, writing them off as hopeless. Mohandas had no such qualms. My grandfather made careful note of this experience. In later years, whenever he embarked on a reformist mission, the first task he assigned to colleagues was to carry and clean buckets of nightsoil.

Bapu believed this was one way to break caste taboos — to emphasise that all honest work was worthy, no essential work was lowly. By this time, Mohandas' pamphlet (known simply as the "Green Pamphlet" because of the colour of its cover), was drawing comment in newspapers and journals all over India.

Mohandas Gandhi's words were making his countrymen aware of the previously ignored plight of Indians in South Africa, and his name was being read for the first time (and remembered) by the Indian public.

In September a reporter for Reuters, the British news agency, cabled a brief account of the Green Pamphlet and the stir it had caused, to the London office.

London then cabled a still briefer version to the Durban office, a three-line summary in which Mohandas was quoted (misquoted, actually) as saying Indians in Natal were "robbed, assaulted, and treated like beasts," with no hope of redress. This distorted report, printed in the *Natal Mercury* caused an uproar in Durban, and would soon lead to repercussions for him and his family.

Kasturbai was uneasy, too, though trying not to show it. She, who had never travelled more than 100 miles beyond the borders of Porbandar and Rajkot, was now facing the immediate reality of crossing the sea in a ship and living thousands of miles away from home and relatives. Who could tell when or if she would ever see her parents and her brothers again?

She kept reminding herself that when the voyage was over she would have her own home with her own family living all together. She was pleased, too, that their nephew was going with them. At ten, Gokaldas was only a few months younger than her firstborn son would be, had he lived. She felt a pang, thinking of poor Raliatben whose husband had recently died.

Grandmother realised she would have to find a dress that would amalgamate western and eastern cultures. She opted for the dress worn by Parsi women: longer saris, long-sleeved blouses, socks and shoes.

Whites in South Africa regarded Parsis as the most civilised of Asians, so Mohandas had decided this costume would give his family the respectability he sought for them.

"What a heavy price one has to pay to be regarded as civilised."

Such was my grandmother's comment, years later, while reminiscing to friends about this period in her life. On board ship, Mohandas insisted that she and the children wear their new shoes and socks from the time they got up till the time they went to bed. This was something they never did in Rajkot, and they hated it. Their feet hurt and their socks got sweaty and smelly. To get his family used to wearing shoes, Mohandas had them spend hours each day walking on the ship's deck. He walked with them, studying Kasturbai's posture.

"Be straight, hold your head high," he kept telling her. For several days she felt as if she would fall at every step.

But she plodded on for Mohandas' sake, waiting for the night, when she could throw off her shoes and soothe her aching feet. Secretly she yearned for the freedom and peace of Rajkot.

There was none of this nonsense there. She could dress in normal fashion, and walk and sit on the floor as she pleased.

Mealtime was worse than walking — a nightmare for them all. In Rajkot, everyone sat on the floor, each with his own brass plate, when they had meals. But now Kasturbai and the boys had to sit at the table with their legs dangling. The china plates were small, and they were prohibited from using their fingers.

Mohandas watched over all of them like a hawk, endlessly chiding them for not holding the spoon or fork correctly and not using the knife as it should be used. "You must keep your mouth shut when you chew," he would say.

For Kasturbai, struggling to get food to her mouth with strange implements, this last instruction was too much. Impossible! How could you eat with your mouth shut without making forbidden slurping noises. And the food was impossible, too. Unlike anything she made at home; it was tasteless.

Boiled vegetables and bread! This they had never even seen, let alone tasted. What Kasturbai wanted, above all else, was to cook a proper meal again, one they could eat in the way they enjoyed. She began counting the days until the end of the voyage.

But there came a time when she feared the voyage would never end. They were barely five days from Durban when a violent storm seized them at sea, one of the great summer monsoons common in December in the Southern hemisphere. Both ships were tossed about by gigantic waves. No one could stay on the gale-swept decks. Terrified passengers, most of who were on their first sea voyage, were sent below. Prayers of many religions were said. Almost everyone, including Kasturbai and the boys, soon became extremely ill as the ship's pitching and rolling turned stomachs inside out. Apart from the ship's crew, the only person on the *Courland* who remained unaffected by the turbulent weather was Mohandas. He got his family settled in their cabin, consoled them as best he could, then toured the ship, at the captain's request, reassuring the other passengers.

Left alone with the whimpering children, Kasturbai tried to comfort them, but her own misery was too great. For what seemed like the longest 24 hours of her life, she lay in the cabin, waiting for the end to come. Each time the ship rolled on its side, she thought it was about to sink. She was convinced they would all drown in this dreadful sea; her only consolation was they would all die together. She vowed she would never set foot on a ship again, if by any chance, she came off this one alive.

At last, the skies cleared and the sun appeared. With fear of death gone and appetites returned, the passengers celebrated their survival. The Gandhis resumed their daily walks on deck. A few days later, on December 19, 1896, there was great excitement aboard both ships when the *Courland* and *Nadir* arrived at the port of Durban.

But the festive mood vanished when health authorities boarded the ships before they entered the harbour and declared that no one would be allowed to disembark. The vessels were to be held in quarantine for at least the next five days, because of the outbreak of plague earlier that year in Bombay.

The enforced confinement while the *Courland* lay at anchor just outside the harbour was nerve-wracking. Mohandas tried to divert the passengers. Games were organised to pass the time, and the Gandhi boys joined in. On Christmas day the Gandhi family was invited to join other cabin passengers and the ship's officers. Speaking in English, Mohandas celebrated the fact that Christianity, like other great religions of the world, taught peace and nonviolence, but deplored the paradox that Western civilisation often seemed to be based on force. I've often wondered what it was like for a pious Hindu wife like Kasturbai to find herself publicly observing the most sacred day of an unfamiliar religion by listening to her husband make a speech to strangers in an unintelligible foreign tongue. Surely this was as bewildering and unsettling as anything that had happened thus far on her first sea voyage.

But there was more to come.

The day after Christmas the quarantine was extended. No explanations were given. But it was becoming clear that the true cause for the docking delay was not plague in Bombay, but an epidemic in Durban — an epidemic of indignation among the whites of Natal. From the offices of Dada Abdullah & Company, Mohandas got reports of what was happening in the city. News had spread that the author of the infamous Green Pamphlet published in India was coming to Durban bent on making trouble.

Garbled press reports had created the impression that Mohandas had condemned all Europeans for ill-treating the Indians. Now the rumour was that Mohandas had arrived in Natal, bringing with him two shiploads of unindentured Indians (more than 800 new immigrants, according to the latest exaggerations). It was said that he intended to swamp the country with these free Indians, these hordes of brown Asiatics fighting for equal rights. Government officials were disturbed. Even some of Mohandas' white friends, among them his neighbour Harry Escombe, who was Natal's Attorney General, had come to doubt his good intentions, or, at the very least, to see him as a threat to law, order, and tranquillity in South Africa. Public protest meetings were being held nightly, angry whites were castigating Mohandas and demanding his expulsion.

There was even talk of expelling all Indians from Natal. Most immediately, there were demands that the *Courland* and *Nadir* be turned back. There were hints that the government was prepared to pay Dada Abdullah & Company the full cost of returning the passengers to India. Some whites were reportedly offering the ticket refunds directly.

As these reports spread among passengers on the *Courland*, there was great consternation. Some were ready to go home to India. Others, with homes in South Africa, worried about being separated from their families. Mohandas sought to reassure them all, and sent messages of encouragement to passengers on the *Nadir* as well.

"Don't be frightened by these threats," he told them. "You have as much right to be in South Africa as the whites do."

But it was harder to reassure Kasturbai. She was dismayed by the news they were receiving; indeed, she was petrified. So many people were so very angry. She couldn't understand it. She feared for the children, for herself, but most of all for her husband. Kasturbai realised that the anger of the whites was directed mainly at Mohandas and she asked him why they were so agitated. What had he done?

"I've done nothing wrong," Mohandas said. "The facts I reported are true. The demands I made are just — the same demands I have been making in Natal for two years. If only I could explain to them ..."

"But they would not hear you — they are too angry," she said. "How can you make angry people listen to explanations?"

Mohandas had been asking himself the same question.

"We must have faith in God to see us through this crisis." That was his only answer, but it was answer enough for Kasturbai. So the crisis continued for another 2½ weeks. The S.S. *Courland* and S.S. *Nadir* lay at anchor just outside Durban harbour, becalmed by the Natal government's gamble that passengers could be intimidated into returning to India; or, failing that, could be prevented from landing until public unrest in Durban subsided. With each succeeding day on board, tension mounted, hardships increased. Water and provisions ran low; fresh supplies were tardy in arriving.

Finally, on January 13, 1897, the waiting game was over. The government, its pretexts for delay exhausted, lifted the quarantine. Forty-four days out of Bombay (19 at sea and 25 quarantine) the *Courland* and *Nadir* were at last allowed to enter the harbour and dock in Durban.

# 9

It was late afternoon. Kasturbai and the boys, dressed in their fine new clothes, were waiting in the cabin with bags packed. They had been ready to disembark since noon, but Mohandas was nowhere in sight. Summoned to the captain's cabin by a grave-faced crewman, he had been gone for what seemed an eternity.

Kasturbai was sick of this ship and sick of the endless delays. She wanted to get off. She wanted to place her feet on firm ground. Yet even now, even as the last stragglers among the other passengers were making their way down the gangway of the *Courland* the Gandhi family was still on board, still waiting. The children were as impatient as she was. Five-year-old Manilal was sleepy and fretful; eight-year-old Harilal and ten-year-old Gokaldas were restless and unruly. And why not? Wouldn't any normal young boys be miserable, cooped up for hours in this suffocating little cabin?

For what must have been the tenth time, a plaintive Harilal asked, "How much longer do we have to stay here?"

And for what must have been the tenth time Kasturbai told him she didn't know, and gave him a soothing pat on the shoulder.

A few minutes later, when Mohandas at last returned to the cabin, he was bringing news they did not want to hear. No, he said, they couldn't leave the ship yet — not for several hours: not until after dark. Disregarding the children's groans, he tried to explain the situation to Kasturbai, but without alarming her. Earlier that day, he said, when word had spread through the city that the ships were berthing, a crowd of irate whites had gathered on the docks. Don't worry, he hastened to add. They had all been dispersed by now. But his friend Harry Escombe, a government official who should know about these things, had sent word that the atmosphere in Durban was still too hostile for Mohandas to venture out during daylight hours.

Kasturbai caught her breath at this. What kind of people live in Durban? Why had they ever come to this wretched land?

After talking it over with the captain, Mohandas said he had agreed to accept Mr. Escombe's suggestion: to avoid trouble, the Gandhis were to wait until nightfall, and then quietly leave the *Courland* under cover of darkness. What Mohandas did not tell Kasturbai was how much the idea rankled — sneaking ashore in the dark, hiding from his adversaries. That was not his way. But he had no wish to put his family in jeopardy, or to endanger the other passengers. He knew what hatred the racists were capable of. He could never forget that night on the train in Transvaal when he had been cursed and manhandled by the white coach attendant.

Mohandas was still trying to calm the boys and allay his wife's misgivings when the captain sent for him again.

What could it be now? All sorts of dire thoughts went through Kasturbai's mind. After another wait, a shorter one this time, Mohandas was back again, bringing startling news. Everything had changed, he said. They must leave the ship at once.

The boys were overjoyed, but Kasturbai was perplexed. As Mohandas gathered their baggage, and began shepherding them out of the cabin, he explained. The ship's agent and legal adviser, a Mr. F. A. Laughton, had just come on board. Speaking on behalf of Dada Abdullah & Company, he had advised Mohandas that he was not bound to accept Harry Escombe's advice.

The Attorney General had officially supported or, at the very least, condoned the recent anti-Gandhi, anti-Indian sentiment in Natal, and no one was certain where he now stood. Speaking for himself, Mr. Laughton said he felt it was not only unnecessary but also unwise for Mohandas to wait until after dark and enter the city like a thief in the night.

Since the unfriendly crowds were gone there was little risk of danger, and such cowardly behaviour would surely lend credence to all the false rumours about him. Mohandas agreed entirely. Arrangements had therefore been made. The Durban port commander had provided a carriage that was now waiting to take Kasturbai and the boys to the nearby home of Mohandas' good friend, Jivanji Rustomji, a wealthy Parsi merchant and a trusted member of the Natal Indian Congress.

"And what about you?" Kasturbai asked.

"I will follow on foot with Mr. Laughton," Mohandas replied. "He says we have nothing to fear. We will have no problems."

"Then I will come with you," Kasturbai said.

"You can't. It is a long way to walk, almost two miles. And the children can't go to the Rustomji's alone. You must go with them."

Kasturbai wanted to argue the point. Although Mohandas had tried not to reveal too much, she sensed that all was not well. If her husband was facing possible danger, she wanted to be by his side. She had no fears if they were together. What she did fear, what all her long-held beliefs made her dread, was exactly what he was asking her to do — to go out alone, unshielded from the public gaze, and allow herself to be driven by strangers through the streets of an unfamiliar and hostile city.

Kasturbai's carefully conditioned reflex told her that, for a virtuous woman, such behaviour would be both shameful and hazardous. And how could she take her children into the home of people she had never met? If the Rustomjis were not Hindus, they must have a very different way of life. Surely Mohandas knew that she couldn't go there, not without him. Surely he must realise ...

Then suddenly, shockingly, came the awareness that Mohandas did know. He fully realised what he was asking her to do; and it made no difference to him. Therefore, it could make no difference to her. She must do it. Because of the children, for their safety, she must put aside her own fears and do the unthinkable.

Without further protest, Kasturbai followed her husband and the excited little boys out onto the deck. She let herself be hurried down the gangway and helped into the waiting carriage. As the carriage began to move, she leaned forward to take one last look at the *Courland* and saw Mohandas standing at the rail beside a European man who must be Mr. Laughton. Then she sat up straight and proud and covered her face with her new Parsi-style sari.

A few minutes later, with Mr. Laughton by his side, Mohandas began his journey to the Rustomji home on foot, walking along a straight road that led past the docks to the Esplanade. Normally, there was little traffic on this road except for vehicles carrying merchandise, and seldom any pedestrians, other than dockworkers loading and unloading cargo. But this was not a normal day.

The two men had walked no more than a few hundred yards from the *Courland* when several rowdy young white men who had been loitering around the dock area all day, ever since police had earlier dispersed the crowd of protesters, saw and recognised Mohandas.

"Gandhi! Gandhi!" they shouted, running toward him.

Before either man realised what was happening, they were being jostled and taunted by a half-dozen jeering young toughs. Several older men rushed over to join in the harassment. It was clear that Mr. Laughton, well intentioned though he may have been, had delivered Mohandas into the hands of a mob.

At that moment, Laughton spied a passing rickshaw. He ran out and stopped the poor, miserable-looking African who was pulling it, and shouted for Mohandas to get in the rickshaw and flee. But the mob had Mohandas firmly in hand. Someone had snatched off his turban, others were pelting him with rotten eggs. It was the terrified rickshaw-puller who fled the scene. In any case, I am certain my grandfather, even had he been able to break away from his tormentors, would not have chosen to save himself by commandeering a rickshaw. Throughout his life he despised the very idea of riding in a vehicle pulled by a fellow human being.

The mob unleashed all its pent-up fury. They shoved Laughton aside. They punched Mohandas with their fists, they slapped and kicked him. And they showered him with brickbats. Had it not been for the memorably brave act of one lone white woman, they probably would have murdered him on the spot.

Providentially, a certain Mrs. R. C. Alexander, who happened to be the wife of Durban's police superintendent, was walking on the Esplanade that day. When she heard a commotion on the dock road, and saw that someone was being beaten unmercifully, she pushed her way through the crowd. To her dismay, Mrs. Alexander recognised the victim as Mohandas Gandhi, the young Indian barrister whom she and her husband knew and respected. Without a moment's hesitation, she stepped into the melee, opened her parasol and held it above Mohandas' head to shield him from blows and missiles. The crowd fell back momentarily confounded, hesitant to harm a lady.

At about the time Mrs. Alexander made her appearance on this ugly scene, another chance passerby, a young Indian, saw the plight Mohandas was in. The Indian youth ran to the nearby police station and reported the matter to Superintendent Alexander, who promptly dispatched a group of constables to rescue Mohandas from his attackers and escort him to safety. By the time the constables arrived, however, most of the young toughs had scattered. Someone among them had recognised that Gandhi's "guardian angel" was none other than the wife of the Superintendent of Police.

But the day's ordeals were still not over.

At the Rustomji home a worried Kasturbai had been anxiously waiting for her husband. When Mohandas arrived safely, she was vastly relieved. Then she got a good look at him — his bruised and bloodied face, his dishevelled clothing. She was aghast. Her first instinct was to go to him, to comfort him, even though she was acutely conscious of being a stranger in a strange house. According to the tenets of her orthodox Vaishnava upbringing, any immodest display of emotions between husband and wife would be unseemly. But tradition deterred her for only an instant. Some great calamity had befallen them in this terrible land. She could not just stand by and weep.

"Oh, what have they done to you?" she cried, rushing to Mohandas' side, ignoring everyone else.

"It's nothing. I am not badly hurt," he reassured her.

Kasturbai was not so easily put off. She asked for a dish of water and began swabbing his cuts and bruises with her handkerchief. When a doctor arrived to examine and treat Mohandas, he found only one or two abrasions that needed dressing.

But the angry whites were not finished with Mohandas. A few of his attackers had followed him to the Rustomji residence. Word spread, and a boisterous crowd began to gather outside the house. The police superintendent himself arrived, bringing more constables, but he saw they were already greatly outnumbered. Using his wits, not force, Superintendent Alexander tried to defuse the situation by humouring the crowd, hoping to cool tempers by cracking jokes. Yet, despite his efforts, the crowd grew larger. And angrier. By nightfall, it had become a virtual lynch mob, yelling epithets, shouting demands, threatening to break down the bolted doors of the house.

"Send Gandhi out! We must have Gandhi!"

The women and children of both families, Rustomjis and Gandhis, had been sent upstairs for safety. They could hear the shouts clearly. Kasturbai was frantic with fear. What was to become of them in this dreadful city? Why would anyone want to kill her husband? What could she possibly say to comfort Harilal and Manilal? And poor little Gokaldas who had just lost his own father in India and then been brought across the dark waters to this awful place. The boys were trying to be brave, but she knew they were terrified.

Outside, Superintendent Alexander was losing control of the crowd. He sent a message to Mohandas: "If you wish to save your friend's house and the lives of your family, you must escape from here in a disguise. Decide quickly."

Mohandas did not hesitate. He felt he had no choice. The white constable delivering the message had brought with him a parcel containing the uniform of an Indian police constable. Mohandas donned the uniform. Around his head he wrapped a crude Madrasi pugree with a brass plate concealed in its folds to serve as a helmet. He was soon joined by two white detectives, also in disguise. Their faces were darkened and they were dressed as Indian merchants.

Though the detectives said they must leave at once, Mohandas took time to go upstairs and say a word of reassurance to his family. But the sight of her husband in his outlandish costume, and his explanation that he was being taken to the safety of the police station did little to quiet Kasturbai's apprehensions. As she watched him hurry away, her heart was seized by an awful foreboding.

Repercussions from the near-lynching of Mohandas Gandhi were instant and widespread. News of the assault reached India and England the next day. In Bombay, the Queen's Viceroy expressed grave concern. From London, the Queen's Secretary of State for the Colonies, Joseph Chamberlain, cabled Natal demanding that the instigators be prosecuted. But Mohandas, still under friendly protection at the police station, said he had no desire for revenge. He declined to testify or press charges against his assailants, saying they were simply a few hot-headed young men who had been misled by false press reports and incited by anti-Indian political leaders; they would regret their actions once the truth became known. He even provided a grateful (and now contrite) Attorney General Escombe with an affidavit to this effect to send to Secretary Chamberlain in London.

Durban newspapers reported with some amazement Mohandas' refusal to prosecute. The *Natal Advertiser* printed a long interview with him in which he was able to establish, with full quotations, that his writings and speeches in India had contained nothing more inflammatory than what he had said many times over in South Africa. And that he had had no role in bringing two shiploads of unindentured Indian immigrants to Natal — the majority of whom were on their way to the Transvaal, in any event. For Mohandas and his cause, the assault turned out to be something of a "blessing" — at least, that was how he later described it in his autobiography. His courage under attack earned high praise from Indians in South Africa — and new clients for his law practice. His magnanimity to his foes won the esteem of thoughtful whites, and increased their respect for the Indian community he served.

More immediately, after two days, Mohandas was able to leave the police station and return, without incident, to his waiting family at the Rustomji residence. Two days after that, the Gandhis moved into Beach

Grove Villa — Mohandas' own home nearby.

Kasturbai left the Rustomjis with mixed emotions. She was grateful for the safe shelter and unstinting kindness they had offered in a time of trial which had marked a turning point in her life. During the hours she spent with them, she had seen for herself how prominent her husband had become. Witnessing for the first time the passions his public pronouncements, even his reputation could arouse. She had discovered how perilous such prominence could be.

Yet the experience of staying with her children in a Parsi household had been traumatic for her in other ways too. Ways that had nothing to do with the dangers they had faced. From the protected and pious seclusion of her Rajkot home where she never came out of the kitchen or the women's quarters with her face uncovered, Kasturbai had been thrust into an alien everyday world where men and women sat together, talked together, went out together, and the women did not even cover their heads, let alone their faces. And that was not all. Most of the food she had been served was not just unappetising, but inedible.

The Rustomjis, being Parsis, regularly ate meat, fish, and fowl, but this was a violation of an ages-old taboo for a faithful Vaishnava Hindu like Kasturbai. So her gratitude to the Rustomjis for their hospitality was overshadowed by her joy to be leaving them and to go to her own house, her own kitchen, to live life her own way.

Yet, although my grandmother was unable to feel completely at ease with the Rustomjis at first, her misgivings about them were evidently short-lived. The two families became and remained friends for life. As late as 1943, a year before she died, in letters to my parents in South Africa from the Aga Khan Palace in India where she and Bapu were imprisoned during World War II, she often sent her loving greetings to the family of Jalbhai Rustomji. As a child, Jal Rustomji had shared with the Gandhis the terrors of that January night in 1897 when a howling mob besieged his parents' home.

Kasturbai was elated. For the first time in all her 28 years, she was under the authority of no other woman. Her new home was her own domain. And, marking the respected status this conferred, she would again be known by a new name: Kasturba.

But no sooner was she moved into Beach Grove Villa than her elation began to dissolve into uncertainty. True, the ocean views and the pungent scent of sea breezes brought back happy memories of her childhood days in Porbandar, but this spacious, two-storey, five-bedroom house with its iron front gate, its small garden, its big veranda under the balcony facing the bay, was unlike any home she had ever known. Downstairs was equipped with handsome European style furnishings that had been provided, Mohandas told her, by some prosperous Indian merchants among his clients.

In the carpeted living room were a sofa, two lounge chairs, a round library table, and a bookcase filled with books Mohandas had collected: the writings of Tolstoy, publications of the Theosophists and the Vegetarians, literature on Hinduism, the Bible, the *Qur'an* [Koran], and biographies of Indian leaders. The dining room had a rectangular table, eight bentwood chairs, a corner whatnot. Upstairs, the bedrooms were more austere, furnished with nothing more than wardrobes and bare wooden platforms to sleep on.

But nowhere in this house was there a family deity awaiting morning offerings. There was no courtyard for evening prayers. No sacred tulsi plant representing the healing presence of the beautiful Tulsi, one of the Lord Krishna's 16,000 wives. Did Hindus in South Africa have to give up such things? Or, Kasturba asked herself uneasily, was it just Mohandas?

The house had been locked during Mohandas' absence, and Kasturba's sharp eye for detail found innumerable tasks waiting to be done. The rooms required cleaning and airing, furniture needed dusting and polishing. Bags had to be unpacked, provisions bought. Even with the boys' cooperation and the help of a servant or two, it took many days to make her new home acceptably clean and comfortable. At the same time, she was trying to serve her hungry family their favourite dishes, while learning how to cook in an infuriatingly unfamiliar kitchen.

The kitchen, this longed-for kitchen all her own — it was impossible! In this kitchen she was expected to cook standing up! And not just standing, but wearing shoes as Mohandas insisted she do at all times, even though they still made her feet ache. Like other Indian women through the ages, Kasturba had always squatted comfortably on the floor while preparing food and cooking it on a small coalburning sigri. Here she was confronted with waist-high worktables (taller than waist-high for one as tiny as she was) and a gigantic wood-burning stove which had six plates. Mohandas had to show her how to light it.

Only after many weeks of struggle was Kasturba finally able to adapt to these new cooking methods. But keeping house and serving proper meals at Beach Grove Villa never became less than drudgery for her. It was hard work; but most of all, it was lonely work. Standing in her Durban kitchen, peeling fruit or slicing vegetables, Kasturba recalled the easy give-and-take of the Gandhi kitchen back home. There she had always shared with other women the never-ending tasks of preparing meals, minding children, doing chores. She missed their daily exchanges of news and, yes, gossip. Now, her only news of her sisters-in-law and her nieces came in fleeting mentions of the family in letters from Lakshimidas that Mohandas read aloud to her.

She realised for the first time how much she had enjoyed, how much she had relied on the company, the help, and most of all, the friendship of the women she had left behind in Rajkot.

Kasturba asked to be informed about all that was going on. She saw many people who came to Mohandas for advice, how much they depended on him and how much he demanded of himself. It was amazing. She wanted to be able to help her husband in his work to any extent she could. She sensed that somehow this still wasn't enough for Mohandas. Here in Durban, her husband was intent on becoming the complete householder, providing for his family and serving the community.

Just as they were in Porbandar this Gandhi household became an open house. Mohandas, in consultation with Kasturba, invited several of his young law clerks to move into Beach Grove Villa where there was plenty of room. One day, when a leper came to the door begging, Mohandas asked the poor creature in; dressed his wounds and, after consultations with Kasturba, offered him permanent care and shelter. The experiment ended, however, almost before it began. Mohandas realised they lacked the resources to care for a leper and took him to a government hospital for indentured labourers.

What little spare time Mohandas found in his busy schedule, he tried to spend with the boys. Having lived apart from his children for so much of their lives, he now seemed to feel he should be with them whenever possible. Kasturba understood that and she knew the boys needed him. They were lonely, too. Their education was proving to be a great problem in race-conscious South Africa where schools were segregated, the best reserved for whites and the worst for blacks.

Mohandas' sons might well have been able to attend an exclusive European school, but only as an exception not granted to other Indians — an idea he firmly rejected. He felt such favouritism would alienate the boys from Indian society. The Christian mission schools attended by most Indian children, meanwhile, had unqualified teachers and offered instruction Mohandas viewed as totally inadequate. So the boys were not enrolled in any school.

With Manilal it did not matter. He was still too young for school. But Kasturba worried about the older boys. Harilal, so bright and eager; Gokaldas, so quiet and shy.

They shouldn't be at home all day long, missing their schooling. She pleaded with Mohandas to do something. His first solution was a short-lived experiment with private tutoring by a white governess who spoke only English. When that proved unsuccessful, Mohandas decided he himself would teach the boys at home, conducting lessons in their native Gujarati. This, to Kasturba's way of thinking, was no solution at all (the whole thing reminded her of the times he had tried to give her instruction). Mohandas was far too busy to devote enough time to the project. He came home late in the evening when the boys were too tired to concentrate on lessons. Other times he began instruction before dawn when the children were only half-awake. Clearly this would not do, and Kasturba said as much to Mohandas. She was a simple, straightforward woman, and her logic was faultless: some education was better than no education. If there were schools, the children should go to them.

One day, early in 1898, Kasturba's loyalty to her husband and his ideals came into sharp conflict with the traditions in which she had been nurtured. She had just learned, in the final months of 1897 that another child was on the way. The pregnancy was proving difficult. She tired easily, felt uncommonly irritable and yearned to be back home in India. Nevertheless, she tried uncomplainingly to keep her household running smoothly.

Complying with his decree that all residents of Beach Grove Villa must each morning empty the chamber pots from their own rooms — and especially his proviso that she would join him in cleaning any pots that were neglected — filled Kasturba with disgust, anger, and above all, shame. Had Mohandas brought her to this strange land simply to reduce her to the lowest human level? From earliest childhood she had known, undeniably and as a matter of faith, that this was the filthiest of tasks, fit only for Untouchables — those unseen polluting shadows who came and took away the nightsoil from the toilets in the back of the house by the road, without ever setting foot on the family's property. She deeply resented being asked by her own husband to so defile herself. How could one so respectful of everyone else's religious conviction be so heedless of those of his own wife?

Kasturba's breaking point came one morning when a new house guest, a Christian Indian of Untouchable parentage who was unaware of the customs at Beach Grove Villa left his chamber pot under his bed, unemptied. She knew Mohandas would clean it, but the idea of her husband doing such degrading work was just as bad as doing it herself. Weeping and furious, she forced herself to carry the pot down the outside staircase and empty it, unaware that Mohandas was watching her.

In his autobiography, *The Story of my Experiments with Truth*, my grandfather gave a memorable account of what then ensued:

> I was far from being satisfied by her merely carrying the pot. I would have her do it cheerfully. So I said, raising my voice: "I will not stand this nonsense in my house."
>
> The words pierced her like an arrow.
>
> She shouted back: "Keep your house to yourself and let me go." I forgot myself and the spring of compassion dried up in me. I caught her by the hand, dragged the helpless woman to the gate, and proceeded to open it with the intention of pushing her out. The tears were running down her cheeks in torrents and she cried: "Have you no sense of shame? Must you so far forget yourself? Where am I to go? I have no parents or relatives here to harbour me. Being your wife, you think I must put up with your cuffs and kicks. For Heaven's sake behave yourself, and shut the gate. Let us not be found making scenes like this."
>
> I put on a brave face, but was really ashamed and shut the gate. If my wife could not leave me, neither could I leave her. We have had numerous bickering, but the end has always been peace between us. The wife, with her matchless powers of endurance, has always been the victor.

It seems significant to me that my grandfather, 30 years later, would remember this incident so vividly, and describe it in such painful and self-accusatory detail. Earlier in the same passage he says he was still at that stage a "cruelly kind husband", and claims in his own defence, "I regarded myself as my wife's teacher and so harassed her out of my blind love for her." Perhaps so. But it also appears to me that, by the time he wrote this, he wished somehow to make amends to the young wife whose needs he so often misunderstood and whose feelings he so often disregarded.

What I find even more significant, however, is his portrayal of my grandmother's character in this passage. How passionately full of life is the forceful, defiant, and altogether sensible woman he describes here. Especially in contrast to the enigmatic, withdrawn, unfailingly compliant wife who so often appears elsewhere in his autobiography and, even more, in the writings of Gandhi biographers.

I am grateful to Bapu for giving us this glimpse of a very human Ba, a woman who did not always have the patience of a saint — or *for* a saint in the making.

A subtle change had occurred. For the first time in their 16 years of married life, a show of near-violence had occurred between them. To Mohandas, the incident had brought into agonising focus the need to control his temper. If he behaved in this manner with his wife, what could stop him from behaving the same way with friends? And what if Kasturba was his wife, and sworn to obey him? Did she not have a mind of her own? Was he right to expect her or anyone else to accept what he said without argument?

Eager to forget their quarrel, to think of the future, they each vowed that it must not — could not — happen again. Kasturba busied herself with preparations for the birth of another baby. In a new country the event must be handled a new way. There was no birthing room in Beach Grove Villa. Mohandas wanted his wife to have the best medical care available, so they decided together, according to his account, that a doctor would be called when Kasturba's time came. It no doubt took a good deal of persuasion on the part of the "cruelly kind" husband to get Kasturba to agree. She must have felt instinctively that the presence of any male — even a male doctor, even an Indian male doctor — during the female ritual of childbirth was a rude, even a profane intrusion.

They also agreed to hire a nurse to take care of both mother and child after the baby's arrival. "But it must be an Indian nurse," Kasturba insisted. "With you away in the office most of the day, how do you expect me to communicate with a European nurse?"

Mohandas agreed, but pointed out that in Durban an Indian nurse was much more difficult to find than an Indian doctor. "If we cannot find one," Kasturba said, "I will look after the child. After all, I am the mother. And if we were in India no nurse would be helping me."

Mohandas decided he could help too should the need arise. If it was the wife's duty to go through labour and bear the child, it should be the husband's duty, he reasoned, to nurse the mother and help care for the child. This was a radical notion — even more uncommon then than it is today. An Indian husband's participation in these matters was traditionally restricted to impregnating his wife, and surely never included any nappy changing. To ready himself for such duties, Mohandas ordered from India a popular book on childbirth written in Gujarati. Entitled *Advice to a Mother*, it provided a full account of the birth process and detailed instructions on care of newborn babies.

It was fortunate Mohandas had prepared himself.

In May of 1898 when Kasturba gave birth to their third son, Ramdas, in an upstairs bedroom at Beach Grove Villa, the labour was long and the delivery difficult. Mohandas was present to assist the doctor. And, during the next few weeks, while Kasturba was bedridden with anaemia and almost too weak to breast-feed her newborn son, it was Mohandas who attended them both, and also bathed and fed and cared for the older boys, too.

# 10

As Kasturba regained her strength in the months following the birth of Ramdas, she sensed that Mohandas was in the throes of some inner struggle — a turmoil she felt she could help in resolving. In India she worried that her husband was not earning enough to support them. In South Africa, she wondered if he was becoming too prosperous. His legal practice was increasingly lucrative. A dozen people now worked in his office, and his annual income was as much as £75,000. But living the life of a well-to-do barrister seemed to hold less and less satisfaction for him. The ease and comfort enjoyed by the Gandhis at Beach Grove Villa had become oppressive to Mohandas.

Obsessed now with the idea of simplifying their lives, he announced they must reduce household expenses. This would free more of the earnings to be spent on public service, he explained, and, of equal importance, it would encourage them to become more self-reliant. Among his first innovations was the dismissal of all servants. He insisted that everyone, including the children, must help with the household chores. The biggest load, of course, was borne by him and Kasturba, who had to teach the boys what needed to be done and supervise their work. For Kasturba there was the additional duty as cook for the family and their boarders.

Even though she had never been part of a completely servantless household, Kasturba saw this as a way to bring the family closer. In India it was the women who did all the household chores. In South Africa she had to get used to having the male members participate. Living in South Africa, seeing firsthand the loyalty his leadership inspired, had convinced Kasturba that Mohandas knew what he was doing.

Mohandas assumed his share of the labour by getting up early. He volunteered, first of all, to do his own laundry since his court appearances required daily changes of shirts and collars. As was his custom when embarking on a new endeavour, he bought a book of instructions, this time a book on laundering. He studied it carefully, then read it aloud to Kasturba — somewhat to her amusement, I imagine, for she undoubtedly had far less need for laundry instructions than he. His first attempts at washing, starching, and ironing were hilarious.

On a trip to Pretoria, he had been turned away from a white-owned barbershop by the English proprietor who contemptuously disdained to cut "black hair". Mohandas refused to take offence at this insult, acknowledging to himself that the barber would lose customers if he offered his services to non-whites, and reminding himself that similar prejudices existed in India. ("We do not allow our barbers to serve our Untouchable brethren," he later wrote. "I got the reward of this in South Africa.") Instead of getting angry, Mohandas bought a pair of clippers and cut his own hair, using a mirror to trim the back. His initial efforts were ridiculed by his friends in court; they asked if rats had been nibbling at his hair. But his barbering skills improved in time, and he soon took to cutting his sons' hair as well as his own.

Mohandas was now spending so much time and energy in public service that, to Kasturba, he sometimes seemed propelled by an overpowering drive to improve the lives of others. Their behaviour, too, for that matter. To awaken among his fellow expatriates a sense of duty to their homeland, he established a relief fund for India's poor during a terrible famine in 1899. Prosperous South African Indians made sizable donations and, to his satisfaction, indentured workers also gave their share. To disprove the criticisms, all too prevalent among white South Africans, that Indians were slovenly and unclean in their habits, he organised a series of successful "sanitation" campaigns. But it took arduous effort and infinite patience to persuade the Indian community to undertake voluntary sanitary reforms, and he found his preachments were not universally appreciated.

Bapu later wrote that this experience taught him the sobering truth that, often as not, it is the reformer who is anxious for the reform and not society. Still, his interest in public health and his love of medicine endured. He read books on nature cures, and sometimes prescribed treatments for ailing legal clients. He continued his volunteer hospital work. He seemed determined to use not just legal skills, but medical skills as well, to improve the lot of Indians in South Africa.

Just such an opportunity arose (paradoxically, for an apostle of non-violence like my grandfather) with the outbreak of the Boer War. The conflict had been in the making for more than a decade, ever since gold was discovered in the Transvaal in 1886. The Boers and the British tried to claim control of the mines. As hostility between them steadily escalated, the Boer republics denied citizenship to Britons and increased their taxes. The British countered by sending troops to their South African colonies. Finally, in October of 1899 the Boers declared war.

Most Indians in South Africa had no wish to get involved in the white men's war. They believed they were despised by both sides and feared reprisals, whatever the outcome. But Mohandas declared they could not be bystanders. Even though his personal sympathies originally were with the Boers (an instinct confirmed, he later decided, when he learned of the hardships suffered by Boer women and children sent to British internment camps during the conflict), he felt compelled, because of his loyalty to the Empire, to support the British.

Grandfather devised a non-violent plan that would allow Indians to prove their loyalty to the Queen without bearing arms. Mohandas wrote to the government of Natal offering to organise and lead a corps of Indians to serve as stretcher-bearers and medical orderlies at the front. But scornful English officials, sharing the belief commonly held by South African whites that Indians were unreliable and cowardly, rejected the plan.

Mohandas persevered, nonetheless. Working tirelessly during the next few weeks, he recruited 40 leaders and enlisted some 1,100 men: 300 free Indians and 800 indentured labourers released by their employers, for service in an ambulance corps. His friend Dr. Booth, the British medical missionary who was superintendent of Jivanji Rustomji's charitable hospital, volunteered to train the men and help them secure certificates of fitness for medical service. Meanwhile, during those first months of the war, outnumbered British troops had met unexpected and alarming reverses in the field; Natal had been invaded by Boer forces, Ladysmith was under siege. In early December of 1899, the beleaguered government of Natal reversed its decision and accepted the Indians for war service, with offers to provide transport and uniforms. The Indian Ambulance Corps was ready.

They marched 25 miles or more a day across treeless plains under a scorching summer sun, carrying wounded men on stretchers to base hospitals. A British journalist, Vere Stent, later recalled for the *Johannesburg Illustrated Star* his encounters with the Indian Ambulance

Corps during the bloody Spion Kop battle in January of 1900:

> I came across Gandhi in the early morning sitting by the roadside eating a regulation army biscuit. He was stoical in his bearing, cheerful and confident in his conversation, and had a kindly eye. He did one good ... I saw the man and his small disciplined corps on many a battlefield during the Natal Campaign. Their unassuming dauntlessness cost them many lives ...

Mohandas had seen enough senseless carnage to confirm forever his hatred of war and violence. But the goal of the ambulance corps had, in his view, been accomplished. Forgetting all differences of religion, caste, and language, a well-knit group of Indians had worked together in unity during a time of crisis. Their courage and endurance had won the praise of British officers and the respect of the Tommies, the grateful British infantrymen. Indian pride and prestige were at an all-time high. Mohandas and 36 other corpsmen were awarded the War Medal. A new era was bringing new thinking. Surely the British colonial government in South Africa would moderate their policies of discrimination. Such were the hopes of most Indians in that opening year of a new century.

Shortly before the outbreak of war in 1899, Kasturba had realised she was pregnant. During the many weeks Mohandas was away from Beach Grove Villa, she had been alone with the children. For the first time ever, she was in complete charge of her own daily life and she found such independence not at all unpleasant. Kasturba was quite content, moving at her own pace, looking after her own little empire; taking care of the boys, planning for the new baby's arrival, enjoying visits from new friends she had made in Durban, and trying not to worry about Mohandas.

The couple's fourth son, Devadas, arrived on May 23, 1900. Kasturba went into labour so suddenly and the birth came so quickly there was no time to summon doctor or nurse. Once again the birth was difficult and Kasturba's suffering was great, but this time Mohandas delivered the baby safely all by himself. ("I was not nervous," he reported in his autobiography. He disclosed nothing about his wife's state of mind.) With Kasturba's health again in a fragile state, Mohandas again cared for her, their newborn and the other boys. Then, in the midst of these domestic endeavours, 7-year-old Manilal came down with a serious case of smallpox. Mohandas put aside any thought of an early return to India. After many weeks, Kasturba's strength returned; but so too did her worries about Mohandas. She had often seen him struggle with his conscience, wrestle with self-doubt and guilt because of his sexual desires. She realised among all the other changes that Mohandas sought to bring about in his life he would now desire sexual abstinence also. He started bringing work home; working late into the night and coming to bed only after he was completely exhausted. Then he suggested they sleep in separate beds and Kasturba agreed without question or comment.

We can, as I have said, do no more than speculate about what happened in private between my grandparents, for only one side of the story has been told. My grandfather's writings, remarkable for their candour in discussing his own strong sexual passions and strivings for self-control, revealed nothing about his wife's innermost feelings, alluding only to her "reticence" with him about these matters. That reticence seems also to have prevented Ba from confiding in others.

Kasturba had become aware sometime after the birth of their second son Manilal that, while Mohandas still desired her, he despised being a slave to sexual desire. Ever since his student days in London, Mohandas had been pondering the conflicts between family obligations and personal goals — and more specifically, between his responsibility to his wife and children and his wish to devote himself to serving the larger community. One seemed inevitably to impinge upon the other. How then, he had asked himself, did his undiminished desire for Kasturba fit into the equation? What should be his relationship with her? He was forever "wedded to the monogamous ideal", as he put it, but faithfulness to his wife did not prevent conceptions — far from it. Mohandas knew all about contraceptives. The thoroughly modern members of the Vegetarian Society in London had discussed the subject often. Yet this knowledge had only compounded his dilemma, for he could not on principle accept their use.

Aware of his own sexual drive he was convinced that contraceptives would remove any inhibitions the fear of pregnancy imposed on unrestrained sexual indulgence. Mohandas believed that if he used contraceptives regularly he would end up, in his own words, "making my wife the instrument of my lust". Kasturba, on the other hand, probably had little if any knowledge about contraceptives, and remained oblivious to the questions troubling Mohandas. Like many women in many cultures, and particularly during that Victorian age, her information about sexual matters was most likely incomplete, at best. Her premarital instruction from older Hindu women had been about ways to please her husband, not how to control fertility. But even had she understood all the reasons for her husband's ambivalence about their relationship, it is doubtful Kasturba would have shared his concerns. She had accepted her role as Mohandas' wife without reservation, conceiving children with love and bearing them with hope. She had always felt confident that Mohandas' dedication to their marriage was as strong as hers.

Mohandas' ongoing debate with himself had become more intense, taken on new dimensions after the delivery of their fourth son Devadas. Witnessing Kasturba's agony in childbirth, had caused him to contemplate the man's role in the procreation process, and it had affected him profoundly. This came at a time when Mohandas was struggling with the implications of new insights gained in South Africa where his hatred of oppression, his concern for justice, his desire to help alleviate human suffering, led him to challenge a whole array of society's accepted conventions. Among other things, he was examining, perhaps for the first time, the position of women in Indian culture (and, indeed, their fate throughout human history), and was beginning to see a need for radical change in relations between men and women. It was all coming together now in some as yet unresolved fashion.

But Kasturba and Mohandas were growing more and more anxious to visit relatives and friends in India. Friends from India had been calling Mohandas home to work on India's problems, and he longed to escape the seductive affluence of Durban and forget material pursuits. Kasturba yearned achingly to return to friends and family she had not seen for four years, and show off her two South African-born babies.

There was also the matter of the older children's schooling. Aside from lessons at Beach Grove Villa as Mohandas' schedule allowed, no satisfactory arrangements had yet been made.

Now the older boys were in their teens. Manilal was nearly 9 and they were far behind most children their age. What good was it, Kasturba asked herself, that they could sweep floors, wash clothes, and do household chores better than others?

Sometime in October of 1901 Mohandas made the decision that they all needed to go home. But it took his solemn promise to return to South Africa whenever his help was required to convince other Indian leaders that they could carry on without him. There began a round of testimonials, farewell parties and finally, a shower of expensive parting gifts from grateful members of the Indian community — altogether about one thousand pounds worth of silver, gold, and diamond jewellery, including a beautiful gold necklace presented to Kasturba. Suddenly Mohandas and Kasturba found themselves involved in a clash of principles.

At home after the presentation, with presents lying heaped on a table downstairs, Mohandas paced the floor of his room most of the night, unable to sleep. He couldn't refuse to accept the gifts for fear of offending his friends, yet he couldn't very well keep them with a clear conscience, having long ago declared that accepting gifts in return for public service was morally wrong. Besides, he couldn't see himself, his sons, or his wife ever having any use for expensive jewellery. Simplicity had become their way of life. He mulled over the issue for hours, and finally decided that because the gifts were "a tribute to Congress principles", they should be given to the Natal Indian Congress and used for the benefit of the Indians of South Africa. Glad to have arrived at a solution, he wrote up legal papers creating a public trust for the purpose, and naming his Parsi friend Rustomji and several other close associates as trustees.

Next morning, reflecting on how to convince Kasturba he was doing the right thing, he decided to take Harilal and Manilal into his confidence. Without much difficulty, he got his sons to agree to help him explain to their mother why they could not keep the gifts, and he was pleased when Harilal volunteered the suggestion that, if they ever needed jewels, they could buy their own. The lesson on self-reliance had taken hold. With the boys in tow, Mohandas went to Kasturba and announced the gifts must be returned.

What happened next is described in detail in my grandfather's autobiography. He had anticipated objections, but he had badly under-estimated the force of his wife's convictions. Kasturba was a traditionalist at heart. If friends gave gifts out of love, they should be accepted in the same spirit. More than that, she was practical. The gifts added to the family security. She had concern for the future welfare of her own four sons, and for Mohandas' sister's son, too. The boys would grow up and require help to establish themselves in careers, just as Mohandas had. And who knows? She herself might someday need something to fall back upon.

Facing the solid phalanx of family males, Kasturba stated firmly, "I do not agree with you. Gifts given by friends with such affection cannot be rejected."

"But it is immoral to accept gifts given for social service."

"I don't see why."

"What do you propose to do with them then?" Mohandas asked.

"I will keep them for our daughters-in-law," Kasturba declared. It was a reasonable position. In an Indian wedding, the bridegroom's parents are required to make a gift of jewels to the bride.

"But the boys are still young, they won't marry for a long time yet," Mohandas said in exasperation.

"We don't need these things," the boys chimed in.

"Who asked you?!" Kasturba snapped. And to Mohandas she said, "You're trying to make saints out of my boys before they are men."

"But surely we won't choose for our sons brides who are fond of ornaments." Now Mohandas was being reasonable. "And if we do need to provide them with jewels, I will be there. You will ask me then."

"Ask you!" Kasturba's usually melodious voice was strident. "You have already given everything away. Where are you going to get jewels from?"

"But I've already drawn up the trust-deed," Mohandas countered.

"Who asked you to?" She burst into tears. "And what right have you to my necklace? The gifts are as much mine as yours."

"The gifts were given for my services to the people." Mohandas was very patient in making his point.

"I agree, but it's the same thing," Kasturba sobbed. "Service rendered by you is the same as rendered by me. I have toiled for you day and night. Is that no service?"

His wife's last argument struck home. Mohandas was taken aback, but only for a moment. He remained unyielding and, by his own account "somehow extorted a consent from her". Before they sailed from Durban, the gifts, including Kasturba's necklace, went into a bank vault to provide trust funds for the Natal Indian Congress.

My grandfather never regretted his decision and, according to his autobiography, my grandmother eventually saw its wisdom. But she had also learned what became increasingly true: in a battle of wills over what he considered a matter of principle, Bapu was not to be beaten. Yet Ba, too, refused to relinquish dearly held beliefs, except on her own terms and for her own reasons. When the time came, she found ways to give wedding gifts to her daughters-in-law as my mother Sushila and my father Manilal could later attest.

# 11

When the Gandhis reached India in December, 1901, they went immediately to Rajkot. Their homecoming was warmly celebrated with friends and relatives alike, but Kasturba was aware that Mohandas' mind was elsewhere. The Indian National Congress was holding its 17th annual meeting later that month in Calcutta; he wanted to be there, not only to introduce a resolution protesting the wrongs suffered by Indians in South Africa, but also to renew ties with the Indian leaders he had met five years earlier.

On December 17, three days after he had settled his family in Rajkot, Mohandas left for Bombay where he arranged to join a group of leading Congress delegates travelling to Calcutta in a private railway car. He used the time en route to lobby for passage of his resolution, describing at length the deteriorating position of the 100,000 Indians living in South Africa. But a leading Bombay lawyer soon put a damper on his enthusiasm. Nothing would come of a South African resolution, he said. "Conditions in India are just as bad. Our energies must be used to fight our battles at home. So long as we have no power in our own land, Indians in other colonies cannot fare better."'

After the Congress Party session Mohandas stayed with Gokhale to exchange ideas on South Africa. Gokhale wanted Mohandas to prepare to do Congress work in India; he took him to the India Club to meet and play billiards with members of influential Bengali families; he introduced him to distinguished callers who came to his home; he advised him to overcome his shyness, to travel, to become acquainted with people all over India. Mohandas, in turn, spoke of the virtues of self-reliance, recommended the simple life, and, in due course, he even made bold to suggest ways his mentor might simplify his own way of living. Gokhale, he said, should take a tram-car instead of riding in his private carriage; or, better still, he could cultivate the habit of walking for his health. Gokhale did not take offence at such advice, but neither did he heed it.

Mohandas, on the other hand, was acting on Gokhale's advice. His business concluded, he embarked on a travel itinerary that began with a quick trip to neighbouring Burma where he was charmed by the "freedom and energy of the Burmese women", but pained by the "indolence of the men", and disgusted by the sight of rats running around in the Golden Pagoda, Rangoon's famed Buddhist shrine. Back in Calcutta he decided to make his return trip to Rajkot a week-long railway pilgrimage through sections of India he had not seen before and announced he would travel third class to acquaint himself with the hardships poor Indians had to endure. Gokhale ridiculed this notion at first. Although he had advised Mohandas to get in touch with people, these weren't necessarily the people he had in mind. But when the time came for Mohandas to board the train he was appropriately garbed in peasant-style Gujarati coat and dhoti. He was also equipped with a cheap canvas bag containing a towel and a blanket, and carried a jug of water. There on the platform was Gokhale immaculate in silk turban and jacket, who came to deliver his farewell gift, a metal tiffin box filled with ladoos and puris, the traditional Indian sweetballs and bread.

This was the first time my grandfather had travelled third class in India, an experiment which, on principle, would one day become his regular practice. The journey was a daunting one. En route to Rajkot, he made several stopovers. The first one was the holy city of Benares. There, after bathing in the Ganges, he went seeking darshan. (A darshan is the blessing one derives from viewing a sacred object or holy person.) This darshan was at the great Kashi Vishvanath temple where Mohandas was shocked by its bazaar-like atmosphere. The scene at this ancient temple dedicated to the god Shiva was far from sacred: "swarming flies, rotting flowers, cunning shopkeepers selling sweets and toys of latest fashions", and corrupt priests who cursed him because his offering was too small. "I searched here for God," he later wrote, "but failed to find Him."

His railway tour continued westward through Agra, Jaipur and Palanpur, and his distress increased. "Third-class passengers are treated like sheep," he wrote, "and their comforts are sheep's comforts." The cars had no cushioned seats, no sleeping accommodations — standard amenities, he pointed out, for third-class passengers in Europe and even in South Africa! Trains were infrequently cleaned; regulations against overcrowding were seldom if ever enforced. He was appalled by the railway employees' indifference to the needs of third-class passengers, and even more by the passengers' lack of consideration for each other. "They pushed, shouted and yelled, littered, smoked, chewed betel and tobacco, converting the whole carriage into a spittoon." Mohandas saw only one solution: if more educated people travelled third class they would surely complain incessantly to railway authorities until conditions were remedied. They could also reform the behaviour of their fellow passengers by good example.

For Kasturba, the return to India was proving turbulent. From the moment she set foot on her native soil, she had been caught up in cross-currents of emotion. The welcoming festivities went on and on, long after Mohandas had left for Calcutta. And for good reason: this time it was not just Mohandas but his whole family returning home from abroad. Kasturba had been the first woman among her friends and relatives to have travelled to a foreign land, and despite the caste strictures against ocean travel, she found herself enjoying near-unanimous acclaim. For days on end she was busy receiving callers, attending parties, recounting her adventures on the high seas and in faraway South Africa. Her two older sons were treated like heroes; her two young toddlers were hugged and admired.

Yet I believe that my grandmother, through all this excitement, must have been carrying a burden of unrelenting sorrow. Based on what I have learned in tracing her story, the evidence suggests that she was mourning a great loss. During the five years she was away, the deaths of one or, more likely, both of her parents had occurred and she had returned to a world full of constant reminders of their absence. Once again, the history of the Kapadia family is so poorly documented that there are no records to refer to, no correspondence to examine, and few reminiscences to rely on. But Gokaldas and Vrajkunwerba Kapadia seem to have disappeared from their daughter's life after her departure for South Africa in 1896. Kasturba's brothers are the only Kapadia relatives mentioned in writings about the Gandhis after that date. And there is no indication Kasturba visited her parents' home in Porbandar when the Gandhi family returned to India in 1901. Nor, apparently, did the Kapadias come to Rajkot to see their newest grandsons. I think it is also significant that my father, Manilal, who was 9 in 1901, old enough by then to remember, never spoke of first-hand memories of his maternal grandparents. Yet whatever grief Kasturba may have known can only be imagined. Like so much else in her personal life, the full truth of this experience has remained hidden, private — untold.

There were, of course, pleasures for Kasturba in Rajkot: settling back into the familiar routine in the Gandhi household, enjoying long talks with her sisters-in-law, admiring their new babies. While Kasturba was living in South Africa, Nandkunwarben had presented Lakshimidas with two more children — little boys who were perfect playmates for Ramdas and Devadas. Also, Gangaben and Karsandas had become parents of another baby girl. So now there was endless sharing of tales about birthing and teething, and first steps and first words. The older boys were thriving, too; quite as happy to be with uncles and cousins again as Kasturba was to be with sisters-in-law and nieces. She was aware once more of the important role her brothers-in-law had played in the lives of her older sons, especially Harilal. Almost 14 now, and in quest of answers, he seemed able to discuss problems more easily with his uncles than with his own father. Kasturba was pleased that Harilal found an opportunity, while Mohandas was still in Calcutta, to tell Lakshimidas about his great desire to study and his father's reluctance to send him to school. Lakshimidas promised to do what he could to help.

Kasturba was more than ready for the family to settle down in Rajkot, perhaps in their own house, if all went well. She hoped her husband would feel the same. But when Mohandas returned to Rajkot from Calcutta, he seemed unwilling to make that commitment. As she watched him reflecting on what he had seen and learned during his travels, Kasturba could see that this was not the assertive Mohandas of South Africa whose tireless work was set by clear imperatives. She sensed that he was unsure of himself again, wondering where he could fit into India's vast complexities.

While Mohandas was struggling with his indecision, the family's trusted old friend and adviser Mavji Dave, the Rajkot lawyer who had urged the Gandhis to send Mohandas off to London to study law, placed three cases in his lap. Mohandas won all three. Kasturba took it as a sign: clearly, her husband should practice law in Rajkot. But Mohandas was now being pulled in another direction. His new mentor Gokhale, who lived in Bombay for part of the year, was luring him to come there, establish a legal practice, and help with Congress work. Mohandas was tempted, yet remained reluctant. He remembered all too well his previous failure to become a Bombay barrister.

Once again, the wise and faithful Mavji Dave took charge.

He came to Mohandas one day and announced abruptly, "Mohan,

we will not let you vegetate here any longer. You must go to Bombay."

For several seconds Mohandas was speechless. Then, in a shaky voice he said, "How could I survive there?" He murmured something about expenses — Bombay was a big city; the cost of living was high; his family would need a house; and he would need an office. ...

"Don't worry," Dave said. "We will send you cases from here. We can also bring you to Rajkot occasionally for professional advice."

In good humour now, Mohandas said, "You want to get rid of me."

"No, no. It is just that we feel you are wasting your time and talents in this small town. With your ardent love for social and political work, you are destined for public service. Bombay will provide you with more opportunities."

To Mohandas, it seemed as though the words had been plucked from his own mouth. This was precisely what he had been feeling for some weeks, but had not dared to say aloud.

By the end of July, Mohandas had made all arrangements. He had hired office space in the central part of Bombay known as the Fort area, and rented a small bungalow in nearby Girgaum. Heeding advice from his brother Lakshimidas and pleas from his son and nephew, Mohandas still held himself responsible for the upbringing of his widowed sister's son, he had also enrolled Harilal and Gokaldas as boarding students in schools at Gondal and at Benares (the story is told that only one space was open at each school, so Mohandas had the boys select coins with the one picking the coin of higher denomination to be sent to Benares. Harilal went to Gondal).

In early August of 1902 Mohandas moved his wife and his three younger sons to Bombay. Uprooted again, Kasturba had to adjust once more to a new life in an unfamiliar place. But this time she could revel in the change. Bombay, its population then approaching one million, was one of the world's great metropolises. With its magnificent harbour, busy rail centres, and huge cotton factories, its wide palm-bordered boulevards lined with the marble mansions and landscaped gardens of native Indian princes and wealthy Europeans, Bombay was an exciting place, unlike any other she had ever known. Yet Kasturba could feel at home here, always aware that she was in her beloved India. In Bombay was the largest branch of the textile firm her father had established. Her brothers, who had inherited the family business, had homes there; other relatives and friends from Porbandar and Rajkot lived in Bombay. Here were countless bazaars to be explored, bustling markets filled with silk brocades, gold and silver filigree ornaments, beaten brass utensils, lacquered toys, beautifully crafted jewels, finely carved woods, and the colourful gossamer-like textiles for which India was, and still is, famous. Here were splendid temples, great domed buildings, white and gleaming in the sun, filled with the wonders of India's glorious past — a joy for any pious Hindu woman to visit. Here in Bombay, Kasturba's lingering memories of the loneliness of Durban could fade away like a dream, forgotten in the blessed sunlight of a new day.

But even as the Gandhis were moving into the Girgaum house, and long before it was in order, the family faced a grave crisis. Kasturba and Mohandas had been concerned about 9-year-old Manilal's health ever since his bout with smallpox two years earlier which had left his eyesight permanently weakened. Now, suddenly, he became seriously ill again — typhoid this time, complicated by pneumonia. The Parsi doctor called in to examine Manilal said he was extremely weak. The child needed nourishment to fight this double attack, the doctor said. Manilal must be given eggs and chicken soup.

Already agonised over their son's condition, Kasturba and Mohandas were even more deeply troubled by this prescription, and resisted any thought of breaking with the vegetarian tradition of their Vaishnava sect. In this, the two of them were equally resolute.

Taking Kasturba aside, Mohandas said, "It seems to me that God is testing us. Testing our faith in Him."

"Yes, I agree," Kasturba replied. "But what about Manilal? How can we save him?"

"Do you mind if I carry out some experiments?" Mohandas said. "I have read about a water cure involving frequent hip baths, and I have faith in it. I want to try it on Manilal, but I need your support. Manilal is as much your son as mine."

Kasturba did not hesitate. "Of course you have my support."

Mohandas then told the doctor of their dilemma. "His mother and I cannot, in good conscience, give eggs or chicken soup to our child."

"I know," the doctor replied, "but there is nothing else I can suggest. The boy needs nourishment; his survival may depend on it."

"If he were grown up, we would let him decide. We wouldn't stand in his way. But he is still small and incapable of making such a decision. His mother and I must decide for him." Mohandas hesitated for a moment, then continued. His voice was barely audible. "I would like to ask you a favour. I think the hydropathic treatment devised by a German physician, Dr. Ludwig Kuhne, may help our son. I want to try it in combination with another remedy I have seen used with success — fasting except for occasional sips of water and orange juice. But I would like you to come and examine him every day and let me know if his condition improves."

The doctor agreed, and the treatments began at once. For the next three days, Mohandas and Kasturba gave Manilal repeated hipbaths, having him sit in a tub of tepid water for not longer than a minute or two at a time. They also kept him on a diet of orange juice and water. But every day when the doctor came, he would shake his head sadly, and say there was no change for the better.

If anything, Manilal was getting worse. Kasturba and Mohandas could see that for themselves. His high temperature showed no signs of abating; at night, he became delirious. Their apprehensions grew.

For once Mohandas began to wonder whether he was doing the right thing. He was not sure this remedy he had only read about would work. His mind was in turmoil. Did they have the right to gamble with the life of another, even their own son? Should they call in another physician, or perhaps a practitioner of India's ancient Ayurvedic medicine? What if his son should die? Would he ever be able to forgive himself? Would Kasturba forgive him? She appeared to be her calm and gentle self, soothing Manilal, administering his treatments. Mohandas knew she, too, was becoming desperate.

That evening, sitting by Manilal's bedside, Mohandas called Kasturba into the room. It was 10pm. Manilal's temperature had reached 104°F. His skin was parched, burning to the touch. He was more restless and agitated than ever before.

"There is one other treatment I would like to try," Mohandas said. "I don't know if it will reduce the fever, but we must not give up. We must have faith. Would you help me?"

Following Mohandas' instructions, Kasturba got a clean bedsheet and soaked it in cool water. By the time she had it ready, Mohandas had undressed Manilal. They wrapped their child in the wet sheet and then covered him with two blankets, leaving only his head exposed. When they had finished, Kasturba could see that her husband was suffering terrible mental agony.

"I have to get away," he said. "I am going out for a walk. Would you sit at Manilal's side and keep wet packs on his forehead?"

"I will." Never questioning, Kasturba took over. "And remember," she whispered, as he turned to leave. "God gives life and He takes it away. Let us trust Him and abide by His decision."

For the next half-hour, Mohandas paced up and down the dark deserted beach walk near the house. Over and over, his lips silently murmured the name of Rama, Ramanama — a long-standing exercise dating back to the earliest years of his boyhood in Porbandar. In those days, the Gandhi family's faithful nursemaid, an old woman named

Rambha, had taught him that he could overcome his childish fears of the dark and ghosts and spirits by a constant repetition of the name of Rama, an incarnation of the god Vishnu and the heroic ideal of Hindu manhood. Rambha's remedy had worked then for Mohan the child, it worked now for Mohandas the man. (And it would again bring solace to my grandfather in years to come. Ramanama was Mahatma Gandhi's invariable prayer of faith in times of fear and turmoil.) His confidence restored, his hope revived, Mohandas turned back toward home. His heart was beating fast.

In their son's sick room, Kasturba could scarcely believe what was happening. Manilal was perspiring profusely. The fever had broken! Her son, who moments before had been delirious, was himself again. She could feel the anguish drain from her body as she stroked his damp forehead. For the first time in days she was at peace.

As soon as Mohandas entered the house, Manilal called out to him. "Please, Bapu, get me out of these blankets. I'm all wet."

Mohandas rushed to his side. "In a moment, my son." He turned to his wife, his heart full of wonder, his mind full of questions. Kasturba's radiant smile confirmed the miracle.

In later years, my father Manilal had no memory of having lived, even briefly, in the small house in Girgaum. Indeed, his only recollections of the episode that had brought him so close to death were the details recounted to him by his parents (Bapu usually prefaced the story with a declaration that Manilal, after that, became the strongest and healthiest of his four sons).

During Manilal's illness, Kasturba and Mohandas had been too worried about him to think of anything else. Only after he had fully recovered did Kasturba first notice how cramped and uncomfortable their house was; how dank and dark. Surely an unhealthy place for anyone to live. Suddenly she was aware of feeling stifled by the confines of city life in crowded Bombay. She realised no matter what complaints she might have had about South Africa, she very much missed the open spaces in Durban. She told Mohandas she wanted to move again. To her relief, he said he felt the same way.

The search for a home in one of the outer suburbs of Bombay began. One suburb, while pleasant enough, was too far from the sea. Another home, though attractive and conveniently located, was ruled out promptly by Kasturba because there was a slaughterhouse very close to the market where she would have to go to buy vegetables. She knew she could not bear to see the animals being led to slaughter each day. Then, in the inviting suburb of Santa Cruz (an area where Bombay's airport would one day be located), they found an ideal bungalow — roomy and airy, with a garden and plenty of sunshine. It was close to the market, near the railroad stations, and there was a school nearby where Manilal could go in the fall. They rented the bungalow at once, moved in, and felt instantly at home.

Mohandas now settled happily, even complacently, into the daily routine of commuting into the city. He bought a rail season ticket from Santa Cruz into central Bombay, and (this being one of his very rare periods of self-indulgence) "frequently felt a certain pride," as he later confessed, "in being the only first-class passenger in my compartment." His career went well. He received no court cases, but he soon had enough chamber work to live comfortably. He had use of the High Court library, and occasionally attended High Court trials, sitting by the big open windows and enjoying the cool sea breezes as he listened to the courtroom proceedings. His friend Gokhale kept an eye on him, as promised. Gokhale would appear at Mohandas' office several times a week, bringing friends whom he wanted to introduce, or suggesting some work for Congress he wanted Mohandas to undertake. All in all, life in India was proving to be most agreeable.

Kasturba, too, was blissfully content. By training, by habit, and indeed by temperament, she was something of a traditionalist. Yet, despite her protected upbringing, she had always enjoyed talking with people, making new friends, in Santa Cruz and in Bombay, too. She was quite comfortable going out on her own or with friends, and loved doing so. She also liked being mistress of her own home, and was far more at ease in that role than she had ever been in Durban. Most of their Santa Cruz neighbours were Gujarati-speaking Hindus from the Kathiawar region of India. In South Africa their neighbours had been white and English-speaking. Many of Mohandas' friends and co-workers had been Muslim or Christian. Kasturba was glad to welcome all visitors to her home, but in South Africa she had been unable to communicate with some of their guests. Worse still, in extending hospitality to one and all, she had often had to go against the religious teachings of her youth. At her husband's request, she had broken all rules of caste distinction, she had stopped observing many of the strict rules of eating, drinking, washing, bathing, cleaning, not wearing shoes inside the house. These things were second nature to her and to many other Gujaratis of that period.

Kasturba had never acknowledged how much these defections troubled her. Not until she returned from South Africa and was back home in Rajkot. One day in a long talk with her sister-in-law,

Nandkunwarben, Lakshimidas' wife, she had confessed her feelings of guilt. Though Mohandas had proved to her the seriousness of his convictions, Kasturba said she was still not convinced he was right. If the Hindu religion had divided the community into many different castes and assigned specific duties to each caste, the ancient sages must have had very good reasons for doing so. This was straightforward logic; Kasturba was a straightforward woman. She had been brought up in orthodoxy to respect the scriptures and the learned men who expounded them. All the Hindu world accepted these teachings. What reason could she or Mohandas have to doubt them?

Her sister-in-law's response (words of wisdom that my grandmother would recall many times over in the years to come) had been comforting and, in an odd sort of way, liberating.

"In South Africa, you were simply being a good wife," Nandkunwarben assured Kasturba. "As long as you are a good wife, you can do many things that are forbidden by dogma."

Kasturba had then stopped reproaching herself. Still, it was a great relief here in Santa Cruz to be able to live her life without making any of the concessions Mohandas had required of her in Durban.

It appeared that the Gandhis had found their future and were settled in India. In early November 1902 an urgent cable arrived from Durban:

"Chamberlain expected here," the cable said. "Please come immediately." There were no further details, but Mohandas at once understood the significance of the message. This would be the first trip the British colonial secretary had made to South Africa since the Boer War had finally ended in victory for the British earlier that year. The Indians in Natal obviously feared the visit could bode ill for them, and wanted Mohandas to be on hand to represent their cause when discussions took place. His promise to return to South Africa whenever the Indian community needed his help must now be honoured.

Again, plans had to be changed. But the mere mention of moving the family again brought Kasturba's protest. "We can't keep upsetting our lives every time something happens in South Africa! We must think of the effect it will have on the children and their education."

"In that case, I will have to go alone," Mohandas said. "I don't think the work they have for me will take more than a year. We can make arrangements for you to remain here in Santa Cruz."

Next day he sent off a cable saying he was prepared to leave as soon as his ticket was paid for. The South African Indians cabled passage money at once. At that point, Mohandas began worrying in earnest about leaving his family alone and unprotected. Ever since moving to

Bombay, they had been living from month to month. While he was away, he could send Kasturba money to pay for the family's needs, but what if something happened to him? The home in Santa Cruz was rented. The jewellery had long since been sold. If he should die, Kasturba and the family would literally be penniless.

Mohandas then recalled that an American insurance salesman had visited him in the office a couple of times, trying to persuade him to buy a life insurance policy. He had thought it nonsense at the time, but now he hunted the man down and bought a 10,000-rupee policy naming Kasturba as his beneficiary.

When he showed the policy to Kasturba that night, and told her what it said, she pushed it away with contempt. To an Indian woman, becoming a widow is unthinkable. Kasturba, like other Indian wives, often prayed she would die before her husband. But here he was now, giving her a piece of paper, which promised her money if he should die.

"How can you think of such an awful thing on the eve of your departure?" she said.

"There is nothing awful about it," Mohandas said. "It could happen to anyone, and a person like me would be regarded a fool if I did not foresee such a possibility."

Kasturba turned away. "Do be quiet. I don't want to hear any more about it." Like so many women of her generation, my grandmother knew nothing of insurance policies and had no trust in people who insisted that forms be signed, identities be established, and papers be kept track of forever. Gold and jewellery were what they valued — not just as adornment, but also as a form of savings which would never depreciate.

Mohandas smiled, said no more and put the policy away. He then busied himself making all other necessary provisions for his family's welfare: both his immediate family and his extended family. He arranged for his son Harilal and his nephew Gokaldas to continue their schooling as boarders at their respective schools, and asked Lakshimidas to keep an eye on them. He even arranged with a barrister friend in Rajkot for the two boys, when visiting there, to be allowed to use his tennis court. Mohandas also invited a close relative, 23-year-old Chaganlal Gandhi, who was working as a clerk in Bombay, to move his family into the bungalow in Santa Cruz. They could keep Kasturba and the other children company while he was away, and Chaganlal could act as Manilal's tutor. Chaganlal and his wife Kashiben had one little boy who was just a bit younger than Ramdas and Devadas, and for Kasturba, no house could have too many children. More than that, she got along very well with Kashiben. It would be like having a congenial younger sister-in-law in the household.

Mohandas had meantime asked several other young Gandhi relatives, enterprising youths with high hopes for the future to accompany him on this trip to South Africa. They could get started, he said, by helping in his work with the Natal Indian Congress. Of these, the young man Mohandas felt closest to was 19-year-old Maganlal Gandhi, Chaganlal's younger brother. My grandfather always spoke of Chaganlal and Maganlal as his "nephews". They were the sons of one of his favourite cousins, Khushaldas Gandhi. Orphaned as a child, Khushaldas had been raised by Mohandas' parents, Putliba and Karamchand, as their own son. Almost grown by the time Mohandas was born, he had seemed like a respected oldest brother, and Mohandas had always regarded him as something of an exemplar. Khushaldas had been the first young man in the Kathiawar region to complete his high school studies (there would be times when Mohandas' own sons suspected their father felt closer to these "nephews" than he did to them — but that lay in the future).

By the second week of November 1902 when his ship sailed out of Bombay harbour en route to Durban, Mohandas had every reason to be pleased with all the arrangements he had made. In a year or less he would be back again, ready to resume life in India where he had left off.

Such, at least, was the plan.

# 12

In January of 1903, with all due ceremony, Lakshimidas had arranged the betrothal of Harilal, then 14 years old, to 11-year-old Gulab, the daughter of old and trusted Gandhi family friends in Rajkot. Lakshimidas, Kasturba, and Gulab's parents all agreed it was an eminently suitable match. Mohandas had a cordial relationship with her father, Haridas Vohra, a member of the Modh Vania subcaste and a leading lawyer. But they had all underestimated Mohandas' great aversion to child marriages. when notified that the betrothal had actually been announced, he objected strenuously, giving his reluctant consent only when assured that the marriage of the young people, who scarcely knew each other, would not take place for many years.

Sometime in late autumn of 1903, Kasturba and her four sons visited a photographer's studio in Bombay where they posed for a formal portrait. It is probably the best-known photograph ever taken of the Gandhi family, even though Mohandas is not in the picture. Kasturba, looking resolute and serene, stands in the centre of her little brood, her left arm around her youngest son, three-year-old Devadas, and her right hand resting on the little boy's knee to steady him as he sits perched on a tall wooden pedestal. Eleven-year-old Manilal, gravely watchful, is next to Devadas, standing in front of the carved pedestal — the kind that regularly shows up in wedding photos of that era — usually supporting a flower-filled porcelain vase. Beside Kasturba, at her right elbow, is earnest but uncertain five-year-old Ramdas, seated on a sort of stool that appears for all the world to be a tree stump. Standing just behind Ramdas with a hand on his young brother's shoulder is 15-year-old

Harilal — thin-faced, sober, intense.

By all appearances, this handsomely attired little group might well be a prosperous Parsi family of the period. The Gandhis were obviously still abiding by Mohandas' decision, made several years earlier, to follow the lead of the Europeanised Parsis in matters of attire.

In the autumn of 1903 the family was again in a state of flux. Mohandas, instead of returning home after a year's absence, had sent for his wife and sons to join him in South Africa as soon as possible. Departure time was near, and Mohandas had given no hint of when, if ever, they would return to India.

Certainly Kasturba, while appearing unperturbed, was inwardly troubled. While she wanted to take her rightful place beside her husband, she dreaded leaving her son, Harilal, behind. He wanted to stay and continue his education. His desire for learning pleased Kasturba. She had long taken pride in the fact that family and friends regarded Harilal as intellectually gifted.

I believe my devout and strong-minded grandmother understood and respected Harilal's determination. To her, it was fitting for a son to insist on his right to be educated.

Kasturba was silently confronting other uncertainties. Doubts graver in some ways than those she had felt before her first voyage to South Africa. True, her fear of ocean travel had diminished. But her apprehension about what lay in store for her and her family in that distant land had not. According to Mohandas' letters to the family, South Africa was changing rapidly. Their life there would be changing, too, and she did not know what to expect. It was almost as if she had never lived in South Africa at all.

The house that awaited them at the end of this journey was not in Durban, or even in Natal; Mohandas was now practicing law in Transvaal, a place she had only heard about (and what she had heard was quite disconcerting, at least for Indians). They would be living in Johannesburg, a city unknown to her, among people who spoke a different language, different even from English. Mohandas had rented a house for them — to be shared with strangers, no doubt, if she knew her husband. She would again set up a new household; one to be run in accordance with his latest notions about diet, health, housekeeping, and schooling for the boys. All of which was fine. But Mohandas was so unpredictable that his ideas had undoubtedly changed since the last time they were together. Change sometimes seemed the only constant element in her life. But Kasturba refused to fret about it. She had adjusted to changes before, she would adjust again.

Even so, she hated to give up her independence. Living in their pleasant bungalow in Santa Cruz during the past year, managing her own household with the assistance and cooperation of her husband's young relative Chaganlal Gandhi and his wife Kashiben, Kasturba had developed a comfortable self-assurance about her ability to take care of herself and take responsibility for the welfare of others. Now, her first extended experience of complete personal autonomy was coming to an end. Particularly painful was the realisation that she might not meet Chaganlal and his family again. Even though they were also going to South Africa, they were planning to settle in Natal.

In the days before they sailed, as Kashiben helped her with the final shopping and packing, Kasturba realised how much she would miss this young couple. Almost as much as she would miss Harilal.

During the year that had passed since he was summoned back to Natal by his Durban friends, Mohandas had observed many unforeseen changes, some subtle, some ominous, affecting the lives of his fellow countrymen throughout South Africa. Indians in the British crown colonies had expected their situation to improve after the British victory in the Boer War. They had, after all, remained loyal to the crown (as Mohandas had urged), and had been hailed as "sons of the Empire" by their fellow citizens. Transvaal's Indians, and even the Orange Free State's few Indian residents, had also believed cruelties and indignities they had suffered under oppressive Boer rule would be redressed, once those defeated Boer republics came under the British flag. Hadn't the British declared at the war's outset that one cause of the conflict was ill treatment of their Indian citizens by the Boers?

What was actually happening, however, was quite different. By 1903 the position of Indians everywhere in South Africa was deteriorating.

Mohandas had realised this almost as soon as he disembarked in Durban and his friends from the Natal Indian Congress rushed him off to meet with the visiting British colonial secretary, Joseph Chamberlain, heretofore regarded as a champion of Indian rights. Mr. Chamberlain was courteous in receiving Mohandas, preoccupied while listening to his petition on behalf of Natal's industrious and law-abiding Indian community, and casual in dismissing him.

"We do not interfere in the affairs of the colonies," he said. "I shall do what I can, but if you choose to live among the Europeans you must try to win their confidence yourselves." And with that, he was off to inspect war-torn Transvaal.

Such aggravations, Mohandas soon learned, were common everyday experiences for Indians in postwar South Africa — especially in the Transvaal.

The Indian community was shaken. They confronted Mohandas with their disillusionment: "You told us if we cooperated with the British in the war they would be more sympathetic to our cause."

Mohandas had to admit he had made a mistake in his evaluation of British officialdom. But he still had faith in British justice, and was determined to make that justice work for South Africa's Indians. He couldn't give up, not as long as their rights were in jeopardy. He simply had to begin over again, this time in Transvaal.

He decided to set up legal practice in the booming city of Johannesburg where some 12,000 of his fellow countrymen lived. His progress was immediate and encouraging. He applied for admission to the Transvaal Supreme Court and, somewhat to his surprise, was enrolled without challenge. He discovered a vegetarian restaurant in Johannesburg where, as had happened in London, he met many congenial people. One such was Herman Kallenbach, a wealthy and successful German-Jewish architect and something of a free thinker, who had become interested in both vegetarianism and Theosophy through his study of Buddhism. The two men began an instant and mutually satisfying exchange of opinions and advice. Kallenbach introduced Mohandas to a sympathetic English property agent, Louis Ritch, who was a leader of the Theosophical Society of Johannesburg. With Ritch's help, Mohandas leased offices on Risik Street in the legal quarters of the city — also a surprise, as no Indian had ever before been able to do so. He was now ready to confront Transvaal's abusive authorities. After interviewing witnesses and collecting evidence, Mohandas demanded warrants for the arrest and prosecution of two of the Asiatic Department's most notoriously corrupt officers. The white jury, as expected, refused to convict white offenders on the testimony of non-white witnesses. But the trial's exposure of widespread malfeasance embarrassed Transvaal officials, and prodded them into firing the acquitted culprits and ultimately cleaning up the department.

The winning of this small victory reassured Transvaal's Indians, and confirmed their faith in the energetic new barrister from Bombay. It also made the Gandhi name one to be reckoned with among Europeans. Within months, Mohandas' legal practice in Johannesburg was thriving — as lucrative as it had ever been in Durban — and cases of every kind were being brought to him.

Step by step, and without conscious purpose, Mohandas was now approaching the most decisive period of his life. Through personal discipline and professional endeavours, through intellectual discoveries and spiritual explorations, he was formulating a way of action that would transform the world. But Mohandas was not yet ready to act. Still the conscientious private householder but also the emerging public leader, he felt tormented by conflicting loyalties. Painfully aware of family responsibilities yet totally absorbed in the cause of his countrymen in South Africa, he postponed plans to return home to India, but he made no move to send for Kasturba and the boys. For months he continued to live simply in an apartment behind his office. Meanwhile, he dedicated all his excess energy and much of his surplus income to an endeavour just getting underway in Durban.

During a visit to Natal, Mohandas had been approached by a Gujarati businessman, Madanjit Vyavaharik, the proprietor of the first Indian-owned printing press in South Africa. When Madanjit suggested starting a weekly newspaper for Indians in South Africa, Mohandas saw at once what a boon such a journal could be in the campaign for Indian rights. He gave the idea enthusiastic approval and adopted it as his own, agreeing not only to provide generous financial backing, but also to supply much of the editorial content. He even suggested a name for the paper: *Indian Opinion*.

The first issue was published in Durban on June 4, 1903. In order to reach the widest possible audience, not just in Natal, but throughout South Africa, it was printed in four languages: English, Gujarati, Hindi, and Tamil. This proved overly ambitious, and *Indian Opinion* was eventually issued only in English and Gujarati. From the start, however, it managed to achieve Mohandas' main goals. It gave South African Indians a voice of their own. It informed them about common problems. It united them in common purpose. The newspaper also increased the Indian community's credibility with white South Africans. Journalism was something Europeans understood. And the very name *Indian Opinion*, proclaimed that here was a different point of view, one that must be taken into account.

Soon after the launching of *Indian Opinion*, Mohandas began looking for a house for his family in the suburbs of Johannesburg. Now in his 34th year, he was seeing his future and his family's future more clearly. He knew he must complete the work at hand, "even," as he put it, "if that meant living in South Africa all my life." And he knew that Kasturba must be at his side.

Kasturba had expected surprises in Johannesburg, but nothing in her experience had prepared her for her first sight of that sprawling, mile-high city, carved into the slopes of the Witwatersrand mountain ridge.

Johannesburg was some 300 miles north-west of Durban. There had been no town there at all when the world's richest deposits of gold were discovered under these mountains in 1886. By the time Kasturba and her sons arrived early in 1904, less than two decades later, the population of Johannesburg was upward of 100,000. To Kasturba, arriving directly from Bombay, her mind's eye still reflecting the softy burnished patina of that ancient city's vistas, her body and spirit still attuned to its familiar, changeless rhythms, the brash young city of Johannesburg, with its stark, unfinished look and its restless, raucous vigour, must have come as a rude shock.

But on the day of their arrival, Kasturba took little more than passing notice of the Johannesburg landscape. Nor did she linger over her inspection of the large, eight-room house Mohandas had rented for them in Kensington, one of the city's European sections. It was some five miles from his downtown office. Other than being sparsely furnished, it seemed comfortable enough. Her attention was elsewhere that day. Her main concern was Ramdas' broken arm.

She had been worried about her son's arm for several days, ever since he had fractured it on board ship, playing games with the ship's captain. Ramdas had been attended by the ship's doctor who had put the arm in a sling and advised Kasturba that it must be properly set by a qualified doctor as soon as they arrived in Johannesburg. But now, it seemed her husband had other ideas. Mohandas proposed to treat their son himself with earth poultices, he said. Mud packs. Though dubious, Kasturba felt she would go along with the experiment.

And she took heart when Mohandas said he had learned of the remedy through a vegetarian friend who shared his interest in Dr. Kuhne's hydropathic therapy. Remembering how that water treatment had saved Manilal when he was sick with typhoid fever, how could she object to a mud pack treatment for Ramdas? So each day after that, while Kasturba comforted Ramdas, Mohandas gently unwrapped the boy's broken arm, applied a fresh earth poultice, and then bandaged it anew. Once more, her decision to trust in her husband's home remedies was justified. Within a month, Ramdas' arm was completely healed, as strong as new.

By that time, Kasturba was comfortably adjusting to her new home. Her kitchen was in order. She had found the best markets for shopping where she had met and made friends with a few other Indian women. Plans for the boys' schooling were being discussed, and the family was settling into a comfortable routine.

Mohandas left early each morning, sometimes walking, sometimes

114

riding his bicycle, to go to work in the city. He always returned home in time for dinner, often bringing friends or co-workers with him to enjoy Kasturba's cooking. He usually stayed up late each night, writing articles and editorials for *Indian Opinion*, which he sent off the next day to Durban. Though he sometimes crept into Kasturba's bed afterwards seeking the satisfactions only she could give, more often he slept alone in his own room which served as his office. Kasturba was aware, as never before, that she was not the centre of her husband's universe. The weekly newspaper seemed to be his latest preoccupation — and a costly one too, apparently. Mohandas told her the paper needed many more subscribers to become a profitable enterprise. Yet, to close it down, he said, would be both a loss and a disgrace for the Indian community.

What he did not disclose to Kasturba was that he had, by this time, sunk most of his savings into *Indian Opinion*, and was paying subsidies of up to £75 a month to sustain it.

One day in March of 1904, Mohandas sent word by messenger to Kasturba that he would not be able to come home until the next morning.

This was not like Mohandas. Kasturba wondered what urgent work compelled him to remain away from home overnight. But she had no way of finding out, so she and the boys ate an early dinner, completed the daily chores, and went to bed. Not until next morning, when Mohandas came home for a bath and a short rest, did his own family learn of the disaster that had overtaken the Indian community (my father Manilal, years later, could remember listening spellbound to every word, as his father told his mother the fearful news).

"Plague has hit the location," Mohandas announced. "There are already 23 patients. We only hope there won't be more." He had not told her earlier, he said, because he didn't want her to worry.

Mohandas had first learned of the outbreak the previous morning, from his friend Madanjit, the co-founder of *Indian Opinion*, who had been in Johannesburg canvassing for subscriptions, and had been shocked to discover several cases of the dreadful bubonic or black plague in the locations where most of the city's Indians lived.

Convinced the disease would spread throughout the settlement if the sick miners were not isolated, and certain the patients would all die if not cared for, Madanjit had immediately sent for Mohandas.

Bubonic plague (with no known cure before the advent of antibiotics) strikes swiftly and causes great suffering. It is highly contagious and usually kills within days. The outbreak had originated among African gold miners whose welfare seemed to be of no concern to the whites;

then it had spread to Indians who worked with the Africans in the mines, and they had brought the plague to the Indian location. Johannesburg's municipal government provided few if any services in the overcrowded location — a shabby conglomeration of homes in the filthiest conditions (in the African location where the stricken African miners lived, the situation was even worse). Bad sanitation, overflowing gutters, and rotting garbage on street corners provided an ideal breeding ground for epidemics. And there were no hospitals or nursing facilities for Indians anywhere in the city.

By the time Mohandas arrived on the scene, Madanjit, a resourceful person had already broken into a vacant house that could serve as a temporary infirmary. Working together, with the aid of some volunteers, they moved all the plague patients there.

Mohandas had then cycled to the office of the Municipal Corporation of Johannesburg and informed the town clerk of the epidemic. That official, though happy with the prompt steps Mohandas and Madanjit had taken, was worried about the use of the vacant house without the owner's permission, and said it should be vacated as soon as possible. He would try to find another place that might serve as a hospital. He meantime ordered quarantine for the location, placing it off-limits to all except relief workers.

"It was a terrible night," Mohandas concluded, "and it will be worse today. I must get back at once."

"In that case," Kasturba said quietly, "I will come and help."

"And I want to help, too," Manilal said, but his parents did not seem to be listening.

Mohandas was astonished by Kasturba's offer. She had no real experience in community service. Despite his own disregard for danger — he felt, somehow, that he was working as God's instrument of mercy in this emergency — the idea of his wife being exposed to the virulent plague gave him pause. Suddenly apprehensive, his reply was a firm "No." But, seeing her disappointment, he suggested a less hazardous way she might be of service. If she would visit homes in the Indian location, Mohandas said, she could talk to the women about basic health and hygiene measures, and explain how to detect plague symptoms.

Kasturba was not altogether comfortable with the idea of intruding on strangers, giving them advice. But Mohandas was right. She understood how important it was to reach the people in danger. And she knew she must do it.

Later that morning, Kasturba went with Mohandas to the location, leaving Manilal in charge of the younger boys. That was how he could help, she told him. On her own, she met and talked with many women. Even those who did not speak Gujarati seemed to welcome her concern. That afternoon the town clerk notified Mohandas that he had found a big empty warehouse that could be used as a hospital, but the city could provide no staff, supplies, or equipment. Here was something else that had to be done. Kasturba asked some of the women she had met that day to help her clean and scrub the building. Next day, they went from house to house in the location, collecting furniture, mattresses, pillows, bedding, pots and pans. Anything to help turn the warehouse into a functioning hospital. Not until the building was ready to receive patients did Kasturba return home to her own family.

Almost immediately, however, in the wake of the epidemic, a new calamity befell the Indian community — a man-made misfortune that kept Mohandas busy day and night, seeing clients at all hours, seldom getting home for dinner. The Municipal Corporation of Johannesburg, proclaiming that the plague had flourished in the "coolie location" because of unsanitary conditions (for which the city itself, of course, was mostly responsible), decreed the location must be destroyed. The city never provided the settlement with sanitation services. No one was more eager than Mohandas to see disease-breeding conditions eradicated. His campaign to educate Indians about the need for better sanitation had been a ceaseless one. But he was appalled by the callous injustice of this decision and the way it was carried out. The Indians, given almost no advance notice, were evacuated to a camp outside the city. The vacated location was then burned to the ground. Evictees were granted little more than token compensation for loss of their homes and personal belongings, and their only recourse, if they wished to dispute the pittances awarded to them, was an appeal to a special tribunal. Confused and frightened, many of these dispossessed settlers turned to Mohandas for help.

Out of seventy such appeals he handled in the succeeding weeks, only one was lost — justifying to a degree, his faith in legal remedies. He set aside half of his fees, and the costs awarded him by the tribunal, to start a hospice for poor Indians. The other half went to *Indian Opinion*, where financial problems seemed never-ending.

The Johannesburg plague of 1904 made a lasting imprint on Mohandas personally. It was a time when several Europeans, whose lives and fortunes would become merged with his own, first began working for the Indian cause.

Ultimately, though, it was not new-found friends or allies who had made the deepest impression on my grandfather during the plague. It was the one closest to him: his own wife.

Kasturba had become a person he had never known before — a perfect helpmate, revealing hidden strengths, providing unexpected support. For the first time, Mohandas had seen in practice his wife's unique ability to work with other women, to inspire others by her own actions. And he had realised, not for the last time, that Kasturba could no more withhold help from those in distress than he himself could.

But what I believe my grandfather failed to recognise is this: it was not just for him, or even for the community, that his wife had felt impelled to express her compassion, to use her talents during those days of crisis. Kasturba had simply been true to herself.

# 13

With his family comfortably ensconced in their new home, and life in Johannesburg returning to normal, Mohandas addressed the question of schooling for his sons, unconventionally, of course, but seriously. He was still convinced he could give the boys a better education than was offered at any schools available to them in South Africa. He took Manilal and Ramdas along with him on his five-mile walk into the city each day, giving them instruction along the way. At his office, Mohandas kept the boys busy with reading assignments and written lessons while he went about his business, seeing clients, dictating letters to Miss Schlesin. In the afternoon the boys walked home with him, reviewing what they had learned. Kasturba felt this plan for their sons' education, however irregular, was more satisfactory than Mohandas' earlier efforts at home schooling. Besides, the boys got to spend so much time with their father.

One morning, after the long walk from home to office, Mohandas noticed Manilal peering closely at the book he was asked to read.

"Where are your specs?" Mohandas asked his son. Manilal had been wearing glasses for five years, ever since his vision was left impaired by smallpox at the age of seven.

"I forgot them," Manilal replied guiltily. "They're at home."

"Well, you must have your spectacles," Mohandas said sternly. "And to make sure you don't forget them again, I want you to walk home and get them and bring them back here."

It was almost noon when a tired, disconsolate Manilal arrived at the house. Kasturba was surprised to see him.

119

"What happened?" she asked. "Why have you come home alone?"

"I forgot my spectacles," the boy said. "Bapu sent me to get them, and now I have to go back to the office." He sighed deeply, hoping his mother would show sympathy and save him from another ten-mile round-trip trek to the city and back.

Kasturba did not want to countermand Mohandas' order. She quickly prepared some food, then called to Manilal.

"Come," she said. "Your lunch is ready."

While her son ate, Kasturba sat beside him at the kitchen table. How could she impress upon this 12-year-old boy the importance of his father's strong ideals? How could she make him understand?

"I know how it is to feel that Bapu is demanding too much of you." She paused, studying her son's reaction, then continued. "It happened to me once, on a day long ago. You were only five or six years old, then, and we were living in Durban. Remember?"

As Manilal listened in rapt attention, she told him how, in deference to his father's unorthodox ideas, she had forced herself to empty the chamber pot of one of their Christian houseguests. She spoke of how hurt she had been, realising her husband expected her to degrade herself in this way; how furious she had been, knowing he wanted her cheerfully to defy the teachings of generations of religious leaders. She told how she had lashed back at Mohandas, provoking him to greater anger. Even now, Kasturba said, she could not quite see how an argument about the cleaning of one little chamber pot could be so important as to make him want to drive his wife out of his home in a strange land. Yet that incident, she said, had proved one thing to her: the seriousness of Bapu's beliefs. She had vowed, then and there, that even though she could not, on her own account, accept any of her husband's peculiar new notions unless she was convinced he was right, she would try always to understand his way of thinking and, whenever possible, acquiesce to his wishes.

"What I do know," Kasturba concluded, "and what you must understand is this: your father is a good man. He wants you to be a good son, and that is why he asks you to do hard things." Smiling, she ran her fingers through Manilal's unruly hair. "You are a good son, and that is why you must do as he asks — even the hard things. Now finish your lunch quickly and get back to the office before he begins to wonder what has happened to you."

Years later, my father Manilal liked to tell his own children about the day he forgot his spectacles. He would conclude by assuring us that was how he learned not to forget things. But I always sensed that what made him remember the incident so vividly was not his father's stern discipline, but his mother's firm and loving guidance.

By nature and by habit, Kasturba was vigilant in her concern for the welfare of her sons, and constant in her awareness of their individual needs. Harilal, so far away now, became a focus of special anxieties. Since it took up to two months for letters from India to reach Johannesburg, she could never be sure, at any given time, just how he was faring. Kasturba and Mohandas were disturbed when word came that Harilal had changed schools. Bright as he was, he had fallen behind other students his age because of gaps in his earlier education. But there was no mention of trouble with studies after that, so they assumed Harilal's school problems had been solved.

On the day Mohandas told Kasturba that his older brother's latest letter reported that Harilal was seriously ill, she felt especially helpless and frustrated. Lakshimidas had recently moved his own growing family — he and Nandkunwarben now had seven children — back to the ancestral Gandhi home in Porbandar, leaving the family home in Rajkot to their widowed sister Raliatben. He had just received word that Harilal was stricken while visiting her there. But, there was no need to worry, Lakshimidas wrote. Harilal's future father-in-law, Haridas Vohra, realising how difficult the situation was for Raliatben since no adult males lived in her household, had taken Harilal into his own home. They could be assured the boy was receiving the best of care.

There would be repercussions to this incident. While Harilal was convalescing in the Vohra household in Rajkot, he and his intended bride Gulab, the Vohras' beautiful second-born daughter, had come to know and like each other. In a natural sequence of events they had fallen hopelessly in love. After Harilal left, they began a secret correspondence.

In recreating my grandparents' story, I have become intrigued by the way certain patterns of events or circumstances are repeated time and again. (Perhaps this is true for all of us. Who knows?) One recurring pattern in Bapu's life was the pilgrim's revelatory experience: a truth arrived at or a turning point reached during the course of a journey — and in his case, most often, a railroad journey.

It happened to him during the long, dark night he spent in the unheated railway station in Pietermaritzburg, soon after his arrival in Natal in 1893. It occurred again in India on his week-long train trip from Calcutta to Rajkot in 1902, riding as a third-class passenger for the first time. Now, as he travelled on the overnight train from Johannesburg to Durban in October 1904, it happened once more.

For weeks, Mohandas had been receiving disturbing reports about

*Indian Opinion.* The newspaper's office affairs were in turmoil; debts were unpaid, collections in arrears, accounts improperly kept, and losses appeared to be mounting each month. Madanjit Vyavaharik, the paper's co-founder, had become so disheartened that he was returning to India. But hardworking, conscientious Albert West, who had given up a comfortable partnership in a Johannesburg print shop to take charge of the press in Durban, was willing to stay on and try to put things right. He had urged Mohandas to come to Durban and confer with the rest of the staff before deciding the paper's fate.

On the evening Mohandas left Johannesburg, his new friend Henry Polak came to the station to see him and press into his hands a book he had just finished reading. Ever eager to share enthusiasms, the young newspaperman urged Mohandas to look the book over during the 12-hour journey so they could discuss it later. He felt sure Mohandas would find it interesting.

How right Henry Polak was!

The book was John Ruskin's *Unto This Last.* Mohandas sat up most of that night on the train reading it straight through and spent most of the next day contemplating what he had read. A criticism of the cut-throat competitiveness and increasingly prevalent materialism of 19th-century industrial England, *Unto This Last* had stirred great controversy when first published in 1862, and could still rouse passions decades later. Ruskin suggested, among other things, that "what is really desired, under the name of riches, is, essentially, power over men." He argued that a functional, balanced economy should be based on moral principles and cooperative philosophy. "That country is richest which nourishes the greatest number of noble and happy human beings," Ruskin wrote. He urged the rich to give up their luxuries and become servants of the poor, recognising that the true wealth of any society lay in the well-being of all its members — "unto this last as unto."

My grandfather always found his own deepest convictions reflected in any book that appealed to him, whether it was the *Gita* or Tolstoy, or Ruskin. And he himself once noted that it was his habit "to forget what I did not like and to carry out in practice whatever I liked." Certainly, there were reverberations of his own thinking and faint echoes of Hindu teachings as well, in his summary of Ruskin's message. He saw it as threefold: first, that the good of the individual is contained in the good of all (which, to him, meant what he had long believed — a man serves his own best interests by serving the community). Second, that a lawyer's work and a barber's work have the same worth because all useful work has equal value (something Ruskin had merely implied, not declared outright). And thus, that a life of labour with one's hands is the life worth living (which was probably more his own idea than Ruskin's).

By the time the train reached Durban, Mohandas was determined, in his own words, "to change my life in accordance with the ideals of the book." An audacious plan had suggested itself. His mind had gone back to the "quiet little model village" he had visited at Marianhill in Natal some years earlier. The self-sustaining Trappist community with its own gardens, mill, school, even its own printing press, where everyone worked together in peaceful harmony.

Why not move *Indian Opinion* to the country and make it a cooperative village industry — a community of workers sharing chores, growing their own food, and drawing the same living wage? This notion appealed to Mohandas' pragmatism as it did to this idealism. How could the dozen or so workers at the press be persuaded to join in such an experiment?

That morning Mohandas walked into the *Indian Opinion* office and presented his plan to the entire staff. Not everyone was enthusiastic. But those whose support was crucial — the able and irreplaceable Albert West, and the indispensable chief machinist, a man named Govindaswami — encouraged Mohandas to proceed. Most of the others then agreed to go along, at least on a trial basis.

He advertised in the local papers that same afternoon for a suitable piece of land located in the Durban vicinity and near a railroad station. A landowner at Phoenix, a sugarcane growing centre about 18 miles from the city, responded the next day. Mohandas and Albert West went out at once to inspect the property: 20 acres of rich farmland, with a spring, and a small orchard of orange, mango, and guava trees. Mohandas contracted to buy it outright, along with some 80 adjoining acres of uncultivated land, all for a total cost of £1,000.

Just 48 hours after reading John Ruskin's *Unto This Last*, Mohandas Gandhi was turning a dream inspired by that book into a reality. I doubt if the author himself could have imagined or achieved such an instant translation of words into action.

Word of Mohandas' novel plan to save his newspaper spread rapidly in the Indian community and help came from all directions. Parsi philanthropist Rustomji provided building materials, including sheets of corrugated iron from a recently dismantled warehouse. Longtime supporters of Mohandas showed up to erect a sturdy shed 75 feet long and 50 feet wide to house the press itself. Working from dawn to dusk each day, sleeping in tents at night, trying to ignore the many snakes that infested the tall grass and dangled from the branches of fruit trees near the spring, they completed the structures in three weeks. Next, they began to lay out roads, dig irrigation ditches, and cultivate the land for planting.

The printing press and all the cases of type were moved to the farm in November, but getting the first Phoenix-produced issue of *Indian Opinion* printed and dispatched to Durban for distribution as usual involved a breathtaking drama of suspense. The small oil engine which drove the press broke down at a critical moment in the middle of the night, despite Govindaswami's best efforts to keep it going. Fortunately, Albert West had installed a hand-turned wheel for use in just such an emergency, but turning it required the strength of four men. According to West's best estimate, they would have to work in relays, without pause, through the rest of the night to finish the press run on time. The staff was exhausted, they had been hard at work for hours. Yet all present: the compositors, the pressmen, the sleeping carpenters who were awakened and asked to help, and Mohandas himself — took turns at the heavy wheel, while an amazed and gratified Albert West sang Christian hymns to keep their spirits up. They finished the job by 7.00am, just barely in time, with everyone still pitching in, to get the papers folded and carried to the Phoenix railroad station 2½ miles away, before the arrival of the morning train.

With the press functioning in an orderly manner, Mohandas turned his attention to development of the settlement itself. Phoenix was his own creation, a place where he could test principles, exercise his zeal for reforms and invest his vast stores of energy. In the first flush of enthusiasm, he envisioned a community of simple mud huts with thatched roofs (somewhat like huts in the Zulu villages of Natal) erected on three-acre parcels of land assigned to each family. But he soon realised that using wood and the corrugated iron donated by Rustomji to construct the settlers' cottages would be quicker and less expensive. All residents would build their own houses, till their own fields, and learn typesetting. Each worker, regardless of nationality, race, religion, or rank, would earn a standard stipend of three pounds.

From the very beginning, Mohandas planned to retire gradually from his law practice, and move his own family to Phoenix. In any case, he continued to spend most of his time in Johannesburg, since the survival of both the newspaper and the new settlement still depended on generous subsidies he made. Over a period of many months, Kasturba kept their home in Johannesburg running smoothly while he made regular visits to the settlement to work on construction of their house: a simple wood and corrugated iron dwelling consisting of a living-room, two small bedrooms, a tiny kitchen, and an ingenious shower stall with a hole in its roof through which a sprinkling of water from an overhead watering can was released by pulling a string.

Henry Polak, astounded at what his loan of a book to Mohandas had wrought, became a part of the experiment. He moved to Phoenix early in 1905 and became an editor of *Indian Opinion*. Mohandas was delighted.

I have always found it amazing that people of independent mind and spirit, men like Louis Ritch, Albert West and Henry Polak, were so invariably amenable to my grandfather's suggestions, so willing to alter their own lives to conform with his ideas. These men and others who joined forces with Bapu in South Africa did so at a time when his theories were untried, his actions unprecedented, and his name had not yet become a legend. Winning their loyalty and allegiance was, I believe, a clear demonstration of Bapu's innate capacity to inspire others with his vision of truth.

It also provides evidence of something beyond that, something Kasturba and her sons experienced almost daily. Mohandas' inborn determination to guide and shape the lives of others — and his unassailable confidence that he was doing it for their own good.

With the founding of Phoenix Settlement, Mohandas was no longer simply a householder; he had become, in fact and in practice, the complete patriarch, concerned about every aspect of the personal existence of those over whose well-being he presided. When Henry Polak moved back to Johannesburg to work for the law firm, Mohandas invited him to become a member of the Gandhi household. Kasturba, having long since become accustomed to sharing her home with young Indian law clerks, welcomed him without qualms. The fact that the affable young Mr. Polak was a European made no difference to her. Though communication was a problem, she and her sons soon came to enjoy his presence very much. What Kasturba had not bargained for, however, was that she would shortly find herself sharing her home with a young Mrs. Polak, as well.

Kasturba had the advantage of a long history of joint family life and she enjoyed working with people. She liked Millie Polak a great deal and was certain they could work out a plan for kitchen duties if they were able to discuss the problem. So Kasturba asked Mohandas to act as their translator, and together the two women easily agreed that the kitchen chores would alternate between them every day. While one did the cooking, the other would do the washing and cleaning. Things ran more smoothly then. And they soon found an even more satisfactory solution to their communication difficulties. Millie began teaching Kasturba some conversational English.

Having fostered this outbreak of maternity and domesticity among his followers, Mohandas was quite pleased with himself. "At this stage of my life," he later wrote, "I was interested in getting all my friends married."

Later, after his ideas changed, his demands upon his friends and followers — and on Kasturba — would change.

# 14

By 1906 Mohandas Gandhi's law practice became the most lucrative in South Africa, surpassing that of any European attorney, because he was the only Indian barrister in Transvaal (or Natal, for that matter), and his reputation for integrity was unblemished. His prosperity was a measure of how well his enterprising Indian clients were doing as businessmen in South Africa. But it was also indicative of his own growing renown — or, among Europeans, in many instances, notoriety.

Such success brought Mohandas little personal satisfaction. On the contrary, he was feeling as he had earlier in Durban, that he was caught in a meaningless pursuit of material gains, and he feared he was allowing his family to become ensnared also. The *Gita*'s teachings on non-possession and non-attachment, Ruskin's lessons on the dignity of labour suggested a better way.

The obligation to train Kasturba and the boys in self-reliance and frugality was weighing heavily upon Mohandas — one reason he wanted his own family, as soon as possible, to become part of the experiment in self-sustaining communal life at Phoenix Settlement. Until then, their mode of living in the Johannesburg household must be further simplified. As it was, the room's furnishings were spartan; everyone shared in the laundry and housework. There was even a small garden which the boys helped tend.

Mohandas had also been interested in diet and this was reflected in his new household. He had read that fresh, home-baked bread made of hand-ground flour was far more nutritious than baker's bread. One day he brought home a hand-mill, which required two persons to operate, just the sort of thing he appreciated. Turning the wheel provided good, healthy exercise while producing healthy whole-wheat flour from which Kasturba baked delicious bread. The flour was ground once a day, usually by Mohandas and Henry Polak. Occasionally the job fell to the women and children — though Kasturba was exempt for health reasons. But Manilal, Ramdas, even little Devadas, took their turns happily, and without undue urging. Mohandas had recently decided his sons should not be compelled to do chores. He expected them to participate of their own volition when they saw the adults at work; his expectations were usually fulfilled.

Sometimes Kasturba, not yet fully comfortable about letting her husband help with housekeeping duties, was startled to see her sons doing "women's work" also — it seemed against the natural order of things. But Mohandas was adamant: everyone, himself included, must be ready to do anything that needed doing. Since he had dispensed with all paid help, Kasturba found it difficult to argue with him, in the end, the work got done to her satisfaction. Better yet was seeing the pride Mohandas took in their sons' behaviour.

There remained just one vexing problem — the question of the boys' education. Mohandas was so busy with endless public activities that he "was devoting ever less time to teaching them." The daily walks to the office had almost ceased. Mohandas argued that the boys were learning valuable lessons at home through practice in good living. Kasturba believed, as she always had, that such haphazard education was not enough. He declared his sons would become bilingual through contact with his many English-speaking friends. For the Polaks (and for Kasturba) that was licence enough. With Kasturba's smiling approval, the young couple began carrying on long conversations in English with the Gandhi boys, and when Millie, as volunteer governess, started teaching them reading, writing, and simple arithmetic, even Mohandas did not object.

Amidst the prevailing peace and harmony of this well-regulated household, Kasturba was the first one, indeed the only one, to sense that something was amiss. She recognised the signs, she had seen them before. She knew that her husband, outwardly serene, was inwardly seething with unrest. But she could not quite fathom why.

The problem was that Mohandas, seen by others as a successful attorney, now saw himself only as a failed public servant. His tireless attempts to get South Africa's unjust laws changed — all his editorials, petitions, speeches — had, in his despairing view, achieved almost nothing: the government would not change.

Characteristically, Mohandas chose to blame himself. It was not enough, he told himself, merely to cancel insurance and live simply. He must do more. He must ask more profound questions, make more difficult decisions.

Could he free himself for public work only by ridding himself of all vestiges of wealth inherited or earned? If so, would that solve his dilemma? His private wealth earned as a lawyer made his public work possible. Mohandas pondered the questions, and found an answer.

And so it was that Kasturba's husband announced he was taking a vow of poverty for life. She had been expecting some kind of upheaval. She did not protest when he said he — actually, they — were renouncing all wealth. His explanation reassured her: he had not vowed to *earn* no money, he said, but simply to *keep* no money — none, that is, beyond the minimum required for their basic necessities of life. All else would be donated to community service.

What did disturb Kasturba was learning that Mohandas had already written of this vow to Lakshimidas, and had told him to expect no more remittances from South Africa. Any debts his brothers felt he still owed them, Mohandas declared, had long since been settled.

Lakshimidas Gandhi was a patient, conscientious, upright man who took his family obligations very seriously, and expected others to do likewise. Monetary obligations among family members are also rigidly defined. After the head of a family dies, for example, the oldest male child is expected to assume responsibility (as Lakshimidas had) for the entire family's ongoing welfare. But if the older brother runs into bad luck (as Lakshimidas had), and a younger brother is lucky and prospers (as Mohandas had), then the younger brother is obligated to support financially.

When Lakshimidas realised that Mohandas no longer intended to honour these age-old traditions which were the very foundation of Indian family life, he was shocked and deeply hurt. For Mohandas to renounce all wealth now was unthinkable. How could this younger brother, for whom they all had made so many sacrifices, for whose legal education and career he had spent and borrowed so freely, for whose wife and children he had provided food and shelter so long and so unstintingly, even think of shirking his own obligations? His ingratitude was a cruel blow, a humiliation for the whole family. It was not just a matter of paying back money that the family had given him. Mohandas, successful and prosperous at last, should now provide whatever support they needed for as long as it was needed.

Thinking about it, talking it over with Karsandas, Lakshimidas became suspicious. Mohandas' brothers were not prepared to believe he had indeed become some sort of ascetic. The poverty vow, they concluded, was a sham, motivated by personal greed. Mohandas had stopped sending money to his family in India because he was stacking up money for himself and his own family in South Africa. Had Kasturba put him up to it? Her parents had been affluent, she had known riches as a child, her own brothers were wealthy now. Perhaps, feeling deprived, she had influenced Mohandas to cut off the rest of the Gandhi family, and use a vow of poverty as his excuse. Lakshimidas wrote an angry retort to Mohandas, reminding him of the example of their father Karamchand, who had always taken full responsibility for his entire family, and had surely expected his own sons to do so, too. Mohandas, in his brief reply — a letter that began with the coolly formal greeting, "Respected sir" — declared he was doing exactly what their father had done, only he had enlarged the family to include the whole of humanity.

Lakshimidas now became truly alarmed. Mohandas' vow of poverty was real, it was his own — Kasturba was not to blame. There could be only one explanation: his brother was going crazy! Nobody in his right mind would give away so much money, no one would renounce all worldly possessions so early in life. True, there were many sadhus in India, holy men who, sometime after the age of fifty, gave up everything — wealth, family, home — and went away into the forest to live as hermits, to meditate and prepare to die. But Mohandas, not yet 37, was too young to renounce the world. Clearly, Mohandas had lost touch with reality.

What, then, would become of Mohandas' wife and his sons?

On May 2, 1906, Harilal Gandhi, eldest of Kasturba's sons and almost 18, and Gulab Vohra, not yet 15, were united in marriage in Rajkot, India. The elaborate Hindu ceremony was celebrated with the approval and cooperation of the bride's parents and the groom's uncles, but without the knowledge or consent of the groom's parents in South Africa.

Johannesburg newspapers were full of reports of a full-scale "Zulu Rebellion" in Natal. Originally a pastoral people, the Zulus, like other native South Africans over the years, had lost much of their tribal land to an encroaching European civilisation. Now the usurping westerners wanted them to pay oppressive poll taxes and hut-taxes. Already to make ends meet their young men had been forced to leave their families and go to work in what amounted to involuntary servitude in the cities. Their "rebellion" had consisted of a single incident: in February of 1906, a Zulu chieftain, outraged when yet another tax was imposed on his people, had advised them not to pay it, and had run his spear through the tax collector. Fearing the consequences if such defiance went unpunished, the Natal government had begun a series of raids into Zululand, turning the full force of its military firepower against unarmed villagers and burning Zulu kraals.

Though none of this was made clear at the time — newspaper accounts of the "uprising by Zulu warriors" were exaggerated, twisted to fit the preconceptions of a white readership — Mohandas was instinctively sympathetic towards the Zulus, who had done no harm to the Indians. Nevertheless, his loyalty to the British Empire was undiminished; he still believed that, in his words, it "existed for the welfare of the world". When he read that European residents of Natal were volunteering to join the expeditionary force fighting the Zulus, he felt as he had during the Boer War. He and other Indians, as loyal subjects of the British Crown, should do their bit — to protect their own rights of citizenship.

Further legislative restrictions on Indian rights had just been proposed, and Mohandas was acutely aware that many white South Africans still believed that most Indians were knaves, and all were cowards. A correspondent commenting in the *Natal Advertiser*, for example, on what he viewed as the absurd idea of enlisting Indian soldiers to help fight Zulus, had slyly suggested that "the Indians, so that they may not run away, should be placed in the front line, and then the fight between them and the Natives will be a sight for the gods." How, Mohandas asked himself, could such venomous racial hatred be eradicated? How could such degrading stereotypes be dispelled? Perhaps he should advise his countrymen to volunteer for combat and ask for front line duty. Yet, when he contemplated the conflict itself, his only reaction was misery at the thought of so much violence.

At home one night, when the dinner table talk turned to a discussion of the Zulu hostilities, Mohandas spoke of his concern about political implications, his misgivings about military tactics. Listening to her husband, Kasturba did not fully comprehend all the issues involved. But she quickly discerned the nature of his quandary.

"I think you should go and help with the wounded," she said. Mohandas was surprised because Kasturba had expressed the thoughts as if she knew what he was about to say.

He looked around the table, addressing everyone gathered there, "I have, in fact, been thinking of recruiting another Indian Ambulance Corps." His eyes came to rest on Kasturba's face. "But that means we would have to close this house. You would have to move to Phoenix."

Mohandas knew his wife's aversion to moving, and he could not blame her — she had been uprooted so many times. But now, gazing into her eyes, he realised with a surge of gratitude that she had made her suggestion, fully aware of what it meant for her and their sons.

Next day, Mohandas wrote to the Governor of Natal, offering to recruit Indian volunteers to tend the wounded in the Zulu campaign. Kasturba calmly began to pack her belongings. She was certain the Governor would accept the offer, and even if he did not, Mohandas would find some way of getting into the thick of the struggle. For as long as she had known him, nursing the sick and wounded had been a passion with him. She would not stop him from doing what he felt he must do, just because she would have to move again. She had grown so used to Mohandas' quirks, so familiar with his whims and fancies, that she now seemed more comfortable with his convictions than he was. She had learned to live with them peaceably, without turmoil.

When word of the Governor's ready acceptance arrived, everything happened in a rush, Mohandas gave a month's notice to the landlord, and the Johannesburg household was broken up without ceremony. The boarders were dispersed, and Henry and Millie moved to a smaller house. The Polaks were staying on in Johannesburg since Mohandas was leaving his practice in the hands of his staff, and Henry's talents were needed at the law office. Manilal, Ramdas, and Devadas grew more excited each day, helping their mother pack, asking their father endless questions about life at Phoenix Settlement and about the other children there. Mohandas, meanwhile, signed up some Transvaal volunteers for his ambulance corps; others sent word from Natal that they would join when he came there.

On June 2, 1906, when the Gandhi family boarded the train at Johannesburg and set out for Phoenix to start a new life, Mohandas felt as if a heavy burden were being lifted from his soul. For Kasturba, the day marked a change in her life more drastic than any she had yet known. Phoenix was then a wild, snake-infested outpost in the midst of miles and miles of sugar cane fields. The only link with civilisation was the nearest railway station, more than two miles away, and the only way to cover the distance was on foot. Fortunately, Chaganlal, Maganlal and several other men from the Settlement met them at the station to help carry their belongings. Even more fortunately, there had been no recent rains, or they would have had to wade through knee-deep mud and swollen streams.

But none of this seemed to disturb Kasturba. She rejoiced to be reunited with Chaganlal's and Maganlal's families, and to learn from their wives that both were expecting babies — the second for Kashiben, Santokben's first. Then she set about making herself and her own family at home in Phoenix. She was ready to accept any hardships awaiting her in this tiny wood and iron hut in the wilderness with the same equanimity with which she had once adjusted to the comforts and conveniences of a big, modern, well-furnished home in the city. Her only complaint was that the physical strain of packing and unpacking, lifting and carrying had brought on the recurrence of a health problem that had plagued her ever since the birth of her two youngest sons. An excessive loss of blood during her monthly periods sometimes left her quite weak. During the two weeks Mohandas stayed at Phoenix, attending to *Indian Opinion* business and helping his wife get settled, he fretted about how tired and frail she looked. But Kasturba assured him it was nothing serious.

A few days before he was to leave for Durban and join the men who had volunteered for ambulance corps service, a letter from Lakshimidas brought startling news. Reading it, Mohandas felt furious, betrayed — and, worst of all, helpless to do anything about it.

Kasturba, busy in the kitchen, heard him muttering to himself and came to the door. "What has happened? Why are you so upset?"

"Harilal and Gulab are married!"

Kasturba was too stunned to speak.

"Big brother took it on himself to arrange everything," Mohandas said bitterly. "Acting in the boy's best interest, he says." Kasturba heard the anger in her husband's voice, and for a fleeting second felt relieved he was directing it against his brother, not his son. What she herself felt, far more than anger, was a terrible disappointment. For an Indian mother there can be few more important occasions than the marriage of her own son, especially her oldest son. Now, to her great dismay, she and Mohandas had been denied the honour and pleasure of participating in this momentous event in Harilal's life. Not only had his wedding taken place without her being there, it had occurred without her even knowing about it.

"When did it happen?" she murmured.

"Early last month, and according to Lakshimidas, everyone was there." Mohandas recited a list of the wedding guests.

"Everyone came, everyone approved — except me!" Mohandas was still fuming. "Lakshimidas knows my feelings; he acted against my wishes. Gulab and Harilal are too young. Harilal has too much to learn before he begins a family. It's unforgivable!"

But why, Kasturba asked herself, had Lakshimidas said an early marriage was in Harilal's best interest? Why had Gulab's parents agreed? They were all in India, observing things she and Mohandas, in South Africa, could not be aware of; she trusted their judgment, they must have had good reason for allowing the marriage. Intuitively, Kasturba felt she knew what that reason was: Harilal and Gulab were in love, too much in love, and their relatives had recognised the risk. Believing, as most Indians did (as she herself did), that sex before marriage was an unpardonable sin, they would naturally think it best that an engaged couple so desperately in love get married young — before they could get into trouble.

"Perhaps Harilal wanted to be married," Kasturba suggested hesitantly, not wanting to rile her husband further.

"Nonsense!" Mohandas spluttered. "How can he know what he wants at such a young age?"

But our son does know, Kasturba wanted to say. You are his father. You, of all people, should understand. She thought of Harilal — so eager, so impetuous, so single-minded. She thought of Mohandas — so impulsive, so persistent, she remembered how overwhelming had been his early sexual desires, how impossible it had been to deny his passion. She thought of how arduous had been her husband's struggles, in recent years, for mastery over those desires. What if Harilal's feelings for Gulab were just as intense? And what of Gulab and her desire for Harilal? Perhaps the decision to permit them to marry without delay was the wisest action possible.

Kasturba said none of this. Thoughts such as these could not be shared with anyone, not even her husband. She remained silent.

In a letter sent to Lakshimidas the next day, Mohandas wrote, "Harilal's getting married has no meaning for me." It was one of the last letters that would pass between the brothers for many years.

On the first day of winter, June 22, 1906, Mohandas and his small band of stretcher bearers, wearing heavy boots and puttees, and government-issued uniforms that tended to be too large, boarded the train in Durban and headed for the fighting in Zululand. Mohandas had been given the rank of Sergeant Major, and serving under him were three sergeants, one corporal and 19 privates. Some were Gujarati, more were ex-indentured workers from South India. These Indian Ambulance Corpsmen would spend little more than a month in active service in the field. During that time they would discover, as my grandfather later wrote, "this was no war, but a manhunt."

When they arrived at the scene of the "rebellion," they saw no evidence of armed resistance anywhere. There were no wounded troops in the camp hospital, only a few cases of malaria. But the medical officer held their coming as a godsend. Equipping them with bandages and disinfectant, he led them into a nearby stockade where Zulu tribesmen with open, festering wounds, which had been left untreated for days, were lying in their own filth and blood in an improvised infirmary. The doctor, a humane man, told the Indians that he realised their duty as ambulance workers was to carry wounded, not to nurse them, but he was at his wits' end. He had to ask their help, since no white medical attendants would touch the Zulus.

Mohandas and his men went to work. As they cleansed and dressed the ugly wounds — obviously the result of floggings and beatings — the Zulus tried to express their thanks. The Indians found the words unintelligible but understood their meaning. As my grandfather later wrote, "From their gestures and the expression of their eyes, they seemed to feel as if God had sent us to their succour." Meanwhile, white soldiers who had gathered on the other side of the stockade fence to watch the proceedings, were loudly jeering the Indians and cursing the Zulus. Only later did Mohandas realise these were perhaps some of the very soldiers who had inflicted the wounds.

The days that followed were a nightmare. The Indian Ambulance Corps was sent out into the field, accompanying mixed cavalry and infantry units in search of the enemy. Carrying their stretchers, supplies, and equipment on their backs, the corpsmen tried to keep pace on endless marches, a few as long as 40 miles in one day, across rugged terrain. The marches usually wound up in some remote kraal with Zulu "warriors" being dragged out of their huts or chased down like beasts in the nearby countryside, then beaten, kicked, flogged unmercifully. A few were publicly hanged, some were shot — not because they had taken part in any uprising, but as a warning not to participate in future "rebellions." Mohandas had been sickened by the senseless violence he had seen during the Boer War, but having to live with this daily spectacle of man's cruelty to man was far more disturbing. His distress was eased only by the knowledge that the wounded Zulus would have been left uncared for, had it not been for the nursing given them by his corpsmen.

Fortunately, there were military men who shared Mohandas' revulsion. As he learned when he got to know some of the soldiers better, these acts committed by troops under the command of a few ruthless and reckless officers did not go unreported. When news of the atrocities became known, the government, to avoid a scandal, simply declared that the "Zulu Rebellion" had been suppressed. The expeditionary force was disbanded. Volunteers, including the Indian Ambulance Corpsmen, were sent home to their wives and families.

But Mohandas, by then, had made a crucial decision, one that would affect Kasturba as much as himself: he had vowed, for the rest of his life, to observe brahmacharya; to practice celibacy.

That decision, for Mohandas, had become unavoidable. On the long, weary marches between far-flung Zulu kraals, moving through what he called "those solemn solitudes," his mind filled with images of the carnage he was seeing, a revelation seems to have come to him — some intimation of a connection between the nature of armed violence and the nature of human sexuality. In his book *Gandhi's Truth*, psychoanalyst-biographer Erik H. Erikson suggests that "the experience of witnessing the outrages perpetrated on black bodies by white he-men aroused in Gandhi both a deeper identification with the maltreated, and a stronger aversion against all male sadism — including such sexual sadism as he had probably felt from childhood to be part of all exploitation of women by men."

Inevitably, then, Mohandas' thoughts must have gone to Kasturba — the demands he had made on her, the satisfactions he had sought from her. He found himself wondering if his wife was now paying a price in frailty and poor health for his self-indulgence? He thought of his sons, Harilal and Manilal, who had been conceived in passion at a time when his own desires were unchecked. He thought of Ramdas and Devadas, whose difficult births had convinced him he should father no more children. Would his failings be reflected in their lives? Was Harilal, with his early marriage to a young woman who was scarcely more than a child, beginning to repeat mistakes he himself had made?

For many years, Mohandas had been pondering the meaning of existence, searching his heart and mind, seeking to understand the purpose of his life. He had brooded about conflicts between his duty to fulfill family responsibilities, and his yearning to serve the larger community. But now, reflecting on the human brutality he had been witnessing and the human misery he was trying to alleviate, a truth he had only dimly perceived was clearly illuminated for him. His conflict was not between competing loyalties or obligations, but between competing values - between the physical and the spiritual.

If spiritual enlightenment was the goal of his striving (and surely it was — he had already given up any claim on the material things of life), there was one more aspect of physical life he must renounce, one more vow he must take. He must now seek that total non-attachment to worldly pleasures, that "desirelessness" which, according to Hindu scriptures, enables men to enjoy freedom of action in this life, and hope for transcendence to a greater existence beyond.

Here is my grandfather's account of his moment of decision, as related in his autobiography, *The Story of My Experiments with Truth*:

> I clearly saw that [as] one aspires to serve humanity with his whole soul ... I should find myself unequal to my task if I were engaged in the pleasures of family life and in the propagation and rearing of children. In a word, I could not live both after the flesh and the spirit ... The prospect of the vow brought a certain kind of exultation, opened out limitless vistas of service ...
>
> I must confess that I had not then fully realised the magnitude and immensity of the task.

Arriving back at Phoenix Settlement, Mohandas had to inform his wife, the woman to whom he had vowed lifelong fidelity, the only other person in the world directly affected by his vow, that he had forsworn sex for life. Just how uneasy he was at the prospect of facing Kasturba is indicated by the fact, disclosed in his autobiography, that he discussed his vow of brahmacharya with Chaganlal, Maganlal, and Albert West before even mentioning it to her.

Kasturba's reaction, when he did consult with her, is reported in a single sentence: "She had no objection."

Given so little information to work with, Gandhi biographers, over the years, have been equally terse in their accounts of this crucial moment in the relationship between my grandparents. Writing of my grandmother, most say something like, "Faced with an accomplished fact, she acquiesced." Or, "An obedient wife, she accepted this decision as she accepted all the other demands he had made on her." A few venture further. British historian Geoffrey Ashe speculates that Kasturbai may have "suspected the vow applied to herself rather than to women in general."

And American journalist Vincent Sheean, in his book *Lead Kindly Light*, suggests that it may even be that it was a relief to her. "By now she knew that her husband was very far from being an ordinary man, and although in earlier years she may have regretted it, by now she was ready to go with him in whatever way his conscience led."

Most interesting (and most discerning, it seems to me), is the contrast Indian writer B. R. Nanda, in his book *Mahatma Gandhi: A Biography*, draws between Kasturba and another famous man's wife who was confronted with a similar announcement. Count Leo Tolstoy, whose thinking often foreshadowed or paralleled that of my grandfather, declared late in life (after fathering thirteen children) that the Christian ideals of loving God and serving one's fellow men were incompatible with sexual love or marriage, which amounted to serving oneself. Nanda discusses how this "shattered the already weakened vessel" of Tolstoy's marriage; how Tolstoy's wife became hysterical, threatened to kill herself; how their life became a round of recriminations; how "the Countess was totally unable to appreciate, much less adopt, the ideals of her husband."

He then comments on how the Gandhis' marriage was affected:

"But Kasturba was sustained by the faith of a Hindu wife; she followed in the 'footsteps of her husband', however much it went against the grain ... The changed attitude to sex did not introduce a discordant note into the life of the Gandhis; Gandhi himself had no doubt that it sweetened and enriched it."

Like so much else about their intimate relationship, the full truth of what passed between Mohandas and Kasturba when he announced that they would henceforth live together as brother and sister, will remain forever unrevealed. But the facts, as I know them, would support B. R. Nanda's interpretation.

Certainly, there is no discordant note in accounts of an event that took place at Phoenix Settlement shortly after Mohandas told Kasturba of his vow. The story was often told in our family of how my grandmother prepared a homecoming feast for her husband and several of his friends, a few days after his return from the Zulu campaign in July of 1906. My father Manilal, 13 at the time, remembered this celebration in happy detail. And a recollection of the occasion was included in one of the reminiscences of Ba prepared for the "Kasturba Gandhi Memorial Issue" of *Indian Opinion*, published by my father at the time of her death in 1944. It was written by Surendra Medh, one of the Gujarati sergeants serving in the ambulance corps who was present that day, having accepted Bapu's invitation to visit Phoenix after they were discharged. Surendra Medh evidently liked what he saw at Phoenix. He later joined the Settlement as a secretary, and was active in the Satyagraha campaigns.

It seems that Ba had decided to serve her guests one of Bapu's favourite dishes, the sweet Indian bread known as puranpoli, which must be cooked to order. Each round cake is rolled individually, then wrapped around a sweet stuffing and rolled out again, then roasted and eaten hot off the stove. When Mohandas saw Kasturba preparing the dough and stuffing for the puranpoli, he summoned his sons to the kitchen and conspired with them — in a loud whisper. "Why don't we have a contest with your mother today? Let's see if she can bake cakes as fast as we and our guests can eat them."

"That's a good idea! Let's do it," was Manilal's instant reply. Like his father — and his son and grandson, I might add — Manilal was an enthusiastic eater.

Kasturba, of course, had overheard it all. "Well, in that case," she declared amiably, "I challenge *you* to keep up with *me*."

The competition began. Kasturba quickly proved her ability to serve perfectly baked cakes to one and all, indefinitely and without pause — or so it seemed. At last, the guests could eat no more. Then Devadas, Ramdas, even Manilal, gave up, but not their father. Mohandas kept eating the puranpoli long after everyone else had finished. He kept eating until all the dough was gone. Ready to claim victory, he confronted Kasturba.

"Won't you give up? Surely you are ready to concede." Then he saw that she was kneading still more dough. He sighed, made a long face, and prepared to start eating again.

"All right. I admit defeat," Kasturba smiled sweetly. She was humouring him. "But remember," she added softly, "I am not tired of making puranpoli. Not yet." And with that, both of them burst out laughing.

There is no rejected, resentful or long-suffering wife here, nor is there any troubled, guilt-ridden husband. Instead, I believe this story gives a first glimpse of the new life they would be exploring together — the affectionate, playful, teasing relationship that those who knew Ba and Bapu well in later years have so often recalled.

Whatever else may have passed between them at this time of crisis in their lives, one thing is clear: Kasturba's willing acceptance of her husband's vows of poverty and celibacy had quieted his private turmoil of mind and spirit. Mohandas now felt free as never before to answer public calls to action.

It was not a moment too soon.

# 15

In late August, 1906, after spending only a few weeks at Phoenix, Mohandas said goodbye to Kasturba and his sons, and hurried back to Johannesburg. Waiting for him in his office was a copy of the *Transvaal Government Gazette*, dated August 22, which had published the draft of a long-rumoured Asiatic Law Amendment Ordinance. Although its strictures were to apply to all Asiatics, including a tiny minority of Chinese, Indians were clearly the targets of the proposed legislation ("I saw nothing in it except hatred of Indians," Mohandas later wrote). But not until he began translating the text of this new law into Gujarati for publication in *Indian Opinion*, did Mohandas realise how catastrophic its passage could be.

Section by section, the Ordinance established rigorous new legal restrictions on all of Transvaal's Indians. Every man, woman, and child above the age of eight was required to apply in person to the Registrar of Asians for a certificate of registration. For Indians, Muslim and Hindu alike, the very thought of a public registration of women was scandalous; inclusion of children was an added insult. Each applicant must give name, residence, religion, caste, and age.

Mohandas was convinced that if the Transvaal Indians meekly accepted passage of this Ordinance, it would mean their ruin. Next day, he invited a few prominent Indians to meet with him in his office. As he explained the new law's provisions, word by word, they listened with mounting outrage. One man declared that if any official tried to take his wife's fingerprints, or demanded that she show a registration certificate he would shoot him on the spot and take the consequences. Mohandas said he, too, thought it better to die than to submit to the degradation this law would inflict, but he urged them to stay calm, and plan their resistance carefully. He warned that the Ordinance, if passed, would surely be imitated elsewhere.

"We are therefore responsible," he said, "for the safety, not only of the ten or fifteen thousand Indians in the Transvaal, but of the entire Indian community in South Africa."

After some more heated discussion, the group decided the best way to oppose the infamous legislation — already being called "The Black Ordinance" — was to organise a mass protest meeting. They hoped as many as a thousand Indians might gather to hear speeches, pass resolutions and plan action.

At 2.00pm on September 11, 1906, an overflow crowd filled every seat of the old Empire Theatre, and spilled into the aisles. More than 3,000 Indians had come from all over Transvaal. From his place on stage, Mohandas could see the excitement on every face as the meeting was called to order and resolutions were presented.

As speaker after speaker rose and seconded the resolution, tension built. The climax came when a merchant named Haji Habib, one of Johannesburg's most respected Muslim residents, ended his impassioned remarks by swearing, with God as his witness, that he would never submit to the Black Ordinance. He asked all present to take this oath. The crowd cheered wildly.

Mohandas, with quiet intensity, urged his listeners, before making such a commitment, to consider what they would be undertaking — and what it might cost them.

News of the oath taking at the Empire Theatre spread quickly throughout Transvaal, and the notion caught on. Meetings were held, leaflets distributed, and each day more Indians solemnly pledged themselves to peaceful disobedience of the Black Ordinance. This mushrooming movement, being invented as it grew, was based on an idea so new and untried that it had no name. "Passive resistance" was the term originally used to describe the concept. To a man of action like Mohandas, however, those words implied mere nay-saying. He even came to feel that "passive" might suggest weakness or cowardice — an idea that could affect Indians themselves. "The power of suggestion is such," he once wrote, "that a man at last becomes what he believes himself to be." He announced a contest in *Indian Opinion*, inviting readers to suggest a name more reflective of the courageous, dynamic spirit of what was taking shape. The entry most closely expressing what he had in mind came from Phoenix Settlement. Maganlal Gandhi had coined the term Sadagraha from two Gujarati words meaning "firmness in a good cause." Mohandas altered this slightly, to Satyagraha, meaning "firmness for truth" or the pursuit of truth. From then on, the movement was known as Satyagraha and those using the peaceful methods of truth and force to combat injustice were Satyagrahis or Truthseekers.

It was apparent, however, in those waning months of 1906, that no force could keep the Transvaal Legislative Council from passing the Black Ordinance. The act was approved in October with scarcely a dissenting vote. The pledge-takers' campaign of petitions, press notices, and personal appeals to officials, had resulted in only one change in the original draft — deletion of the clause requiring the registration of women. The new law, as enacted, still posed a basic threat to the very existence of South Africa's Indian community.

Events moved swiftly and predictably. On March 21, 1907, when the new Transvaal Parliament was convened in Pretoria, the first piece of legislation passed was the budget; the second was the Asiatic Registration Act, an almost exact replica of the Black Ordinance earlier vetoed by the Imperial British Government. The law would take effect on July 1, and all Indians were required to register no later than July 31.

For the Indians' newly-formed peaceful resistance movement, the first test was at hand.

At Phoenix Settlement during the early months of 1907, Kasturba saw her husband regularly but fleetingly, seldom for more than a few days at a time. Mohandas had become a constant commuter between Johannesburg and Durban, completely caught up in organising a full-scale Satyagraha campaign in Transvaal, while trying, at the same time, to keep all South African Indians informed about that campaign through the columns of *Indian Opinion*, published in Natal.

Isolated though she was at Phoenix Settlement, Kasturba was aware of the importance of Mohandas' work and convinced of the justness of his cause. She was thankful that Harilal and his bride Gulab had heeded her summons and arrived from India a few weeks earlier. Now, finally, Kasturba was getting to know her charming young daughter-in-law Gulab, and becoming reacquainted with her oldest son Harilal — taller, more handsome, more sure of himself than she had remembered. But still, to a mother's eye, as intense and as restless as ever.

This long-awaited reunion had not been easy to achieve. Some months earlier, at Kasturba's urging, Mohandas had finally given his belated blessing to the young couple's marriage, admitting that, in all honesty, he had never been unhappy about the marriage, as such. He liked and respected the Vohra family and Gulab was a most acceptable daughter-in-law. He well remembered her as a small child, sitting on his knee, chattering away whenever he visited her father. What a happy and animated little creature she had been. But he still insisted they had been married at too young an age.

Like every bride arriving at the home of her in-laws, Gulab was nervous at first, a bit apprehensive. She wanted, above all else, to make a good impression on her new mother-in-law who, as she well knew, might prove to be a very forbidding person. But Gulab, far away from home and lonely at times, soon realised that her mother-in-law, the kind and considerate Kasturba, was no such tyrant. Things went well between them from the start.

Kasturba, for her part, loved being a mother-in-law, especially to a daughter-in-law as appealing and — yes, it was true — as much in love with her son as Gulab was. She had always felt the absence of a daughter in her home, and Gulab, still in her teens, bright and curious, eager to please, filled this void. Kasturba took the girl under her wing, made her feel welcome, and helped her adjust to life in a strange new country — she well remembered how hard that could be.

Right on schedule, on July 1, 1907, permit offices where Asiatics were to go to be fingerprinted and apply for certificates of registration were opened in all of Transvaal's principal towns and cities. The Satyagraha volunteers were ready. During the next month, they followed a carefully mapped-out strategy.

Day after day, from campaign headquarters set up in Mohandas' law offices, he and his lieutenants sent out instructions to workers. There was to be no violence, no provocation — just a determined show of resistance by Indians sworn to oppose the registration act fearlessly but peacefully. To emphasise this, all oath-takers were asked to reaffirm their pledges of non-violence: "We do not resist, but suffer for our common good and self-respect."

Frequent mass meetings to explain Satyagraha and build support for the boycott were held, always outdoors, open to all. All actions were publicised well in advance in *Indian Opinion*, which now had many interested readers in Transvaal's governmental offices. My grandfather believed that prior disclosure of plans to adversaries was useful both as a negotiating tool and as a safeguard against unintended confrontations. This would be a hallmark policy of all his Satyagraha campaigns.

Each day, pickets wearing identifying badges lined the streets leading to permit offices, passing out leaflets to any Indians who appeared, trying to dissuade them from registering. Pickets were forbidden to threaten would-be registrants or to be discourteous in any way; they even provided volunteer escorts in and out of permit offices for those who seemed intimidated by the demonstrations. The pickets had also been instructed to surrender themselves cheerfully, if police wished to make arrests. Despite such safeguards, there were a few minor scuffles — from which lessons were learned, that would be useful in future campaigns. For the most part, however, peace prevailed.

The month passed. The boycott held. On the night of July 31, a final mass meeting was held outside a mosque in Pretoria. Some 2,000 unregistered Indians came to sit cross-legged on the ground, listen to speeches, cheer their leaders, and celebrate. As of midnight, they, along with virtually the entire Indian population of Transvaal would be liable to arrest. The jails would not be able to hold them all. Satyagraha was working!

But Transvaal authorities, while they had no intention of rescinding the registration law, had no plans to arrest anyone. The new government, headed by two popular war hero generals who had once led Boer forces into battle against the British — Prime Minister Louis Botha, and his Minister of the Interior in charge of Transvaal's Indian affairs, Jan Christian Smuts — had decided on a war of attrition. They would wait for the Indians' loosely organised and poorly financed campaign to lose steam. Early in August, a one-month extension of the time limit for registration was announced.

The Satyagrahis took this as a heartening vindication of their strategy. Again the posters went up; again the pickets surrounded the permit offices; again few Indians came to register. The boycott still held. Another extension followed, and another after that, until the government at last designated November 30, 1907, as the final cut-off date for registration. The official count on that date showed that in all of Transvaal a total of only 511 Indians had been registered. Generals Botha and Smuts agreed it was time for stronger measures.

On December 28, Mohandas Gandhi and 26 of his colleagues, all prominent in the boycott campaign, were summoned to appear in a magistrate's court in Johannesburg. All were cited for failure to register. All were ordered to leave Transvaal within a fortnight, and warned they would be subject to punishment unless they chose to comply. None so chose. Two weeks later, on the morning of January 10, 1908, Mohandas and his 26 fellow Satyagrahis voluntarily appeared in court for sentencing.

The courtroom was packed. Mohandas' fellow members of the bar were on hand. Standing as the accused in a courtroom, Mohandas was granted permission to make a short statement. As the leader of the resistance movement, he asked that he be given the heaviest penalty. The magistrate, bemused by this unusual demand, ruled that two months' imprisonment without hard labour was a more fitting sentence.

An important and festive event was taking place at the Gandhi home in Phoenix Settlement on that afternoon of January 10, 1908. The traditional Indian ceremony of agarni marking the start of a woman's seventh month of pregnancy, was being celebrated in honour of Kasturba's daughter-in-law Gulab. Looking around the room, seeing so many who were dear to her — Chaganlal's wife Kashiben, Magnalal's wife Santokben, and all the other women of the Settlement who had come to enjoy the occasion and present gifts to the expectant mother — Kasturba wondered at her own excitement. Harilal and Gulab were to be parents! For weeks she had been celebrating in her heart the forthcoming arrival of her first grandchild. Now, the celebration of that happy prospect was being shared.

Kasturba had served everyone present their meal and was about to start eating her own when the celebration was interrupted. A telegram from Johannesburg arrived, delivered by a young man who had carried it on foot from the Phoenix train station.

The grim message was read aloud: Mohandas convicted for failure to register, sentenced to two months' imprisonment.

Suddenly, Kasturba's world changed. Her husband had been hauled off to jail. She had secretly worried about Mohandas' safety — ever since seeing the hatred of the Durban mob that had threatened him on the very first day she set foot on South African soil. Yet, for many years, he had seemed to lead a charmed life. Kasturba had come to believe, just as Mohandas himself seemed to believe, that no real harm could come to him when he was working for a righteous cause.

She had heard that prisoners in South African jails were locked in dark cells, that they had to wear coarse, unwashed clothing, that the only food ever served to them, other than an occasional boiled potato or perhaps a tiny portion of unseasoned rice, was "mealy-pap," a tasteless sort of cornmeal porridge.

Kasturba looked at her plate of flavourful and appetising food. All at once she knew what she must do. She pushed her plate away.

Facing the women gathered there in her home that day, Kasturba quietly made her announcement. Even though she could not share her husband's hardships in jail, she said, she could at least share his diet. Until Mohandas was released, she would eat nothing but unsalted, unsweetened, unflavoured cornmeal mush, the very same food he was being served in Johannesburg jail.

That was her own personal Satyagraha pledge.

# 16

These were agonising weeks for Kasturba. She had always accepted her husband's frequent absences with equanimity, knowing his work as a lawyer required him to be away from home for long periods. But this was different. This time Mohandas was not the wise counsel, the able defender. This time he was the accused, the convicted, locked up with criminals, in the custody of a government bent on punishing him for his leadership of Indian resistance.

For the latest reports from Johannesburg, Phoenix Settlement residents relied on newspapers picked up along with the mail at the railway station each day, and each evening Kasturba waited anxiously for someone to translate the stories for her. She soon learned, to her relief, that Mohandas was not alone. All his co-defendants in the Johannesburg magistrate's court had been given the same sentence as he had — two months of imprisonment with an exemption from hard labour. (Indian Satyagrahis, repeatedly jailed during the long South African struggle, would never again be granted this exemption.) Other protesters, having contrived new ways to court arrest — street hawkers, for example, "lost" their licenses and were convicted for illegal trading — were joining them. Within days there were reports that more than 150 newly arrested Indian prisoners were crammed into the Johannesburg jail, built to accommodate only 50. But the news reports said nothing about what was occurring inside the jail. That was what worried Kasturba.

She knew the intransigence of the ruling white South Africans — she had seen a white mob's fury. She was consumed by fear that physical attacks might as easily take place in a Johannesburg jail as on a Durban dock. And who, she asked herself helplessly, would protect Mohandas this time? But her answer came quickly and surely: God would. God was guiding and protecting them all.

Fortified by this certainty, Kasturba put aside her fears. It was never in her nature to feel sorry for herself, to plague herself with doubts or regrets. She, no less than my grandfather, was the inheritor of an age-old Vania tradition of pragmatism. Whenever Kasturba faced adversity, she accepted those circumstances she could not change, then tried to ameliorate those she could. Now, with her husband in jail, her duty was clear.

The Phoenix Settlement, in a very real sense, was her household — her joint family. She was the matriarch, the one upon whom all depended, the one who held things together. Thus, it was her task in Mohandas' absence to make sure no one became discouraged. She must make them all understand — not just her own sons, but the other settlers as well — that the surest way to keep faith with Mohandas' ideals was to keep up with the work he had outlined for them to do.

I believe this decision, arrived at during the period of her husband's earliest imprisonment, marked a turning point in my grandmother's life. For it was at Phoenix Settlement, working with the diverse, multiracial group of residents of that original Gandhian ashram that she first began to exert the gentle but unquestioned authority which later became so familiar to all who knew her. I have often contemplated how difficult it must have been initially, for her to establish this enlarged role for herself. All of the men and a number of the women at Phoenix were more knowledgeable, more educated than she; she was unable to converse in their language with several of them. Nevertheless, Kasturba made her wishes understood, and she could be firmly persuasive. She won the respect, cooperation, and affection of her colleagues — just as she would in future ashrams — not because of her position as Mohandas' wife, nor because of their shared dedication to his cause, but because of her unassuming natural dignity, her unshakeable belief in herself.

While Ba's attitude was never dictatorial, she was a demanding taskmaster. In South Africa and later in India, I have heard veteran residents of Gandhian ashrams recount stories of how my grandfather always noticed minute details others might miss or ignore, but they all invariably agreed that my grandmother was even sharper. Nothing escaped Ba's eyes. She always saw what needed to be done. She never failed to note what was left undone. Words like "forget" or "overlook" were just not part of her working vocabulary — not for herself, not for those around her. My grandparents' long-time friends liked to recall how meticulous Bapu was in his daily financial accounting, but they always pointed out that Ba was equally as painstaking. Even though she had no formal knowledge of arithmetic, she developed a remarkable talent for precise calculation. Ba taught herself to keep in her head throughout the day a running record of every penny she received or spent. Later, in the evening, she would report these memorised figures to whoever was in charge of the community's bookkeeping — most often, at Phoenix Settlement, this was Albert West or Maganlal Gandhi. I might point out that my grandmother, perhaps as a result of these nightly conferences, usually had a very accurate idea of the current state of the ashram's finances.

Exacting though she was, Kasturba could also be surprisingly lenient. My father Manilal never forgot an experience he had at Phoenix Settlement in that January of 1908, shortly after his father was sent off to jail for the first time in Johannesburg. As part of a new agricultural experiment, pineapples had been planted on a number of acres, and the first crop ripened late that month. Thousands of big, juicy, thorny-crowned pineapples, ready for harvesting, had to be cut from their stalks and packed for market, a task that kept all available Phoenix adults, and even some of the older children busy from dawn until dusk for more than a week. The settlers needed few reminders from Kasturba to realise how vital this work was for the ashram's future. Mohandas was counting on profits from this cash crop to help subsidise the continued publication of *Indian Opinion*.

Taking a break from the kitchen chores late one hot afternoon, Kasturba sent her pregnant daughter-in-law Gulab off to have a rest before dinner, and walked out to the pineapple field behind their home. While Harilal worked at the press, the other boys had been harvesting pineapples and she was concerned about Manilal. His younger brothers Ramdas and Devadas, aged nine and seven respectively, had come back to the house several hours earlier, utterly exhausted by their labours. But Manilal, large and strong at 15, and priding himself on being a tireless worker, had continued cutting pineapples from their stalks without pause. Now, however, at the sight of his mother, Manual stood erect and wiped his brow with his shirtsleeve.

"Oh, I am so thirsty!" he moaned.

"You have all these juicy pineapples to quench your thirst," Kasturba said. "What are you waiting for?"

"But ... but I thought they all had to be taken to the market." Manilal was amazed. "You mean I can really eat one?"

"Of course," Kasturba said, patting him on the shoulder as she turned to go back to the house. "They are meant to be eaten."

Manilal sat down beside the pile of pineapples he had just harvested, used his sharp knife to slice one open, and started eating.

When Kasturba returned to the field a half-hour later, it was her turn to be amazed — and amused. Her son was still at it, so busy peeling and eating pineapples he did not see or hear her approach.

"Still thirsty?" she asked softly.

Manilal looked up sheepishly. But he saw his mother's smile and was reassured. When he struggled to stand up, Kasturba's smile gave way to laughter, and Manilal had to join in. He was so full he could barely bend forward to work. I feel bound to report that my father claimed he consumed 18 pineapples that day.

In her demands upon others, Kasturba might occasionally lapse into leniency, but her self-discipline was steadfast, in good times or bad, as she proved one afternoon a few days later. Manilal was again in the field, cutting the last of the pineapples, but when the day's mail arrived, he stopped work to read the newspaper headlines. The next minute he was rushing toward the house.

"Ba, Ba!" he shouted.

"What is it?" Kasturba, looking troubled, came outside. Gulab was close behind, and Devadas and Ramdas, too. "What has happened?"

"Bapu has been freed!" Manilal announced excitedly.

Kasturba felt a surge of joy. She was almost afraid to believe it. Mohandas had served only three weeks of his two-month sentence. Yet despite her excitement, and her impatience to hear more, she was determined not to lose her composure.

"That is very good," she said quietly. "But we must get back to work now. Have you boys finished your chores?"

Not until late that afternoon did Kasturba allow herself time to hear the story read aloud — a brief statement about how, during a face-to-face meeting in Pretoria between the government leader, General J. C. Smuts, and the Indian barrister Mr. M. K. Gandhi, the release of all the imprisoned Indian protesters had been negotiated. Mr. Gandhi, the report said, had been freed on the spot.

Kasturba, in due course, would learn much more about this entire episode from Mohandas himself, starting with his assurance that his weeks in jail had not been as bad as she had imagined. The jailers had permitted the Indian prisoners to exercise together and to prepare food to their own liking; he had been allowed to have books and writing materials.

Then one morning he had been taken from his cell in Johannesburg and transported under police escort to Pretoria to meet with General

Smuts in his office and consider a proposal for ending the registration deadlock. The Boer general seemed friendly, reminding Mohandas that he, too, was an English-trained barrister. "I could never entertain a dislike for you people," Smuts declared. "I had some Indian fellow students in my time." After a good deal of discussion, the two men had settled on terms of an agreement — a simple understanding that, if the majority of Transvaal's Indians (at Gandhi's urging) would register voluntarily, the government (at the general's behest) would respond by repealing the Black Act. They exchanged mutual assurances of compliance, but nothing was put in writing.

Mohandas did not object ("A Satyagrahi bids goodbye to fear," he later explained. "He is therefore never afraid of trusting the opponent.") Smuts ordered the release of the other prisoners, told Mohandas he was free to go, and excused himself. The meeting was over. It was 7 o'clock in the evening and Mohandas, still in his prison uniform without a penny in his pocket, borrowed the railway fare from the general's secretary to get back to Johannesburg.

Though details were scarce in the first news reports reaching Phoenix, everyone knew it was time to celebrate. They regarded the prisoners' early release as a great victory for the Satyagraha cause. Kasturba rejoiced because Mohandas would now be able to come home, even if only for a few days. And, as she cheerfully reminded one and all, his release had freed her, too: from her flavourless diet of cornmeal mush. With Gulab's help, Kasturba prepared a huge dinner that night for her family, her neighbours and — most of all, this time — for herself.

The celebratory mood at Phoenix was short-lived. Ten days later, a telegram from Johannesburg brought alarming news. Mohandas had been assaulted on the street near his office — beaten, kicked, and knocked unsciousness. But the brief message gave no information about the extent of his injuries or any indication of who had attacked him, or why. Again, they were left wondering — in limbo.

Kasturba was frantic with anxiety. Someone suggested she should rush to Johannesburg to be at her husband's side.

"No. No, I cannot," she said at once. "Phoenix is short of money as it is. I can't spend what little we have for my selfish needs."

"But we'll manage to tide things over somehow," Albert West said. "I think you should go to him."

"There is really no need," Kasturba said firmly. "He has many friends there to take good care of him. Besides,", she added, leaving no room for further argument, "you know how concerned he always is about the proper use of public money."

Kasturba's awful uncertainty was finally relieved a few days later when a long letter arrived from their good friend Henry Polak, reporting that Mohandas was safe and recovering slowly from his wounds — mostly cuts, bruises, and abrasions, but no broken bones. Since he had been summoned to the scene immediately, Polak was able to provide a detailed, first-hand account of how and why the attack had occurred. His most surprising disclosure was that Mohandas was not the victim of a ferocious white mob, as Kasturba had feared. Instead, his assailant, who was arrested on the spot, had been one of his own countrymen who had misunderstood the agreement that Mohandas had reached with the government. The Indian could not understand why Indians should now voluntarily register themselves when the struggle was to avoid registration all together. He concluded that Mohandas had probably taken money from the government and "sold out" the community.

To Kasturba, the very idea of anyone believing Mohandas would engage in some kind of underhanded treachery — and for money! — was preposterous, infuriating. But she pushed her anger aside, and concentrated on the assurance that her husband was being nursed back to health. Polak reported that Mohandas, on regaining consciousness, had been carried to the nearby home of a Baptist clergyman, the Reverend Mr. Joseph Doke, and a doctor had come to treat his injuries. The police were waiting to take his statement, but Mohandas had flatly refused to give testimony or press charges against his attacker Mir Alam. He had, however, insisted that the Registrar of Asiatics come to his bedside that day with all the necessary forms, take down the required information, and issue him a certificate forthwith.

He was still determined to be the first Indian to register. Kasturba was no doubt heartened by this evidence that her husband was behaving just like the stubborn, unpredictable Mohandas she had always known. Henry Polak concluded his letter by saying he and Millie hoped to move Mohandas to their house soon to continue his convalescence, but at present he was in good hands with the Doke family, and all was well.

What Polak may not have known is that the Reverend Mr. Doke's white parishioners were in an uproar, horrified at the mere thought of their pastor caring for a black man in his own home, alarmed at the spectacle of the Dokes allowing this well-known agitator to receive a daily stream of visitors of all races and religions, coming there, no doubt, to plot against the government. They predicted the scandal would create havoc in the community, and have dire consequences for the congregation. By all accounts, they were soon proved right. Joseph Doke, this latter-day Good Samaritan, this kindly Christian clergyman who had previously had only a passing acquaintance with my grandfather, was forever changed by this experience, transformed into a firm believer in the Gandhian philosophy, and an active supporter of the Satyagraha cause. At the height of the struggle a year or so later, when many Phoenix residents were in prison, he would serve a stint as editor of *Indian Opinion*. And he would eventually go on to write the first full-length Gandhi biography ever published.

Once Mohandas recovered from his injuries, he wanted to return to Phoenix, but his homebound journey was marred by renewed threats of violence. Stopping off in Durban to address a meeting held to enlist the support of Natal's Indians for the struggle of their fellow countrymen in the Transvaal, he had to be whisked away to safety when a mob of angry dissidents seemed ready to storm the platform. The rioters, again mostly Pathans, were repeating the false charges of "selling out" that had circulated in Johannesburg. The quick spread of these rumours to Natal convinced some of Mohandas' friends that agents of the Transvaal government were trying to disrupt the Indian resistance by sowing seeds of dissension among the Pathans. This theory, though never proven, can lead to interesting speculation: was this the beginning of the unofficial divide-and-rule policy, which later became so commonplace in South Africa?

Mohandas did not share these suspicions. He blamed himself for the hostility he was encountering — he had failed to win over those who opposed him. Rejecting suggestions he remain in Durban where the police (still under the command of his old friend Superintendent Alexander) could be quickly summoned in case of trouble, Mohandas decided to go on to Phoenix as planned, and write a series of articles for *Indian Opinion* to explain his controversial position. Four of his strong young rescuers — one, a Natal-born Tamil, was a trained boxer — wanted to go along to protect him, but he scoffed at the idea.

"I can't remain in fear all the time," Mohandas replied while Kasturba was listening.

"I understand," Kasturba said in a quiet tone, "and I am prepared for the worst. I've been preparing myself to face the worst ever since you took to public life." She paused a second, her eyes searching his face. 'Your mind must not be burdened with worries about me or the family. We will be all right. That's what I want you to know."

Kasturba was saying what she had truly come to believe. She knew, too, from his grateful look of relief, it was what her husband wanted to hear.

Only when she was alone in the retreat of her room did she shed the tears she could not show to Mohandas or anyone else.

For the Gandhi family, a pattern was being set during the long months of that first Satyagraha campaign. Events both public and private moved so swiftly, crisis followed crisis so relentlessly, that Kasturba sometimes felt they were caught up in a whirlwind of conflicting emotions, living through endlessly recurring cycles of fear and hope, anxiety and deliverance.

On April 10, 1908, a healthy baby girl was safely born to Harilal's wife Gulab. In the absence of doctor or midwife, Kasturba and the other Gandhi women at Phoenix assisted at the delivery, and Kasturba found special satisfaction in the fact that her first grandchild was a granddaughter. Rami was the name Gulab and Harilal chose for the infant, and the proud parents accepted congratulations at a traditional naming ceremony held the following week, when Mohandas arrived at the Settlement for one of his periodic visits.

But in the same week that a birth was being celebrated by the Gandhis in South Africa, death had come suddenly and cruelly to a member of the Gandhi family in India — Raliatben's only son Gokaldas. This eager and able nephew who had been like another son to Mohandas and Kasturba when he lived with them in Durban, had continued his studies in India, planning to rejoin them at Phoenix as soon as he was finished. More than that, Gokaldas had recently sent word he intended to bring a bride with him. But on April 14, 1908, only a few days after his marriage, the young man died in a freak accident. While playing cricket in Rajkot, Gokaldas was hit in the groin by a hard-thrown ball and fatally injured.

News of his death grieved them all. Mohandas, who had foreseen a long life of public service for his promising young nephew, was devastated. But Kasturba noticed that Harilal, who had been closer to Gokaldas than the younger boys, was deeply affected too. When he decided, some weeks later, to leave Gulab and little Rami in her care at Phoenix, and go to Johannesburg to join the Satyagraha struggle, Kasturba did not try to dissuade him. Harilal, like his father, had always been sensitive to the suffering of others, and she realised he hoped somehow to console Mohandas, to make up for the loss of one for whom he had held such high hopes.

By July, the campaign for repeal of the Black Ordinance was stalemated. Although Mohandas had fulfilled his promise — he had managed to convince the vast majority of Transvaal Indians to register voluntarily — Smuts was either unwilling or unable to uphold his part of the bargain. Mohandas had written the General many letters asking about the delay, but had received temporising replies, or no answers at all. The Black Act not only remained on the books, but the Transvaal legislature, adding insult to injury, was now considering a new law that would further restrict Indian immigration. In protest, the Satyagrahis had started another push to fill Transvaal's jails, and Harilal, with his father's encouragement, enlisted for duty. On July 24, while selling fruit on the street without a hawker's license, he was arrested for illegal trading.

Just two days later, on July 26, 1908, Mohandas sent off a somewhat cryptic message to relatives in India, in response to recent inquiries about his own safety. The letter which is addressed to his esteemed older cousin Khushaldas, the father of Maganlal and Chaganlal Gandhi, says:

I am writing this letter at midnight, I do not have much time. You ask me to take care, but we are taught that the soul does not die nor kill, and cannot be killed. If the body is to be taken care of, our Lord considers it to be just attachment. I consider the soul to be more important, and therefore I will strive to take care of it ...

Respectful regards,
Mohandas

Mohandas was present in the magistrate's court the next morning, July 27, when Harilal was convicted and ordered to pay a fine of one pound, or, failing that, to serve a sentence of seven days' hard labour. When Harilal refused to pay the fine and accepted the jail sentence, his father was the first to congratulate him.

A few days later, on July 31, 1908, Mohandas gave up the practice of law. Or, more accurately, he turned his practice over to associates (including Louis Ritch, now a barrister, who had recently returned from England), thus making official a decision that, for all practical purposes, had already gone into effect.

The next week, on August 3, Harilal was released from Johannesburg jail and ordered to leave the Transvaal in seven days. He did not leave. For his failure to do so, he was arrested again on August 10. And Mohandas was again a silent observer at the court hearing, as Harilal, offering no defence, was sentenced to one month's hard labour and led off to jail again.

Less than a week after that, in Johannesburg, the most significant Satyagraha protest to date took place. India's renowned modern statesman Jawaharlal Nehru, who was both protégé and successor to my grandfather in Indian politics, would one day observe that Mahatma Gandhi's unique success in creating a mass movement could be attributed primarily to "a curious knack for doing the right thing at the psychological moment." Such a moment had now arrived. Mohandas learned that the new immigration law was to be voted on (and inevitably passed) by the Transvaal legislature on August 16, making repeal of the registration law more unlikely than ever. He knew something must be done to give vent to Indian outrage, to dramatise Indian resentment. He sent General Smuts one more message, a cautionary one announcing that, unless the Black Act was repealed on or before August 16, Indians who had voluntarily applied for certificates were prepared publicly to destroy their registration cards and "humbly take the consequences". Smuts called this odd pronouncement an "ultimatum" he could not honour and curtly dismissed it. Legislators, incensed at such impudence on the part of an Indian, simply ignored the matter. Thus, the stage was set.

On August 16, 1908, on the grounds of the Hamida Mosque in Johannesburg, some three thousand Indians — Hindus, Muslims, Parsis, Christians — gathered for a carefully planned ceremony. In the centre of a hastily constructed platform sat a huge African cooking pot; more than two thousand registration certificates collected in advance from Transvaal Indians were piled up beside this four-legged iron cauldron; a can of kerosene was nearby.

At precisely 4.00pm, the deadline Mohandas had set for a response to the demands, a bicycle messenger arrived with the expected bad news. The government's stiffly formal telegram was read aloud to the crowd: there could be no change in the present line of action. The Black Act stood.

On the platform, men immediately began tossing registration cards into the cauldron, to the delight of the applauding audience. The certificates were doused with kerosene, amidst cries of "Burn them, burn them!" A lighted match was thrown into the cauldron. As the flames leaped up, the crowd cheered wildly. Their enthusiasm grew even more boisterous when Indians who had arrived late, or had withheld their decision until now, began filing up to the platform, one by one, and consigning their registration cards to the bonfire.

But the meeting's climax was unplanned. One of the last men to come forward from the audience was Mir Alam, the Pathan who had attacked Mohandas. Convicted on the testimony of other witnesses, despite Mohandas' refusal to press charges against him, Mir Alam had recently been released from prison after serving a three-month sentence for the assault. He now mounted the platform, announced who he was, loudly proclaimed he had been wrong to doubt Mr. Gandhi's integrity, and handed over his own certificate to be burned. The applause was tumultuous. And when Mohandas stepped forward to shake Mir Alam's hand, and assure him he had never harboured any resentment against him, the crowd's jubilation knew no bounds. For a Satyagraha celebration, this was indeed a crowning moment.

Next day, the *Daily Mail* of London compared the certificate burning bonfire staged by protesting Indians in Johannesburg to the famous Boston Tea Party of the American Revolution.

For some time Kasturba had been having difficult menstrual periods — a recurring problem for her, ever since the births of her two youngest sons. The excessive loss of blood each month left her quite weak. Constant worries about the safety and welfare of her husband and her oldest son during confrontations and jailing were also taking an emotional toll on her. But Kasturba was uncomplaining by nature, and she regularly went about her daily chores with such calm efficiency that it was easy to forget how small and frail she was, how delicately built. So it is understandable how Mohandas, whose overriding concern at this time was the Satyagraha movement, might have failed to notice, during his visits to Phoenix, how his wife's health was deteriorating. ("A Satyagrahi" he once wrote, "has to be, if possible, more single-minded than a rope dancer.") Truth was the Satyagraha campaign was lagging. The card burning ceremony had attracted attention, but it had changed nothing.

In early October, after spending two hectic weeks at Phoenix, Mohandas set off for Johannesburg convinced that the best way to bolster faith in the faltering movement was to get himself jailed once more, this time in protest against the new Immigration Act. He announced the news in a telegram sent to Phoenix Settlement that same day, and added a message to be printed in *Indian Opinion*. His words must have brought little comfort to an already distressed Kasturba: "Keep absolutely firm to the end. Suffering is our only remedy. Victory is certain." Years later, one of my father Manilal's prized possessions was the small identification card issued to my grandfather in Volksrust Prison at that time. It mistakenly lists his name as "M. S. Gandhi" rather than "M. K. Gandhi," and provides the following information:

"Trade: Solicitor. Sentence: £25 or two months. Date Imprisoned: October 10, 1908. Due for Discharge: December 13, 1908."

On the reverse side, in the space headed "Prison Offences" are no entries whatsoever. Mohandas was obviously a model prisoner.

He was permitted to have occasional visitors. On October 28, according to a diary notation, he enjoyed a reunion with his son Harilal, and his friend Herman Kallenbach.

Soon after this he received in the mail an urgent letter from Albert West giving news of Kasturba's excessive bleeding. Mr. West felt she needed hospitalisation and wanted Grandfather presumably to pay the fine, cut short his sentence, and return to Phoenix. Bapu's letter to Kasturba shows both the tender yearning and the harsh self-denial that were present in almost equal parts in his love for his wife. And it documents the soul-searching stress Bapu suffered whenever his conscience demanded that he make (and then try to explain) difficult decisions he knew would adversely affect those dear to him:

My dearest Kastur,

Mr. West has just given me the news of your ill-health. Though I feel anxious about your health, I am not in a position to come and nurse you. I hope you will understand that I have renounced everything in life for the sake of the struggle. Now if l am to come to you I would have to plead guilty of breaking the law and pay the fine so that I can be released from jail. You know this is not possible. It would reduce the struggle to a farce.

However, I am sure you will feel better if you keep courage and eat well. Even so, if it is destined that you shall die, I think it is preferable that you should go before me. You know I love you very much. And you must know that I will continue to love you just as much even after you are gone. Even if you die, for me you will be eternally alive. Your soul is deathless.

On my part, I would like to assure you that I have no intentions of marrying another woman after your death. I have told you this a number of times. You must have faith in God and set your soul free. Your death will be another great sacrifice for the cause of Satyagraha.

My struggle is not merely against the authorities, but against nature itself. I hope you will understand this and not feel offended. This is all I ask of you.

Yours,
Mohandas

At the bottom of the letter, Mohandas added a post-script addressed to his son, Manilal, and to his daughter-in-law, Gulab:

> I want you both to read the above letter yourselves and read it aloud to your mother ... I feel very worried, but I am helpless. You must keep me informed of Mother's health regularly. Look after Ramdas and Devadas, and I shall pray that Ba is up and about soon.

Blessings from Mohandas

Kasturba's condition did improve, at least temporarily. But when Mohandas hurried to Phoenix soon after his release from prison, he was surprised to see how haggard she looked, how tired and listless she had become. And when word came, not long afterwards, that Harilal had been arrested yet again, Mohandas was disturbed at how the news affected Kasturba. Distraught, weaker than ever, she seemed unable to carry on her daily schedule. After much pleading, Mohandas convinced his wife that she should have a medical check-up.

Early in January they travelled to Durban together and consulted with Dr. Nanji, a Parsi physician who was one of Mohandas' trusted personal friends. After an examination, the doctor told them Kasturba's haemorrhaging could be cured surgically. He advised that the operation be done at once, and Kasturba agreed, even though the doctor explained that he could not risk giving her an anaesthetic because of her emaciated state. The surgery, a curetting procedure, went well, and Kasturba endured the pain courageously. Afterwards, Dr. Nanji and his wife (who was a nurse), took Mohandas aside and suggested that Kasturba stay on in their Durban home, rather than returning to Phoenix for her recuperation.

"We'll take good care of her," the doctor told Mohandas. "She will get the rest she needs, I will keep a watchful eye on her, and you may go to Johannesburg and attend to your work with a free mind."

Mohandas was only too conscious of his long-neglected Satyagraha duties. He consulted Kasturba about the plan a few days later. When she made no objection, he took the train to Johannesburg. But the doctor had been overconfident. Kasturba continued to lose blood, and heavy dosages of medicine given to relieve pain made her feeble and lethargic. Dr. Nanji, a non-vegetarian, decided that a strictly vegetarian diet could not give his patient the nourishment she needed to make up for the loss of blood and regain her strength.

One morning, about two weeks after Mohandas returned to Johannesburg, the telephone in his office rang — a somewhat unexpected sound, since it had only recently been installed. Dr. Nanji, calling long-distance from Durban, got right to the point: "Kasturba is very weak," he said. "I feel she must be given beef broth."

"But that is unthinkable," was Mohandas' first reaction.

"I fear for her life," the doctor insisted. You will lose her if you don't listen to me."

"I cannot give you permission on Kasturba's behalf," Mohandas said. "Have you asked her about it?"

"I cannot ask her. She's in no condition to decide such matters."

Mohandas said he would take the next train to Durban. He asked the doctor to withhold any decision until he arrived and they could discuss the matter. But when he reached Durban the next morning, and rushed to the doctor's home, he learned that Kasturba had already been given a bowl of beef broth, without her knowledge.

Mohandas was shocked. Whatever the doctor had done was done with good intentions. But he was a close friend, he knew of the Gandhis' strict vegetarian beliefs, yet he had ignored them. Mohandas felt betrayed, and said so, adding that a trustful Kasturba had been betrayed even more than he.

"I am a doctor, and I don't have to consult my patients about the mode of treatment I prescribe," the doctor argued, "not when it is a matter of life or death."

Mohandas could see for himself that Kasturba's condition was critical. But this was no time to tell her what had already happened — it would break her heart to know she was made to drink beef broth. Yet choices affecting her own life had to be made, and he felt he must speak to her.

"The doctor says you must have beef broth to give you strength," he explained gently.

"Never!" Kasturba said in a barely audible voice. She reached for his hand. "Take me home. I will get better there."

Mohandas was relieved. He had lost faith in his medical friend, and Kasturba had suggested the best possible solution. But when he told Dr. Nanji, in whispered consultation, he was moving Kasturba to Phoenix he was taken aback by the physician's strong objections.

"What a callous man you are! I tell you that your wife is in no state to be moved anywhere. She cannot stand the least bit of jostling."

"Whatever the consequences," Mohandas said, "I must move her."

"Do what you feel you must do," the doctor said, "but be aware that you are acting against my best medical advice."

Kasturba, sensing that something was amiss, thanked the doctor and his wife for their kindness and hospitality. Then she tried to reassure Mohandas, "You need not worry about me, nothing will happen. At Phoenix, I promise you, I will soon get better."

That was all very well, but the problem was how to get her to Phoenix, a long and arduous journey which exhausted even the healthy.

Mohandas made a plan. He remembered an unused hammock at the Settlement which, if attached to two bamboo poles, would form a stretcher on which Kasturba could easily be carried. He dispatched a messenger to Phoenix to explain this to Albert West, and to inform him what train they would arrive on. He asked that West have the hammock and four men to serve as stretcher-bearers waiting at the station. The men should bring along a flask of hot milk, too.

Later that afternoon, Mohandas summoned a rickshaw. He despised the thought of riding in a contraption pulled by another human being. But this was an emergency. There was no other transportation available to reach the train station in time to catch the train.

Mohandas gently carried Kasturba out to the rickshaw and climbed in, holding her in his arms. He was amazed at how light she was — no more than skin and bones. He realised again the gravity of her illness and this made him more worried than ever.

Kasturba was not worried, she was mortified. To her it seemed an unpardonable breach of proprieties for a wife to be seen in public in her husband's embrace. But here she was, sitting in her husband's lap, riding through the streets of Durban, and there was nothing she could do about it. She was totally drained of all strength.

When the rickshaw arrived at the station, Mohandas had to carry Kasturba down the length of the platform to board their train. Fortunately, there were few passengers, so she was able to sleep on the seat until they reached Phoenix station. The men from the Settlement were waiting there with everything Mohandas had asked for. He gave Kasturba some of the warm milk to drink, then placed her on the makeshift stretcher. The two-mile trek through the sugar cane fields was treacherous; it had rained that morning, and the track was slippery and muddy. But Kasturba's spirits seemed to lift with each cautious step. They reached home at last, and after a reunion with family and friends, she claimed she was feeling almost well again.

Kasturba was never a devout believer in Mohandas' medical experiments — "health fads," she sometimes called them. But this time she made no objection when he insisted on giving her mudpack treatments. Over the next few weeks at Phoenix, whether due to the mudpacks, or because of the normal course of healing after an operation, Kasturba's strength slowly began to return — just as she had predicted it would.

Meanwhile, news of her grave illness, and reports of the resolute way she and Mohandas had rejected the doctor's beef tea treatment, had become known among Hindus in Natal. In his autobiography, in a chapter entitled "Kasturba's Courage", my grandfather related with obvious relish an incident that occurred soon after he brought his wife back to Phoenix.

One day, a Swami or religious teacher, appeared at their door, explaining he had come, prompted by sympathy, to plead with Mohandas on Kasturba's behalf, in her presence, and with two of the Gandhi sons, Manilal and Ramdas, listening in engrossed silence. The Swami held forth at length on why there were no real religious strictures against eating meat. He cited verses from the writings of Manu, the ancient lawgiver, to prove it — verses Mohandas knew were regarded by most Hindu scholars as interpolations. The two men fell into a serious argument, Mohandas pointing out that his own vegetarianism, in any case, was not based on scriptures or theology, but on ethical principles and medical knowledge. This fruitless dialogue was going nowhere — until Kasturba firmly put an end to it.

"Swamiji," she said, "whatever you may say, I do not want to recover by means of beef tea. You may discuss this with my husband and children if you like, but please don't worry me any more. My mind is made up."

# 17

For the Gandhi family, the arrests, the sentencing, the imprisonments continued without respite. In one year alone, the 12-month period following Kasturba's return to Phoenix after surgery, she received word, on eight different occasions, of the arrest of her husband or of one of her sons. Indeed, by the time the Satyagraha struggle reached its culmination in South Africa five years later, members of Kasturba's immediate family would have served a total of 18 jail terms.

Sometimes Kasturba's husband and her son were in prison at the same time, even at the same place. This happened when Mohandas, on returning to the Transvaal on February 25, 1909, was arrested for the third time, given a three-month sentence, and taken to Volksrust Prison where Harilal had just been sent to serve his third sentence — six months hard labour. But the two Gandhis were soon separated. The government, determined to chasten Mohandas, and demoralise the many Satyagrahis then imprisoned at Volksrust, transferred him to Pretoria Central Jail where conditions were the worst he had yet encountered.

When Mohandas was permitted to write a letter, he addressed it to his son Manilal, just turned 16, who had suddenly become the man of the family at Phoenix. Dated March 25, 1909, that lengthy letter from my grandfather to my father has been preserved over the years — five long sheets of prison stationery covered on both sides with crowded handwriting, first in purple ink and then in pencil. He writes:

My dear son:

   I have a right to write one letter per month and receive also one letter per month. It became a question with me as to whom I should write to. I thought of Mr. Ritch, Mr. Polak, and you. I chose you, as you have been nearest to my thoughts ...

Then, after explaining that he is not allowed to write anything about himself, Mohandas launches into a series of inquiries about, and messages for, nearly every one of dozens of persons residing at or visiting Phoenix, plus a number of his colleagues in Johannesburg. He hopes Ba is now quite well and able to walk about freely; he urges that she continue taking sago pudding and milk each morning. He thinks about Gulab and little Rami daily; he hopes Ramdas and Devadas are learning their lessons and that Ramdas has got rid of his cough. He trusts Mrs. West is well, he wonders how Miss Ada West is keeping. He hopes the evening services continue and that Manilal and the entire family attend the Sunday services at Mr. West's. He expresses gratitude for the handmade socks and gloves that have been sent to him. He thinks the verandah should be fenced, and asks how the new school is progressing. If the building is being constructed, he wants Chaganlal to see to it that tanks are put at each of the four corners to collect rain water for drinking. He inquires about some outstanding debts to be collected, and wonders about the articles Miss Schlesin is preparing for *Indian Opinion*. He reports he is allowed only one visitor each month and says he wants Mr. Polak to come, adding (and probably not as an afterthought) that "he has not yet sent the books I asked for."
   After that comes a special message to Maganlal Gandhi. Having just been introduced (through the jail library) to the works of yet another American author, Bapu advises Maganlal to buy and read a book by Ralph Waldo Emerson adding that, to his mind, Emerson's writings "contain the teaching of Indian wisdom by a Western philosopher." He particularly recommends Emerson's essays which, he reports, "can be had for nine pence in Durban — there is a cheap reprint out."
   But, to me, the letter's most interesting (and most heart-wrenching) passages are those addressed directly and personally to my father Manilal. Reading them, I am ever aware that this lengthy letter (to me) was composed in solitude at a time when my grandfather was still engaged in his personal battle for mastery over his natural desires and inclinations, and was addressed to a son who was undoubtedly enmeshed in his own personal struggle to cope with all the natural

urgencies and uncertainties that puberty brings. My grandmother had told her husband, years earlier, that he was trying to turn his sons into sadhus, or saints, before they had become men. By the time Bapu wrote this letter, his wife's discerning observation had become more apt than ever. His stern, constricted, yet awkwardly affectionate words show just how unrealistic were his expectations for his sons, how impossible were his demands upon them:

> ... And now about yourself: how are you? Although I think that you are well able to bear all the burdens I have placed on your shoulders and that you are doing it quite cheerfully, I have often felt that you required greater personal guidance than I have been able to give you. I know too that you have sometimes felt that your education was being neglected ... Now I have read a great deal in prison, and [my readings] all conform to the view that education does not mean knowledge of letters, it means character building, it means knowledge of duty ... What can be better than that you should have the opportunity of nursing your mother, and looking after Gulab and behaving to her so as not to make her feel the want of Harilal, or again, being guardian to Ramdas and Devadas?

Bapu goes on to say he has also been giving special attention to the *Upanishads*, that collection of ancient discourses on the meaning of sacred Hindu scriptures and the nature of man and the universe. In an attempt to forge a bond of mutual understanding with his son, Bapu then comments on a passage in the *Upanishads* about the observance of celibacy during two stages of Hinduism's ideal life cycle — the stage of youth and the sanyasin stage of old age:

> ... This is true. Amusement continues only during the age of innocence, i.e., up to twelve years. As soon as the boy reaches the age of discretion he is taught to realise his responsibility. Every boy from such age onwards should practice continence in thought and deed. This to him must not be an irksome learning and practice, but it should be natural to him. It should be his enjoyment ... Let me tell you that when I was younger than you are, my keenest enjoyment was to nurse my father. Of amusement after I was twelve I had little or none ...

Finally, Bapu offers his closing words of fatherly advice — a long list of very explicit directions:

> ... Do give ample time to gardening, actual digging, hoeing, etc.
> Keep your tools in their respective places and absolutely clean. In
> your lessons you should give a great deal of attention to
> mathematics and Sanskrit. You will not neglect your music. You
> should make a selection of all the good passages, hymns and
> verses, whether in English, Gujarati, or Hindi, and write them out
> in your best hand in a book. The collection at the end of a year
> will be most valuable. All these things you can do easily if you are
> methodical, never get agitated, and think you have too much to
> do, and then worry over what to do first. I hope you are keeping
> an accurate account, as it should be kept for every penny spent on
> the household ... Please send me a copy of algebra, any edition
> will do. And now I close with love to all and kisses to Ramdas,
> Devadas, and Rami.
>
> From Father.

When Mohandas was released from Pretoria Central Jail on May 24,
1909, he needed all the strength he could muster. After only the briefest
of visits to Phoenix Settlement, he was sent off to London on a mission
he would later describe as "thankless and fruitless." The movement,
now in its third year, was faltering; Indian resistance forces were
dwindling in the face of punitive measures, economic hardships, and
internal disputes. Meanwhile, their adversaries in what Mohandas liked
to call the war between the ants and the elephants" were gaining in
unity and power. The provincial governments of Natal, the Transvaal,
the Cape Colony, and the Orange Free State were about to come together
in a long-anticipated Union of South Africa. Official envoys (including
the Boer Generals Botha and Smuts) were already en route to London to
negotiate final approval of the proposed constitution for an autonomous
federal government, one which would enjoy dominion status within the
British Empire. To South Africa's small Indian minority, under siege in
the Transvaal and virtually excluded from the Orange Free State, the
danger inherent in such unification was clear. The anti-Indian statutes in
these Boer provinces could well become the laws of the land throughout
the new Union, replacing the somewhat less repressive measures in the
British colonies. In desperation, the Indians had decided to send their
own advocates to London to plead their cause one last time, and
Mohandas was again the inevitable choice to head such a deputation.

On June 23, he sailed out of Cape Town on the S.S. *Kenilworth Castle*, bound for England. He was accompanied this time by Haji Habib, the prominent Muslim merchant who, during the historic Empire Theatre meeting in Johannesburg, had been the first solemnly to vow resistance to the infamous Black Ordinance. Habib had originally emigrated to South Africa from Mohandas' home town of Porbandar, and despite their differences in religion and, to some degree, in politics — Haji Habib had never become a fully-fledged Satyagrahi — the two men had much in common and got along well. Some of their fellow-passengers even assumed they were brothers.

They arrived in London on July 10, and settled into a two-room suite at the Westminster Palace Hotel, a prestigious address that lent dignity to their cause. My grandfather would later regret that the money this cost his supporters had not been invested in the Satyagraha campaign itself.

At Phoenix Settlement, meanwhile, Bapu had remained a dominating presence — even during his absence. Everyone would gather to share the news when one of his frequent letters arrived from London. I have wondered, for example, what Kasturba made of a brief note dated August 25, and addressed to her young sons Ramdas and Devadas. Enclosed was a photograph of some of the militant English suffragettes whose vigorous "Votes for Women" crusade had attracted her husband's attention. "Many of the ladies in the picture have been to jail," he noted with obvious approval.

To Manilal, who cared for Albert West during a recent illness, Bapu wrote a fatherly commendation: "I am thankful to God for giving me such a son. I pray that you will always remain like that."

Manilal, hoping to emulate his older brother, wanted to go to Johannesburg, join the resistance, get arrested. Bapu was not ready as yet to see another son jailed (a view Ba undoubtedly shared), and tried to scotch the notion. His next letter to Manilal was a long treatise that contrasted the rural virtues of a quiet place like Phoenix where "one can search for soul and truth without the perils of city life in a place like Johannesburg, where people have very little space to grow, where there are many temptations, [making] it very difficult to attain integrity and honesty."

In England, meanwhile, as the months passed, nothing was resolved. The South Africans refused to make concessions; the British were reluctant to intervene on behalf of the Indians. Looking for a way to bring additional pressure to bear on the negotiators in London, Mohandas asked Henry Polak to travel to India and seek help from his friend and mentor G. K. Gokhale, now a member of the Viceroy's Legislative Council. Polak was warmly received, Gokhale and other Indian leaders sent strong messages to London, but all to no avail. In October, when the Union of South Africa Act was at last passed by Parliament, it included no guarantee whatsoever of rights for South African Indians.

Frustrated and disillusioned, Mohandas and Haji Habib sailed for Cape Town aboard the S.S. *Kildonan Castle* on November 13, 1909. Mohandas closed himself in his cabin during most of the seventeen-day homeward voyage. In a furious explosion of creative energy, writing so fast he used first his right hand and then his left to keep up with his thoughts, he scribbled on ship's stationery the 30,000-word manuscript of his now famous pamphlet "Hind Swaraj" (Indian Home Rule). In this work my grandfather took vehement issue with the Indian revolutionaries he had encountered in London, radical nationalists who equated terrorism with patriotism, and regarded assassination as an acceptable tool for achieving the immediate overthrow of British rule in India. But with equal bitterness he also lashed out, not so much at England (he still clung to his belief in the essential decency of the British people and the ultimate justice of British law), as at all of Western civilisation, condemning what he saw as an ever-spreading blight of Western materialism and greed. A less bitter but equally trenchant version of this judgment was later offered to a reporter who had asked, "What do you think of Western civilisation?" Gandhi's oft-quoted reply: "I think it would be a very good idea." Finally, he urged India to reclaim its national soul by returning to the ancient and enduring ideals of simple village life. This, too, was a theme he would later develop in more reasoned form.

Even while immersed in the writing of his pamphlet on Indian Home Rule, my grandfather still found time to correspond with family and colleagues. His letters mirrored his mood at that time. One revealing note, addressed to his eleven-year-old son Ramdas, seemed to restate in simple, personal terms some of the arguments he was then setting forth in the Hind Swaraj manifesto. "Please do not be angry with me for not bringing anything for you," he wrote. "I did not find anything to my liking. European souvenirs did not attract me. I prefer Indian made things. European people are alright, but their lifestyle is not very appealing."

It has often been noted that my grandfather, in all his writings, including his candid autobiography, *The Story of My Experiments with Truth*, discloses a great deal about himself but remarkably little about his wife. What he clearly though perhaps unintentionally does reveal, however — and what became obvious to me as I gathered information for this story of my grandmother's life — is simply this: while Mohandas experimented with truth, Kasturba experienced it.

Kasturba Gandhi spent virtually her entire life living with the daily, all-encompassing reality of Mahatma Gandhi's search for truth. If his experiments required heroic deeds of renunciation, self-denial, and perseverance to attain the spiritual ideal of non-attachment, then her experiences called for equally valiant acts of relinquishment, self-sacrifice, and magnanimity to sustain the human hope of love. The true wonder is that she was able to meet this test on her own terms — with patient conciliation or, when she felt the occasion so demanded, with lively, defiant, sometimes even playful confrontation.

Such an occasion arose one February day in 1910 when Mohandas, on his first visit to Phoenix following his ill-fated London mission, became concerned once more about Kasturba's health. In the year since her surgery, she had slowly regained her strength; she insisted on doing her usual household chores. But her weight had not increased, and she had recently suffered a slight reoccurrence of haemorrhaging, enough to worry Mohandas when he learned of it.

Naturally, he had a treatment to prescribe — another of his experimental diets. He had read somewhere that, to regain their health, frail people should avoid eating all forms of beans, peas, lentils, or other legumes. Though this made sense to him, he was not sure he could convince Kasturba. Both of them loved good food, but while he, in recent months, had been learning to curb his taste buds — mostly because he had come to regard our eating habits as primarily pandering to our sensory pleasure — Kasturba saw no connection between food and desires. She believed tasty food helped build the body, and if one ate food one liked, the body was better able to assimilate the nourishment. Thus, when Mohandas suggested she try a diet that excluded one of her favourite dishes, she was sceptical. In fact, she refused to take him seriously.

"Why don't you try your experiments on yourself?" she asked. "Why don't you give up lentils before advising others to do so?"

Mohandas knew his wife was teasing him; she was well aware that he rarely had a meal without at least one kind of beans, and lentils, especially, were his weakness. Nevertheless, he realised the validity of Kasturba's position.

"All right," he said, accepting the challenge, "I will give up all such dishes for one year — starting today. Now, what about you?"

Kasturba was caught off guard. "Oh, no! You cannot do that. Why should you suffer because of me? I was joking."

"You might be joking, but you have taught me an important lesson," Mohandas declared. "If I ask others to give up things they like, I should be able to give up things I like. It is only fair."

"But I can't let you do this. Take back your vow," Kasturba pleaded, "and I'll do as you wish!"

"How can I take back words that have left my lips?" Mohandas said. "Once they are uttered they are beyond my control, and what good are words if they are spoken without conviction? I have no doubt you will be better off on such a diet. And I will benefit, too," he added. "Restraint, whatever prompts it, is good for the soul." Kasturba knew how to resist. But she also knew Mohandas.

Together, they began their new diet that same day. Kasturba's condition soon improved, and shortly thereafter, somewhat to her surprise, the haemorrhaging stopped completely. Mohandas assigned full credit for her recovery to the diet he had prescribed. But years later, when he recalled the incident, he wryly acknowledged that it may have "added somewhat to my reputation as a quack."

Kasturba was feeling great tension in those early months of 1910 and with far more at stake than just her enjoyment of some favourite food. Increasingly, her allegiance to her husband, her desire to see him achieve his ideals, seemed in conflict with her devotion to her family. She had long since accepted the need for Mohandas to take risks, suffer hardships, face peril. But she found herself ill prepared to do the same with her sons. First, it had been Harilal. In the year and a half since her oldest son had joined the Satyagraha campaign, he had spent even less time at Phoenix than Mohandas had and more time in prison — almost 14 months at hard labour, to date. Kasturba was concerned that Harilal's wife Gulab, once so cheerful and lighthearted, was becoming ever more despondent.

Remembering her own years of loneliness as a young wife and mother separated from her husband, Kasturba tried to comfort her daughter-in-law. Meanwhile, she worried incessantly about her second son Manilal. Though he had left Phoenix to join the "agitation" with her approval, news of his repeated arrests had come as a shock. The thought of her quiet, gentle son Manilal in jail made Kasturba heartsick, and he was now serving his third sentence, three months at hard labour. Looking at Ramdas and Devadas, she dreaded the inevitable day when they, too, would decide they wanted to join their father's Satyagraha protests.

Meanwhile the struggle in South Africa had taken a new turn. Faced with having to house and feed thousands of coal miners who had gone on strike on his advice, Grandfather sought a way out. This was an opportunity, he realised, to lead a march of men, women and children into the Transvaal in defiance of the law prohibiting the free movement of black people. If they were arrested the Government would have to house and feed them. If they were not arrested they would have demonstrated the inefficacy of the unjust law. In the latter case Grandfather decided they would all march up to the property that Herman Kallenbach had donated, to establish the Tolstoy Farm as a settlement for the unemployed coal mine workers.

Kasturba's move to Tolstoy Farm was delayed for many weeks until adequate living quarters were built. It turned out to be more difficult than she had anticipated. After living in her little house at Phoenix for more than four years it had become a home. Now she was required to move again and the only consolation was that Phoenix itself was not being abandoned; the house and her neighbours would be there, and she would return from time to time.

But Kasturba's arrival at Tolstoy Farm on October 9, 1910 was eventful. First, she and her two younger sons, accompanied by Henry Polak, were stopped at the Transvaal border, questioned rudely, and allowed to continue their journey only after the immigration officers realised Kasturba was M. K. Gandhi's wife. Then, at Tolstoy Farm she learned that Harilal had been arrested again and was due to be sentenced the next day.

This disturbed Kasturba for reasons beyond mere worry about the harsh conditions awaiting her son in prison. She was worried about Harilal and hoped she would be able to talk to him in person. Reports she had received indicated Harilal had changed because of his recent disappointments.

The last time Harilal had been at Phoenix, some six months earlier, he learned that Chaganlal Gandhi was about to go to London on a scholarship offered by Dr. P. J. Mehta, the Gandhi family's longtime friend who, years earlier, had greeted Mohandas on his arrival in England as a student. Knowing that Mohandas had taken a vow of poverty, Dr. Mehta had fully expected him to offer this opportunity to one of his own sons. But Bapu, ever scrupulous to avoid even the appearance of favouritism toward his sons, had chosen Chaganlal. Though stunned and hurt, Harilal had managed to hide his dejection (from everyone but Gulab and Kasturba), and had returned to Johannesburg to get himself arrested again.

Another blow came in September when Harilal, just released from prison, instead of coming home to Phoenix had gone to Tolstoy Farm to seek his father's permission, and funding, to return to India. His beloved Gulab and little Rami had already gone to India where Gulab would be delivering their second child. Mohandas had refused, saying no funds were available, and that Harilal should stay on in South Africa. In a huff Harilal left Tolstoy Farm and, once again, deliberately sought imprisonment.

She yearned above all else to see Harilal, to talk to him, to tell him she knew how much he missed Gulab and Rami and, above all, that she was concerned Harilal might consider Mohandas' decision arbitrary, unfeeling. Harilal appeared to be directing his anger not only at his father, but also at his father's cause. Kasturba was hoping that her presence would help heal Harilal's wounds but that could not be, not until Harilal was free again.

Mohandas was meanwhile giving himself to his new project with all his usual intense dedication. He was successful in making a mockery of the unjust law that prohibited the movement of black people. The miners were allowed to come to Tolstoy Farm although they did not have valid travel documents. Mohandas would write, "My faith and courage were at their highest at Tolstoy Farm."

Ba found life at Tolstoy Farm very different from life at Phoenix Settlement, even though both were self-sustaining rural communities. There were, first of all, many more residents at Tolstoy Farm — Hindus, Muslims, Parsis, and Christians, including many children. Each person was issued two blankets and a pillow; when weather allowed, everyone slept outside on a veranda or on the ground. All the men, including Mohandas, wore cheap, ready-made workmen's trousers and shirts — much like the clothing they wore in prison. All cooking and baking was done in a central kitchen. But she could always find comfort, as at Phoenix, in the daily prayers; indeed, prayer services were twice a day at Tolstoy — "the key of the morning and the bolt of the evening", Mohandas called them.

Tolstoy Farm was not without problems, the most serious, in Kasturba's view, being one which threatened her own sons. Several of the older boys came from hard-pressed families with little or no education or economic opportunities and no discipline. Wild, quarrelsome, dishonest, and arrogant, these boys were "hard cases" who needed love and guidance. But Kasturba worried that her sons, meanwhile, were being influenced by their bad behaviour. Remembering how her husband, in his zeal for reform, had once ignored her warnings and refused to give up his own boyhood friendship with that most unsuitable companion Sheik Mehtab, Kasturba decided it would be futile for her to caution him now about the dangers to which he was exposing his sons. Instead, she confided her fears to Herman Kallenbach, and found an ally. Kallenbach said he, too, had been perturbed about the example set by these boys.

A day or two later, he discussed the matter with Mohandas, emphasising his concern for the welfare of Mohandas' own sons. After thinking about it for a moment, Mohandas turned the question back to Kallenbach. "What would you have me do?"

"Send these boys away, if you cannot isolate your own sons," Kallenbach suggested.

"And give my boys the impression that they are special and need to be protected?"

"You could explain that these older boys are being sent away, not because they are bad, but because what they are doing is wrong."

"Would that not make my sons more curious," Mohandas persisted, "make them eager to experiment with these bad habits?"

Kallenbach and Mohandas argued the point at length, but Mohandas would not be swayed. He believed his sons, given time, would themselves realise the behaviour of the other boys was wrong and reject it totally. The offending youths remained at Tolstoy Farm for many months, and with no disastrous results.

Meanwhile, the long-smouldering conflict between Mohandas and Harilal, the dissension that Kasturba had for so long been trying to resolve, was reignited in the early months of 1911. But this time there was no way to contain the resulting conflagration.

It began when Chaganlal Gandhi, who had become ill soon after his arrival in England, gave up his legal studies and returned home to his family in Phoenix Settlement. Indian leaders in South Africa were greatly concerned. Mohandas was still the only one of their number trained in the law, and they worried that he would be summoned home by his friends in the Indian National Congress to work in the struggle in India. They sought a replacement for Chaganlal and gave additional money to continue the London scholarship. An open essay competition was announced and since Mohandas was the only one qualified by knowledge of the law to select the winner, he served as the competition's sole judge.

After careful consideration of examination results, he chose Sorabji Shapurji Adajania, an well-educated young Parsi, originally from Natal, who had been among the first to journey to Transvaal, court arrest, and be imprisoned as a Satyagrahi. Sorabji would prove worthy of the trust placed in him. After completing his legal studies in London, he would return to the Transvaal, ready to work hard in the community, and fearlessly oppose unjust laws. Yet, within months, this capable young barrister was stricken with a sudden respiratory infection and died — something no one could have foreseen. It was sheer bad luck that the efforts of the Indian community were thus wasted.

To another brilliant young Indian, meanwhile, the choice of Sorabji Shapurji Adajania as winner of the London scholarship came as a personal catastrophe. He was the candidate who had scored highest on the examination, ahead of Sorabji, but whose application had not even been considered. His name was Harilal Gandhi. For the second time he became a victim of a father who did not want to be accused of nepotism.

On May 8, 1911, Harilal disappeared from Tolstoy Farm, leaving a note that said the time had come for him to break all ties with his father. Kasturba was distraught, but not surprised. Several days of foreboding and premonitions passed; no one knew where Harilal was. Kasturba grew frantic. Then, one of his friends in Johannesburg disclosed that he was in Delagoa Bay in neighbouring Mozambique, awaiting passage to India. Herman Kallenbach volunteered to go to Mozambique and try to persuade him to come back to Tolstoy Farm.

The climax came on May 15, 1911, the night of Harilal's return. All through that night, walking up and down in the fields and orchards of the farm, Harilal and Mohandas talked to each other. They argued, accused, justified; they listened yet did not hear each other. Kasturba never knew what passed between her husband and her son that night.

Two days later, she watched them leave Tolstoy Farm together, on their way to the Johannesburg railroad station where Mohandas would say farewell to Harilal, departing for India to be with his wife and family, to seek his education. Kasturba knew her son was trying to find his future in his own way. And she was trying to find it in her heart to forgive her husband.

Over and over, Harilal's words repeated themselves in her mind: "He just does not care for us, any of us."

# 18

For Kasturba too many things were happening all at once. If Harilal's going back to India caused any anxiety it was only that he went with bitterness against his father in his heart. Kasturba prayed that he would find solace and comfort in India and that, someday, he might see the wisdom in what his father was trying to teach him. In 1912, Gopal Krishna Gokhale, an eminent leader of the Congress Party in India, came on a month-long tour of South Africa. He was attempting to groom Mohandas for leadership of the movement for independence in India.

Gokhale was following Mohandas closely, and had adopted the problems of South African Indians as his own. As a ranking member of the Viceroy of India's Legislative Council he was entitled to the Union of South Africa's official respect and attention, and he intended to press for reforms in talks with the Union's ruling powers. Thus, the Satyagrahis were hopeful that Gokhale's well-publicised visit might bring the changes they were seeking. But Kasturba did not share that optimism. She knew change did not come so easily.

On his arrival in Cape Town on October 20, 1912, Gokhale was greeted by Europeans as well as Indians and given a red carpet welcome. A state railway car was put at his disposal, and, with Mohandas and Herman Kallenbach in attendance, he embarked on an exhausting train tour, meeting community leaders and addressing crowds. In Johannesburg, where the tour ended, a large ornamental arch of welcome (designed by architect Kallenbach) had been erected at the Park Station terminal.

Later, when Gokhale emerged from his two-hour meeting with the government officials he was beaming. "Everything has been settled," he told Mohandas. "The Black Act will be repealed, the racial bar will be removed, the three-pound tax will be abolished."

Mohandas was sceptical. "I doubt it very much. You do not know the ministers as I do." He asked if there was a written agreement.

"What I have told you will happen, General Botha has promised me it will," Gokhale assured him. "And you, my friend, will be able to return to India within a year. I will have no more of your excuses."

"I am not as hopeful as you are," Mohandas replied sombrely. "I think many more Indians will have to go to jail in South Africa before I can return to India."

Mohandas was soon proved right — Gokhale's intervention had changed nothing. Following his departure, the laws he had discussed with Botha and Smuts either remained on the books, or were replaced by even more objectionable measures. In the case of the three-pound tax, General Smuts declined to sponsor any kind of repeal legislation, declaring that Europeans in Natal would not sanction such a move.

The astute and observant Gokhale, while still in South Africa, had one day gently criticised Mohandas for being too stubborn, too domineering. "You will always have your own way," he chided. Based perhaps on his experiences at Tolstoy Farm, Gokhale had warned his friend against letting his own example of disciplined and relentless self-denial become a tyranny he imposed on others. This was straightforward brotherly advice. But a few months later, back in India, when Gokhale learned that the South African government was not honouring its pledges to him, he saw his friend's strong-willed moral leadership in a new and admiring light. He told a Bombay audience: "Gandhi has in him the marvellous spiritual power to turn ordinary men around him into heroes and martyrs."

When Mohandas announced, in January of 1913, that he was moving the base of operations for Satyagraha activities from Tolstoy Farm in the Transvaal to Phoenix Settlement in Natal, Kasturba was happier than she had been in months. No matter that she had to pack up and move again. This time, it was as if she were going home.

"Do you know you will soon cease to be my wife?"

The conversation was taking place in the kitchen of the little house at Phoenix on a fine autumn day. Kasturba was preparing dinner, and Mohandas was helping peel and slice the vegetables.

Taken aback by her husband's question, Kasturba at first thought she had not heard right. "What did you say?"

"I said, you will soon cease to be my legally married wife. You will be regarded by law as my mistress — my concubine."

She realised then that he was teasing her. "What utter nonsense," Kasturba said. "You do come out with gems at times."

"It isn't I." Mohandas announced coolly. "It is General Smuts who says our marriage is not legal."

"He doesn't know what he's talking about. How on earth do such ideas come into his brain?" Kasturba's manner indicated she was not prepared to discuss the general's foolish pronouncements.

"Whatever you think," her husband persisted, "he is quite serious about it, and so is the government." Kasturba's disbelief turned to indignation.

On March 14, 1913, the Supreme Court ruled that any marriage not solemnised according to Christian rites would no longer be legally recognised in South Africa. With a stroke of the pen, existing marriages of tens of thousands of Muslim, Hindu, and Parsi Indians were being invalidated. Children of such unions were deemed illegitimate, ineligible to inherit property; wives might even be subject to deportation. Mohandas said he had written to General Smuts, pointing out that marriages of all religions were legally recognised in India, and thus, by dominion law, should be honoured in South Africa. But his request that the Court's ruling be rescinded had been ignored.

Kasturba was appalled: "What can we do about it?" she asked.

"You women must raise your voices, you must protest this insult." A pause, and then, in solemn tones, Mohandas declared, 'You must go to jail, just as the men do."

Suddenly, Kasturba relaxed. Women go to prison! Ridiculous! Mohandas was joking. "So, you want to send your wife to jail, is that it?"

"Why shouldn't women share the joys and sorrows of men? Sita shared Rama's struggles. Taramati suffered with Harishchandra. They underwent untold hardships to uphold their honour and defend truth."

"They were divine beings," Kasturba countered. "We are mortal!"

"But would they be worshipped as they are today, if they had not been willing to make sacrifices for truth?" Mohandas was enjoying this discourse. "We are descendants of Rama and Sita. If we were prepared to do as they did, we could also become divine."

Kasturba decided it was time to bring the discussion down to earth. "But how could I live on a jail diet?"

"That is no problem." Her husband was nonchalant. "Demand fruit and live on a fruit diet."

"After everything you've told me about prison authorities, you expect me to believe they will give me fruit just for the asking?"

"Perhaps not." Mohandas gazed at her pensively. "You might have to fast unto death to make them understand your needs."

"First you want to send your wife to prison. Now you want me to die. What sort of man are you?"

"If you die in jail, I shall worship you like a goddess!"

"Well, in that case," Kasturba announced, "I shall go to jail!" And the two of them were laughing together like happy children.

Kasturba thought of that conversation often in the weeks that followed. How could she forget it? Everyone was talking about it, everyone was furious. Mohandas, in that mischievous manner she knew so well, had of course been teasing her. Nevertheless, the words they had spoken in the kitchen that day were finding echoes in Kasturba's innermost being.

She kept recalling the ancient legends she had heard as a little girl: how Sita's faithfulness to her husband Rama helped him defeat Ravana, the demon king of Ceylon, who had kidnapped her. How the loyal Taramati, by giving up her own freedom, rescued Harishchandra from an evil fate and reclaimed their son from death. Her thoughts kept returning to the true story of Rani Laxmibai of Jhansi. Kasturba could still hear her mother's voice, telling of that great queen who led her troops into battle — that modern Indian heroine who proved that a woman protecting those in her care, defending those she loved, was as courageous as any man and as invincible as a goddess.

She had long ago acknowledged in her own mind that what Mohandas was fighting for was important. Now, for the first time, Kasturba understood in her heart why it was important. And she knew in her very soul why she believed in it. It was her fight, too.

For Satyagraha, the critical moment had come. If the peaceful resistance movement was to succeed, it was now or never. The Union government's failure to repeal the three-pound tax in Natal had created a new reservoir of potential protesters. The invalidation of non-Christian marriages, threatening countless Indian families, rich and poor alike, with indiscriminate penalties and humiliation, had loosed a flood of outrage throughout South Africa. Yet autumn had turned to winter, winter was turning into spring, and still there was no governmental response to the growing Indian unrest. Mohandas, sensing that a new force had been born, a new energy released in the land, concluded that a radical new tactic was in order. The participation of Indian women in the non-violent protest movement, fantastically improbable just months ago, had now become virtually inevitable. The women demanded it. To be fully-fledged Satyagrahi, however, they must get themselves arrested, and this was a problem.

The campaign got underway almost of its own accord when a number of volunteers, all women who had lived at Tolstoy Farm and needed little instruction in Satyagraha methods, took to the streets and began hawking fruit without trading permits. The police, wary of the public outcry that would almost surely greet the arrest, let alone the imprisonment, of these Indian women — one was pregnant and several carried babies in their arms — simply ignored them.

Mohandas decided to invite all Phoenix residents to join the "invasion party" — all, that is, except the few adults needed to bring out weekly editions of *Indian Opinion*, children under sixteen, and his own wife.

Not having consulted with his wife in making this decision, Mohandas had not reckoned with her reaction. One day in early September, Kasturba overheard her husband quietly explaining his "invasion" plan to several other women at Phoenix, and realised she was being excluded. She called him aside and asked a blunt question.

"What defect is there in me which disqualifies me for jail?'

"There is no question of my distrusting you," Mohandas quickly replied. "But if I asked you to go to prison, you might go just for the sake of complying with my request. And then, if you fell ill or were unable to withstand the hardships of jail, I could not find fault with you, but I would not forgive myself."

Kasturba was not one to be put off so glibly. "If you can endure prison hardships, and so can my boys, then why can't I?"

Still dubious, he begged her to consider, thinking of the risks.

"I have nothing to think about," Kasturba declared. "I am fully determined to join the struggle." And so the matter was settled.

On September 23, 1913, a party of sixteen Gujarati-speaking Indians, twelve men and four women, boarded a northbound train at Phoenix Station and headed for the Transvaal border with the express purpose of getting arrested. They were led by Mrs. Kasturba Gandhi, and among their number were several other Gandhis — Mrs. Kashiben Gandhi and her husband Chaganlal Gandhi, Mrs. Santokben Gandhi, and Ramdas Gandhi. The only one of the group who was not a Phoenix resident was Jivanji Rustomji, the Gandhis' generous Parsi friend from Durban days, who was now a dedicated Satyagrahi.

Mohandas saw them off without ceremony and walked back to the Settlement to rejoin those left behind, including Maganlal Gandhi, who was sharing with Albert West the task of getting *Indian Opinion* published, and Devadas Gandhi, who at age thirteen was big enough to do press work and to help Miss Ada West mind the younger children. The excursion had received no publicity, not even in *Indian Opinion*, nor had officials been given the customary advance notice of a planned protest action. It was feared that the border police, if forewarned of the arrival of this particular group of would-be prisoners, might not arrest them.

On reaching the border, the "invaders" remained silent as planned, refusing to show permits or any other kind of identification, refusing even to give their names. The strategy worked. All were taken into custody — women as well as men — and police did not discover their identity until after they had been brought before a magistrate, tried, and found guilty. By that time, they had all been sentenced to three months' hard labour.

No one recorded the prisoners' reactions as they were led out of the courtroom that day. Yet I can easily imagine the mixture of pride and anxiety my grandmother felt, not just for herself, but also for her companions, the younger Phoenix women. They had achieved their goal — to become the first women arrested as Satyagrahis — but what lay ahead? I know, too, how painful must have been Ba's last, fleeting glimpse of 15-year-old Ramdas being marched off with the men. Her third son, looking brave, determined, and (to a mother's eye, a bit apprehensive), was also about to experience his first imprisonment.

The Phoenix women were taken to Maritzburg jail to serve their sentences. There, in the ensuing weeks, Kasturba helped her younger companions find the will and the courage to survive the harsh prison routine. She encouraged them to finish the heavy laundry work and endless sewing tasks assigned daily. She attempted, with little success, to convince disdainful wardens that she and her fellow vegetarians could eat almost none of the jail food (which was abominable), that they had special dietary needs. She made a calendar of sorts and, by crossing off one square each day, kept count of how many days were left in their sentences. And every evening, she led all the women in prayers and hymn singing.

News that peaceful women protesters, among them Kasturba Gandhi, wife of Mohandas Gandhi, were in prison in Natal, stirred deep emotions among Indians (Indian women, especially) throughout South Africa. Inspired by their example, and acting with Mohandas' advice, eleven of the Tolstoy Farm women who had unsuccessfully courted arrest as street-traders in the Transvaal, set out in mid October for the border town of Volksrust where they hoped to be jailed trying to cross over into Natal. But the "Tolstoy sisters" (as Mohandas called them), unlike the Phoenix women, were neither detained nor arrested when they refused to show permits at the Transvaal border. There was conjecture at the time that this unequal treatment before the law was a cynical attempt by the government to foment discord among protesters. Such speculation was never proved or disproved. But years later, in the early 1950s, Africans, Indians, and Coloureds, (the designation in South Africa for those of mixed race) tried briefly to wage a joint battle against the so-called apartheid system of colour discrimination. A white-controlled South African government used the same tactic (giving members of different groups differing punishments or no punishment at all for the same alleged offence) to disrupt and ultimately destroy the coalition.

Satyagrahis everywhere were stepping up protests, tirelessly trying to fill the South African prisons. My father Manilal Gandhi, who had been working for the movement in Johannesburg, served two brief sentences in rapid succession in Transvaal jails before finally, in late October, being sentenced to serve three months at hard labour — his sixth imprisonment, to date. From Phoenix, Albert West and Maganlal Gandhi, with the help of young Devadas, published *Indian Opinion* on schedule, complete with dispatches from India where Gokhale was keeping the viceroy and the public informed about the grievances in South Africa. Even the children at Phoenix Settlement, some no more than five years old, were doing their bit, trudging the two miles through sugar cane fields to Phoenix Station each day to pick up heavy bags of mail and supplies and carry them home, slung litter-like between long bamboo poles resting on their young shoulders.

Back in Natal, the situation of the women Satyagrahis in Maritzburg jail was steadily deteriorating. They were hectored and harassed by warders, their illnesses went unattended, their food, especially that served to vegetarians, was often rancid or spoiled. Some women offered to pay for meals to be brought in from outside, but were told that jail was no hotel. Several prisoners contracted a debilitating fever — a fatal fever in the case of one emaciated young woman who eventually died, just days after her release from prison.

Kasturba was looking more weary and worn each day. Though she always finished her work and never missed evening prayers, the younger women, especially Santokben and Kashiben who had known her so well for so long, could see she was suffering.

Kasturba, in truth, was heartsick. Her calm, enduring optimism was being tested as never before by circumstances she had never anticipated.

From the day of their arrest, Ba had been anxious about her son Ramdas. Then letters from Phoenix brought word of her son Manilal's imprisonment in the Transvaal, and now came the latest news that Mohandas had been arrested and sentenced to nine long months in jail in a place she had never heard of. She, her husband, and two of their sons were all in prison — in different prisons — all at the same time.

The government, convinced that Phoenix was the nerve centre of continued Indian resistance, and hoping to halt the spread of unrest by silencing *Indian Opinion*, sent police to the Settlement to arrest Albert West. But Maganlal Gandhi and his young cousin Devadas, working up to twenty hours a day, kept the paper coming off the presses. And before the crisis passed, one legendary issue of *Indian Opinion* would be published by the children at Phoenix, working alone.

Events had now taken on a momentum of their own. The plight of South African Indians was the topic of the day. From Bombay, the Viceroy of India, Lord Hardinge, startled South Africans and riled the British Cabinet by declaring, in an unprecedented public criticism of another member government of the Empire, that "this movement of passive resistance has been dealt with by measures which would not for one moment be tolerated by any country that calls itself civilised."

London, after due reflection, communicated to the South African government its displeasure with the handling of Indian affairs. In Pretoria, General Smuts, the hapless minister in charge of Indian Affairs, was caught between his genuine abhorrence of the atrocities committed in the name of the "blood and iron" policy which he himself had helped create, and his need to accommodate the intransigence of South African Europeans which he himself had encouraged. Smuts was, as my grandfather later wrote, "in the same predicament as a snake which has made a mouthful of a rat but can neither gulp it down nor cast it out."

On December 18, 1913, General Smuts ordered the unconditional release of Mohandas Gandhi, Henry Polak, and Herman Kallenbach — so they could prepare to testify before the commission.

Three days later, Mohandas appeared before a mass meeting in Durban looking gaunt and solemn. The man who was to become the Mahatma, in a visual declaration of identification with his oppressed countrymen, no longer wore European attire; instead, he was dressed in the plain, knee-length white cotton tunic, and the long, skirt-like lungi or loincloth, worn by poor labourers in South India. His feet were bare; his mustache, a familiar feature during all his years in South Africa, was gone. His unturbaned head, except for a close-cropped ridge of hair on top, was shaven, as a sign of mourning for the ten Indians who had been killed in confrontations with the police or had died in prison. when he rose to speak, he attacked the inquiry commission as a "packed body" from which Indians could expect no justice, and asked his audience to prepare for "still greater purifying suffering."

The following day, still wearing his mourning clothes, my grandfather was at the gates of Maritzburg prison. He was awaiting the release of Ba and the other Phoenix women who, as of that date, December 22, 1913, had completed their three-month sentences. Also on hand were Herman Kallenbach, Henry and Millie Polak, several other friends, and a crowd of curious strangers. When the freed prisoners came through the gates, many bystanders assumed that the tiny, frail, careworn woman who was the first to emerge and was greeted with such tender respect by Bapu and his friends, was Mr. Gandhi's mother.

The reunion had to be brief for the long struggle was reaching a climax. While Kasturba and her companions returned to Phoenix, Mohandas and his friends sent off a letter to General Smuts asking that the government, as an indication of good will, release all imprisoned Satyagrahis, and replace the anti-Indian members of the inquiry commission, if not with Indians, then at least with impartial Europeans with "a sense of justice". In his brief reply, General Smuts said that the first request had already been acted upon, the prisoners were being freed; the second request could not be granted. Mohandas countered with a public announcement. There would be another mass demonstration: on January 1, 1914, a party of Indians courting arrest would commence a march for justice from Durban to Pretoria.

An irresistible force, in the person of a tenacious Indian lawyer-turned-protest-leader, was confronting an immovable object, in the person of an implacable Boer soldier-turned-statesman.

Just at this juncture, however, the unexpected intervened. South Africa's white railway workers, long dissatisfied with their working conditions, launched a nationwide strike. Suddenly, the Union government was in a very delicate position, its very existence imperiled by this new disruption. The government declared martial law. Mohandas, in turn, postponed the planned march. He declared it would be "clearly out of place" for non-violent protesters to pursue tactics, which would humiliate, harass, or take advantage of the government's weaknesses. In a Satyagraha campaign, he explained, "the adversary is not to be destroyed, but to be won over."

It was a master stroke. General Smuts and General Botha, relieved of the most immediate threat to their government, agreed to sit down with Mohandas for serious talks aimed at resolving Indian grievances. The news, cabled by Reuters, was received in England with amazement and satisfaction. In India, a hopeful Gokhale asked his trusted friend Rev. Charles Andrews, a well-connected, young British clergyman who had become a Gandhi admirer from afar, to go to South Africa as his special envoy to assist in achieving a just settlement. Meanwhile, in South Africa, many Europeans understood for the first time what the Indians' nonviolent resistance movement was trying to accomplish, and many Indians realised for the first time what the sacrifices their leader had called for could achieve.

But the negotiations, when they got underway, went slowly, and were interrupted when Mohandas was urgently summoned to Phoenix: Ba was gravely ill. For most of the month of February and part of March, Bapu stayed at his wife's side. It was a time of dread and self-recriminations; in a letter written to a friend during this period he reported that, "All of us are mentally prepared for Kasturba's death." In another letter, he seemed to be reproaching himself for her suffering, blaming himself for sorrows he may have brought to her and to others. "I do not know what evil there is in me," he wrote. "I have a strain of cruelty in me, such that people force themselves to do things, even attempt impossible things, in order to please me." Yet as his wife's health improved, along with her good spirits, Bapu's mood lifted. To his great relief Ba was herself again — well enough, in fact, to insist on going with him when he travelled to Cape Town to resume talks with General Smuts and leaders of the Union Parliament. Apparently, Ba was just as concerned about Bapu's well-being as he was about hers.

Gandhi and Smuts, the two leaders so long wary of each other, had by this time developed a grudging mutual respect that could lead to mutual concessions. The general's attitude was reflected in a jocular yet half-serious complaint his secretary once voiced to Mohandas — that the Satyagrahi's desire for victory by self-suffering alone "reduces us to sheer helplessness."

By June, an agreement had been hammered out. As passed by the Union Parliament, the Indian Relief Bill was a compromise for both sides. The hated three-pound tax was abolished, non-Christian marriages were recognised, the importation of indentured labour from India was to cease by 1920. Immigration laws were somewhat relaxed, but only for educated Indians. Still, the main provision of the "Black Act" remained in force: free movement of Indians from one province to another in the Union was not permitted.

Other reforms remained to be won. Most Indians still had to live in "locations", and Indians were not allowed to buy or own land in the Transvaal.

Yet, compromise or no, the agreement was a victory for the principle of racial equality — the adversaries had negotiated as equals. And the victory had been won by non-violence — a vindication of Satyagraha. Mohandas at last felt free to fulfill his promise to Gokhale to return to India, and Gokhale, as it happened, was then en route to London, and was eager for them to meet there and discuss the future. So Mohandas booked passage to sail to England with Kasturba. The ever-faithful Herman Kallenbach would accompany them; later on, other Phoenix residents would join them in India.

Kasturba's last days in South Africa were spent in a triumphal round of celebrations. She stood with her husband in reception lines, sat by his side at banquets. They were garlanded with flowers, presented with mementos, photographed with smiling officials, embraced by tearful friends, hailed by cheerful crowds everywhere. She remembered the long-ago crowds in Durban, taunting and jeering her husband on their arrival in South Africa. She reflected, with a degree of wonder, on how different these crowds were, how different this departure was — and, most of all, how different they themselves were. Everyone was saying how much Mohandas had changed South Africa. But it seemed to her that only she could know how much South Africa had changed Mohandas. And it had changed her, too — she recognised that. They were both new people, going home to a new life.

On July 18, 1914, my grandparents boarded the R.M.S. *Kilfauns Castle* in Cape Town and sailed for England. General Smuts, in a much-quoted statement, summed up his reaction: "The saint has left our shores, I hope forever."

The general's sentiments would change with time. A few days later he received a pair of sandals that my grandfather had made while in prison. Bapu had left instructions for Sonja Schlesin to have them delivered to Smuts as a farewell gift. Many years later, on Bapu's seventieth birthday in 1939, General Smuts, who had himself grown in stature in the world's opinion, returned the sandals to my grandfather as a token of regard and friendship for an old adversary. The general's message on that occasion has also been much quoted: "I have worn these sandals for many a summer," Smuts wrote, "even though I may feel that I am not worthy to stand in the shoes of so great a man."

There were other prominent white South Africans who had been much quicker to appreciate my grandfather's pioneering experiments in the use of nonviolence to resolve conflicts. They had responded instinctively to Satyagraha campaigns to bring change to their own country, and had sensed intuitively Satyagraha's powerful potential to bring reforms elsewhere. One of the most prescient of these early Gandhi supporters was the gifted novelist Olive Schreiner.

"Have you ever known a whole nation to speak at the same time?" she once wrote. "Mr. Gandhi, I knew, was India, and India was Mr. Gandhi. How could I remain deaf to this vastness?"

But even Olive Schreiner, far-sighted as she was, could not fully understand the hidden strength of the Gandhis' appeal to non-violence, much less anticipate the dormant forces it would awaken when my grandparents, working together, introduced it to their homeland. Olive Schreiner never had the opportunity to become well acquainted with my grandmother. I believe, if she had, this perceptive South African woman would have recognised immediately that, while Mr. Gandhi might be the voice of India, Mrs. Gandhi represented its heart.

# 19

A leisurely 19-day sea voyage, even in the tiny, third-class cabin which was Mohandas' choice of accommodations, offered a welcome respite for the homebound travellers. Exhausted from the stresses and upheavals of recent months, Mohandas and Kasturba kept mostly to themselves, eating all meals in their cabin. By special arrangement, the Steamship Company provided ample supplies of dried fruits and nuts, the "fruitarian" diet.

As the *Kilfauns Castle* moved northward across the vast emptiness of the South Atlantic, Mohandas kept busy sorting papers, writing letters. He set aside an hour each day for teaching Gujarati to their fellow passenger Herman Kallenbach, who planned to travel to India with them after their brief London stopover. He spent another hour with Kasturba, reciting favourite passages from the *Bhagavad Gita* or verses from the *Ramayana*. Though her ever-busy hands were at rest for once, her thoughts roamed restlessly. She had left South Africa behind without regrets. She was approaching her first visit to England, that unknown land where her young husband had gone long ago for his education, with some apprehension, to be sure, but also with much curiosity and excitement. Above all, she was anticipating the joys that awaited her in India — to be able to embrace Harilal and Gulab again, to hug her small granddaughter Rami, to hold in her arms her two little grandsons Kanti and Rasik, whom she had never seen.

There was also a sense of poignancy in their journey to India. Many dear ones had died during their absence. Her husband was now the only surviving son of Karamchand and Putliba Gandhi. Word had come, in

1913, that Mohandas' brother Karsandas had died. The news brought a flood of memories of three young couples sharing a long-ago wedding day in Porbandar. There had been little time to grieve; the Satyagraha struggle was then in its final stages. Early in 1914, a cable had announced that Lakshimidas, too, had died.

Then there was the news that her brother — Khushaldas Kapadia, his wife, and their daughter — had all succumbed to a common fever, dying within days of each other. With Khushaldas gone, she was now left with only her younger brother Madhavdas.

During the days my grandparents were at sea in that fateful summer of 1914, events which at first seemed remote and unrelated to their lives were changing the course of world history. In late July, when the *Kilfauns Castle* put in at the island of Madeira off the coast of Morocco, passengers got news of the war clouds gathering over Europe, in places with names that were unpronounceable, at least to Kasturba.

It took two more disconcerting days to reach Southampton; the ship had to be towed through submarine mines laid down in the Channel. When passengers disembarked on British soil on August 6, the country was in a state of fevered excitement. As her introduction to London in subsequent days, Kasturba witnessed a medley of sights and sounds astonishing even to Londoners themselves — streets decorated with colourful bunting and banners, bands playing patriotic tunes, parades of newly enlisted volunteers marching off to military training camps, and throngs of cheering onlookers waving Union Jacks.

Still, the Gandhis' arrival in London did not go unreported. British journalists were intrigued by this new Indian leader. Many news accounts of the Satyagraha struggle also mentioned Mrs. M. K. Gandhi as one who had endured hardship and imprisonment to win redress of Indian grievances in South Africa.

A welcoming reception held for them at the Hotel Cecil was attended by many of Mohandas' English and Indian friends, but Gokhale, who had summoned them to London, was not among them. He was stranded in Paris, having gone to France to take the waters at Vichy as treatment for his diabetes. Mohandas and Kasturba realised they would have to wait in England until Gokhale got back. To their dismay, they also learned that Herman Kallenbach would not be allowed to go on to India with them. Confirmed pacifist though he was, Kallenbach was considered suspect in Great Britain because of his German birth; he might even be interned. To avoid this fate, Kallenbach returned to Johannesburg a few months later, where he resumed his career as an architect.

Mohandas rented lodgings in an inexpensive rooming house in

Kensington. Kasturba welcomed the move. A few days in a hotel had been all that anyone could stand. Mohandas was now grappling with a familiar moral dilemma. With the British at war, where did an Indian's duty lie? He was seized by the idea of organising an Indian Ambulance Corps, just as he had done in South Africa, and for the same reasons: he believed that Indians, as subjects of the Crown enjoying the benefits of the British Empire's system of laws (even though, granted, the laws were not always administered justly), had an obligation to uphold that system against hostile attack.

Mohandas issued appeals to all Indian residents in London, and soon, dozens of his compatriots — doctors, lawyers, students, others — joined him in sending a letter to the Under Secretary of State for India, pledging loyal cooperation with the wartime British government. (One of the names signed to the letter, it should be noted, was that of Mrs. M. K Gandhi.)

In a special plea to Indian women, Mohandas asked for help in making uniforms for the corpsmen. The Lyceum Club, composed of wives, daughters, and sisters of diplomats, princes, and other high-ranking Indians in London, adopted the project and set to work cutting bolts of khaki cloth to patterns of Mohandas' own design.

Mohandas spent much of September encouraging the ambulance corps volunteers in their medical training at Regent Street Polytechnic. Meanwhile, he and Kasturba together enrolled in a hospital training course for nurse's aides. Then an attack of pleurisy brought on by a weak physical condition and soggy English weather confined Mohandas to his rooms, kept a worried Kasturba at his bedside, and dampened the enthusiasm of the ambulance corpsmen. When the young Indians were sent on to an Army hospital for their military training, they were reluctant to accept orders from anyone but Mohandas. Their feud with their officers would ultimately be defused only when the first British wounded began to arrive from France, requiring everyone's complete attention.

Kasturba tried valiantly to keep up with changes in his self-prescribed diets, and to follow instructions given by the English doctor he finally consulted — a confirmed vegetarian who, besides recommending frequent oil massages and the consumption of quantities of uncooked vegetables, advised his patient to bathe in tepid water, and to keep all windows open twenty-four hours a day. Kasturba tried leaving the French windows in their rooms open wide, but it rained in; Mohandas decided to open them only a crack and break several of the small glass panes to let in the fresh air. The experiment failed. Kasturba came down with a bad cold that left her feeling miserable while Mohandas became sicker than ever.

An Indian physician was called in, and his advice left no room for argument: if they remained in London, with winter coming on and colder weather ahead, Mohandas' pleurisy could not be cured. It was time, at last, for the Gandhis to go home.

On January 9, 1915, when the S.S. *Arabia* steamed into Bombay harbour, a huge crowd was waiting patiently in the midday sun. Mohandas, much revived by the voyage, had expected to be met by no more than a handful of well-wishers, but when he and Kasturba descended the gangplank they were amazed to discover that this multitude was waiting to greet them. The stories of their sacrifices during the struggle for Indian rights in South Africa had obviously seized the national imagination.

This spontaneous outpouring of humanity did, in fact, give a first intimation of how deeply the Gandhian principles of non-violence, voluntary poverty, and selfless community service could stir India's collective consciousness.

More surprises followed during the next few days. The British colonial government took benevolent notice of the Gandhis' homecoming. Mohandas, once snubbed even by low-ranking British administrators in India, was now courteously invited to a most cordial meeting with the Governor of Bombay, Lord Willingdon. Kasturba, graceful in her plain sari and wearing no jewellery beyond the traditional glass bangles given to her on her wedding day, was introduced as "the heroine of South Africa." Mohandas, dressed in humble Kathiawadi attire: a cloak, turban, and dhoti made of ordinary Indian mill cloth was hailed as "a hero in the cause of Indian Independence." But he protested, saying he and his wife, more at home these days among the indentured Indian labourers of Natal than the westernised elite of Bombay, felt like "complete rustics".

Next, came a blur of cross-country travel. They hurried on to Rajkot and Porbandar for a visit with their relatives, especially the bereaved families of Lakshimidas and Karsandas. It was a sad encounter especially for Kasturba to see the once vivacious and vibrant sisters-in-law now living the shadowed half-life of Indian widows.

Finally, they were able to go on to West Bengal to meet their own family — their sons, relatives, and friends from Phoenix Settlement. The Phoenix party, minus Mr. Albert West and Mr. Henry Polak who were taking care of the Phoenix Settlement, had arrived in India some weeks before Mohandas and Kasturba reached Bombay. They had found a temporary home at Shantiniketan near Calcutta, a unique school for study of the arts, which had been established by India's distinguished Nobel Prize-winning poet, Rabindranath Tagore. A kind of world in itself, with its own dairy, hospital, even post office, Shantiniketan (meaning "abode of peace") was home to one hundred and twenty-five pupils who, with their teachers, spent their days singing, dancing, acting, painting, reading literature and poetry, learning music, and seeking to make the school, in Tagore's words, "a home for the spirit of India."

Tagore was away when Kasturba and Mohandas arrived, but Charlie Andrews, a sometime teacher at Shantiniketan, was on hand to greet them and show them to the special quarters that had been assigned to the Phoenix group. While Ba was rejoicing in the reunion with her sons, and trying to answer all the women's questions about her stay in London, Bapu was consulting with Maganlal Gandhi and learning, to his gratification, that the Phoenix Settlers at Shantiniketan were still scrupulously observing their own austere rules concerning self-reliance and simple living. Overtaken by his reformist tendencies and ignoring his visitor's status, Bapu was soon making energetic efforts to extend those rules to Shantiniketan proper.

When Tagore returned he was astonished to find the school's students busily engaged in such novel and unlikely pastimes as cooking, washing dishes, scrubbing floors, doing laundry, and emptying rubbish. A tolerant man, Gurudev — as my grandfather always respectfully referred to Tagore — ignored objections from disgruntled teachers and allowed the experiment to continue. He even speculated, as a dedicated nationalist, that India's "key to self-government" might well be found in the kind of self-reliance advocated by the Mahatma — which is what Tagore always called my grandfather. But the do-it-yourself regimen, predictably perhaps, was to be short-lived. As soon as Bapu's visit ended Shantiniketan's cooks and servants would resume their regular duties permanently — except during the school's celebration of an annual "Gandhi Day" when servants were all given a holiday and students and staff did the chores.

Mohandas and Kasturba had been at Shantiniketan little more than two weeks when they received a telegram from Poona: G. K. Gokhale had died. To my grandparents, who had seen Gokhale so recently, the news came as a shock. That afternoon, accompanied by Maganlal Gandhi, they took the train to Poona.

Kasturba had first experienced third-class train travel in South Africa when, as a matter of principle, it had become a Satyagraha tradition.

Now, back home again, my grandparents were continuing the practice, but each journey was a reminder that such travel in India was not the same as in a westernised country like South Africa. My grandfather would later conclude, writing in his autobiography, that a third class train trip exposed the worst flaws of his homeland and its people — the arrogance, the cruel indifference, the random corruption of petty railway officials, and, in his words, "the rudeness, dirty habits, selfishness and ignorance of the passengers themselves." As a case in point, Bapu described their train trip to Poona to attend Gokhale's funeral. They stood endlessly in line to buy tickets, then had to join the crush of frantic, shoving passengers in a futile effort to board one of the packed, filthy, third-class cars. Finally, just as the train was leaving the platform, they managed to push their way into a compartment, but an insulting guard threatened to throw them off the train unless they paid him an excess fare which, to reach Poona in time for the funeral, they paid.

All this while, my grandmother was at her husband's side. Even today, I find it hard to picture the gentle, fastidious Ba that I knew, facing the rude indignities and physical discomforts of third class train travel in the India of her day. Apparently Bapu was troubled, too, and her fortitude weighed on his conscience. But it also won his heartfelt admiration. His account of one incident on their journey to Poona ends with a confession of his own unrepentant untruthfulness that, to me, reads like a declaration of true love — Mahatma fashion:

> ... We reached Kalyan dead tired. Maganlal and I got some water from the station water pipe and had our bath. As I was proceeding to arrange for my wife's bath, Shrijut Kaul [one of Gokhale's co-workers, also on his way to the funeral] recognising us, came up, and offered to take my wife to the second-class bathroom ... I knew my wife had no right to avail herself of the second-class bathroom, but I ultimately connived at the impropriety.
>
> This, I know, does not become a votary of truth. Not that my wife was eager to use the bathroom, but a husband's partiality for his wife got the better of his partiality for truth.

Mohandas Gandhi, in 1915, had lived less than half of his forty-six years in India. He had counted on his "sure pilot" Gokhale to see him safely launched on a career of public service in his unfamiliar homeland, but with Gokhale gone, he felt lost. His only guideline was a promise he had made to this trusted friend and mentor during their last brief visit.

Although certain that Mohandas was destined for national leadership, Gokhale had not been sure that all of his protégé's ideas were suitable for India, or that India was ready for all of his ideas. He had asked Mohandas not to participate in Indian politics for at least a year.

"Go around the country, see, observe, listen," Gokhale had said. "Our views will correct themselves, and then you can get involved."

For Mohandas, that pledge to observe a "year of silence" had now become a sacred vow. The promise to get reacquainted with India coincided, fortuitously, with his need to find a suitable location for his own ashram. Leaving his little band of followers in residence at Shantiniketan, Mohandas roamed the country.

Mohandas, much to Kasturba's satisfaction, sometimes asked Ramdas or Manilal to join him in his travels. And when Harilal, who had quit school and was visiting them at Shantiniketan, went along on one short trip, she was delighted. But Ba's hope that this brief encounter would mark an end to the grievous breach between father and son was soon dashed. Harilal announced late in March that he intended to go his own way permanently.

Whenever she could, Kasturba herself accompanied her husband on his journeys. She did not enjoy travelling, but she very much wanted to help choose their permanent home. The more they saw of India, the more convinced she became that they should settle in their native state of Gujarat. After so many years of living as a stranger abroad, she wanted to feel at home in India, to live among people who spoke her own language. Mohandas, too, had a strong attachment to his home territory. He particularly favoured the Gujarat capital of Ahmadabad for two reasons.

First, Ahmadabad, a beautiful old city famous for its mosques and medieval ruins, had been a centre of handloom weaving in ancient times, and Mohandas already had dreams of reviving spinning and weaving as a cottage industry in India to help millions of his countrymen escape poverty. Second, in modern times Ahmadabad had become the hub of India's thriving textile industry, and he felt sure some of the city's rich textile magnates could be persuaded to give financial backing to the ashram.

A chance meeting settled the issue. Kasturba and Mohandas were in Ahmadabad, telling several of Mohandas' long-time friends of their wish to settle there. A local attorney interrupted to say he owned a house in the village of Kochrab, a few miles outside the city.

"You can start your ashram there if you like," he said.

Next day, after visiting the property, my grandparents accepted the offer. The bungalow, comfortable but modest, had not been built for community living, and was not large enough to house the entire Phoenix group. But there was room on the grounds for additional buildings. Kochrab seemed as good a place to start as any.

Mohandas met with a group of wealthy Ahmadabad citizens to explain his plans. As he had hoped, they seemed eager to support the project, but he wanted to make sure there was no misunderstanding.

"My ashram will be open to families of all religions and all castes," he told them. Then, to make his position even clearer, he added, "I will admit Untouchables if they wish to join."

The prospective backers laughed. They foresaw no problem. "You will first have to find a family who will be willing to stay with you," they said. They were confident that Untouchables, aware that the wrath of society could destroy any who attempted such a breakdown of ancient social barriers, would never join the ashram.

On May 25, 1915, members of India's first permanent Gandhian settlement arrived at Kochrab — 25 men and women (including several who had joined the group only recently in India), plus a number of children. Kasturba, full of hope, felt it was a time of renewal. They were in their own home once more; they could again live a quiet, harmonious life together as one family.

Life at Kochrab ashram was also demanding, and even more austere than at Phoenix or Tolstoy Farm in South Africa. My grandfather had devised his most stringent code of behaviour yet, nine rules of conduct which residents solemnly swore to observe. Most of the vows were familiar ones — to be ever truthful, to be nonviolent, to live celibate lives, to control the palate, to refrain from stealing, to possess nothing. Someone had suggested a vow to be ever humble, but Bapu rejected the idea; he feared humility would cease to be humility once it became the subject of a vow. He did, however, include three vows designed to address some of India's more intractable problems. Residents swore to wear no foreign cloth (Indians must support Indian-owned enterprises), to fear nothing (Indians needed great courage to oppose nonviolently the injustices of colonial rule), and, most crucial of all, to accept Untouchables.

For several months, all went smoothly. Then, in September, an unexpected letter arrived, and Bapu showed it to all the adults at Kochrab. The news came as a shock. One of Gokhale's colleagues in Bombay had found an honest and respectable Untouchable family that was willing to join the ashram — the husband, a schoolteacher, his wife, and their small daughter. Suddenly, the community was facing its first real test. Would they agree to welcome the family? All the residents had signed a vow to accept Untouchables; now, however, they were faced with the reality. Like the ashram's financial backers, they had assumed no Untouchables would ever wish to join. Yet knowing this was what Bapu had always wanted, those with personal reservations did not have the heart to object — not at this point.

On the day the Untouchable family arrived, things got off to a confused start. They were directed to Bapu's room, where they found a small man wearing a loincloth and nothing else, sitting in a corner writing. The husband Dudhabhai, a man of some education, decided this must be the great Gandhi's secretary.

"Where can we meet Gandhiji?" he asked.

"Right here, of course," Bapu answered with a smile. "And you are Dudhabhai and Daniben from Bombay?" He urged the embarrassed man and his wife to sit down; he admired their little daughter Lakshimi, patting her on the head, and calling her "a mere, toddling babe". After several more questions to put them at ease, Bapu asked the couple to vow to abide by the rules of the ashram, and then announced, "Today, you will dine with us as our guests."

Dudhabhai and Daniben were reluctant, still unsure how others would react to Untouchables sitting among them for dinner. But Bapu insisted. Soon, the unsuspecting newcomers found themselves being served a typical ashram meal. That day's menu featured boiled bittergourd, which had been cooked, as was customary, without salt, spices, or seasoning. They put up a brave front and gulped it down.

Afterwards, Dudhabhai asked Bapu where he could go to wash their plates. Bapu called his son "Rama", short for Ramdas, and asked him to wash the guests' dishes. Dudhabhai protested. In his home city of Bombay, "Rama" was a colloquial term used for a domestic servant, but he felt even a servant might object to washing the utensils of an Untouchable. Bapu again was insistent, so Dudhabhai did not argue.

Outside the ashram the reactions of the orthodox community to the arrival of Untouchables were not so benign. First came a threat to their water supply — not surprising in a country where every community had to have separate wells for Muslims and Hindus, and Hindus of every caste believed they would be contaminated if so much as one drop of water from an Untouchable's bucket spilled on them. Although the Kochrab community well was on property owned by their landlord, the well keeper cursed and abused the ashram residents. But they neither retreated nor retaliated, and the harassment eventually stopped.

More ominous threats were brewing in Ahmadabad, threats to the ashram's very existence. Wealthy backers, one by one, began withdrawing their financial support. A day came when Maganlal Gandhi, as bookkeeper, had to announce the bad news.

"We are out of funds," he reported. "Nothing is left for next month." That was not all. Maganlal had heard that the ashram, as a "settlement of Untouchables", was about to be subjected to a social boycott, meaning their neighbours planned to deny them access to all community services, as a way of forcing them to leave the region.

Mohandas seemed strangely unperturbed. Faced with adversity, his faith in providence always grew stronger. It was his serene belief that if he was doing God's work, God would show him the way.

"In that case," he said quietly, "we shall move to Ahmadabad's Untouchable quarter, and live on what we can earn by manual labour."

But it did not come to that. A day or so later, one of the children came running to tell Bapu that someone waiting outside in a car had asked to see him. When Mohandas went out to the car he was greeted by a handsome young man he did not recognise. The visitor, announcing that he wished to help the ashram pressed an envelope into Bapu's hands and drove away without another word. Inside the envelope, Bapu found 25,000 rupees in bank notes — more than enough to keep the ashram safe for at least another year.

My grandfather would soon discover that the generous and mysterious stranger was Ambalal Sarabhai, owner of one of the biggest textile mills in Ahmadabad. For the moment, he knew only that this anonymous donor had brought the divine guidance he sought, the miracle he had so confidently expected. "On all such occasions," he later wrote, "God has sent help at the last moment."

But the crisis had not yet run its course. Inside the Kochrab ashram all was not well. For many days, Mohandas had been too busy dealing with the group's financial woes to see a subtle kind of discrimination being practiced by some of the women residents. Now, for the first time, he began to observe how Daniben was never permitted to help with the cooking, how Dudhabhai was always stopped outside the kitchen door when he asked for a drink of water. One day little Lakshimi happened to stray into the kitchen, and Mohandas noticed that any utensils the child touched were immediately washed, and the entire kitchen was scrubbed. He was also dismayed to observe that among those most scrupulous in their avoidance of any personal contact with the Untouchables were Maganlal's wife Santokben — and, shockingly, his own wife Kasturba.

My grandfather had anticipated adverse reactions from outsiders, but he had never expected this kind of prejudiced behaviour among those he loved and trusted the most. A confrontation was unavoidable. That evening, at the regular prayer meeting, he delivered his ultimatum: ashram rules required acceptance of Untouchables. All those unable to accept the family of Untouchables could pack up and leave. No one, least of all Ba, had any doubt that Bapu meant what he said.

There was much soul-searching that night. Several residents, men and women, went to Bapu's room to say they had not meant to cause trouble, but they had never realised how deeply the concept of Untouchability had been planted in their minds. All their lives they had thought of an Untouchable as a person who carried buckets of nightsoil to be emptied and replaced, and had felt they could never be sure that a person doing such extremely dirty work had subsequently bathed and put on clean clothes. Most swore to change their way of thinking, and some even went to Dudhabhai and Daniben to apologise for any hurt they may have caused them. But a few confessed that they still found it impossible to ignore the injunctions imposed by their religion over a period of several thousand years. Even Maganlal, whom Bapu considered his most devoted disciple, acknowledged that he, like his wife, still felt an unreasoning fear of "pollution" from contact with Untouchables. Maganlal said he and Santokben had decided they should leave; they would go to Madras and spend a few months trying to learn weaving — and to unlearn their prejudices.

Kasturba's dilemma was not so easily resolved. Mohandas, she realised, had taken it for granted that her years of living abroad had broadened her vision. He believed she had long since been cleansed of her bias against Untouchables, and he had therefore found her actions the most hurtful of all.

In South Africa, where the Indian community had been united in a single purpose (thanks mostly to Mohandas, she had to admit), it had been easy for her, as a good wife supporting her husband, to forget all differences of religion, region, and caste. But back among her own people in India, it was almost impossible not to slip into the old ways of living — of knowing. She had grown up "knowing" that Untouchables. lived their present lives in the most loathsome circumstances as a just punishment for unpardonable sins committed in some previous existence. Her religion had taught her that Untouchables therefore deserved to be outcasts, given the foulest jobs, and shunned as unclean. That was their karma, and their only hope for a better future life was meekly to accept their fate. To believe otherwise was heresy. As a good Hindu wife back home again in India, Kasturba worried that her husband's future would be jeopardised, and all his reforms would be rejected if it became known that he brought Untouchables into his own home to live as members of his family.

Yet, Kasturba knew how determined Mohandas had been to establish his complete rejection of the ancient ban on Untouchables, which he considered a perversion of the *Gita*'s true teachings.

He had even stopped referring to India's outcasts as Untouchables, calling them harijans or Children of God, instead. That word harijan was now echoing in some inner recess of her soul. She knew that it was wrong to treat any of God's children with hate and contempt. Could she truly think of Untouchables — even such relatively acceptable Untouchables as Dudhabhai and Daniben — as children of God? Mohandas demanded nothing less.

For several days Kasturba went about her work silently, avoiding all contact with her husband. She could not let him decide the outcome for her. She must look to God for her own answers.

One morning, watching little Lakshimi at play, Kasturba realised she had never really noticed what an exceptionally appealing child she was, and what a sunny disposition she had. Kasturba found herself remembering the children she had known at Tolstoy Farm, the ones she had loved and cared for while their parents were serving prison terms as Satyagrahis. She had been like a mother to them, and they had called her Ba; those children had taught her to think of herself as Ba, a woman who cherished children. But she had never thought of them as Untouchables, even though many of them were.

And she suddenly understood if those Tolstoy Farm children were Children of God, then Dudhabhai and Daniben had always been children of God. Little Lakshimi was surely a Child of God, and, more than that, a messenger of divine truth. Mohandas was right. All of us must love each other, for all of us are God's children.

Ba gathered little Lakshimi into her arms and hugged her more tightly than she had ever hugged her own little granddaughter Rami.

# 20

Grandfather's self-imposed year of political silence was drawing to a close, but he still had no clear notion of what kind of role, if any, he could play in Indian public life. In the months since Gokhale's death, the country's fast-changing political scene had been in flux. But so had Mohandas' own thinking.

Most of his adult life had been spent in a distant land where Indians were an alien and oppressed minority with many grievances in common, where choices between good and evil seemed simple, and appeals for unity and self-sacrifice proved effective. Now he had to attune himself once more to the complex nuances of life in his own homeland — this sprawling subcontinent where the huge and heterogeneous Indian population was an oppressed majority, ruled nominally by their own privileged overlords, yet governed in fact by a tiny cadre of foreign officials. It was an India — fragmented politically, exploited economically, divided religiously — that spoke in many contradictory voices; a society with an ancient and densely layered spiritual heritage, where consensus, even on the nature of reality, was elusive.

Thus, when Mohandas travelled to Bombay in December 1915, to be an observer at the annual meeting of the Indian National Congress, he went as a pilgrim seeking new pathways to progress in an old familiar landscape. What he found, to his surprise, was an ad hoc united front in the making. Nationalist leaders, Muslim as well as Hindu were all in Bombay debating ways to make the most of England's preoccupation with the European war.

Kasturba sometimes felt that her husband's "year of silence" was being succeeded by a "year of speeches". Immediately following the outspoken speech at the Benares Hindu University it was commonly believed that Mohandas Gandhi, having insulted the Indian princes, offended the British officials, and disturbed the Congress elite, was politically finished. But when reports of the address appeared in newspapers, invitations to speak poured in from all over the country. Mohandas had obviously struck a resonant chord, especially among younger Indians. Scarcely a month passed now that he did not leave the Kochrab ashram and travel to distant towns to address college or high school audiences, or speak at some local branch of the international Young Men's Christian Association.

Whenever she could put aside her duties at the ashram for a few days, Ba liked to go along. Such trips gave her a rare chance to be alone with Bapu and discuss family or ashram matters — the news from Calcutta that Harilal and Gulab were expecting another child, their fifth; the return of Maganlal and Santokben from Madras, ready to renew the ashram vows; the departure of Dudhabhai and his family for Bombay, so he could resume his teaching duties. Saying goodbye to little Lakshimi had been painful for Ba; she hadn't realised how dear to her that small Untouchable girl had become. But the child's parents had assured her they would all come back on holidays, and promised that as soon as their daughter was a bit older, she could stay at the ashram for a long visit.

In those days my grandparents were still able to travel on trains and move about the country anonymously; even on arrival at their destination they sometimes were not recognised by welcoming committees. On one memorable occasion, a group of students meeting them at the railway station in Madras searched through all the first and second-class cars before finding them at last in a third-class car at the end of the train, looking tired and dusty after four days' travel. This novel example of renunciation in action won instant acclaim from the student idealists. Amid cries of "Long live Mr. and Mrs. Gandhi!" a surprised Kasturba found herself being led with her husband to a waiting carriage. The students unyoked the horses and my grandparents were pulled through the streets in triumph by the admiring students.

The talks Mohandas gave were no longer provocative. Instead, he spoke about the virtues of simple life, or advocated a revival of Indian values and culture, or delivered unexceptionable homilies about character building. Yet the radiance of his vision, the purity of his desire to identify himself with "the least, the lowliest, the lost", shone through; he attracted adherents wherever he went. It was during this year of 1916 that several young men who would play crucial roles in his and India's future were first drawn into my grandfather's orbit. Speeches alone, Grandfather said, could not make Indians fit for self-government — nor, for that matter, help them win it. Certain that his active brand of non-violence, already tested in South Africa, offered an ideal alternative to bomb-throwing and speech-making, Mohandas was casting about for some way to bring the power of Satyagraha to bear in his country's quest for self-rule. He was looking for some place where reforms could be won by 'Truth Force'. He would find it in the remote foothills of northern Bihar province.

For many weeks, an irksome, insistent peasant, named Rajkumar Shukla had been shadowing Mohandas, showing up wherever he went, complaining about the plight of tenant farmers in his home district of Champaran, a land where indigo, a plant from which natural blue dye is made, was the principal crop. Shukla, himself an indigo farmer, was certain Gandhi could help them — he had heard people say that Gandhi was some sort of a Mahatma. But Mohandas, who had never heard of Champaran and knew nothing about indigo cultivation, found Shukla's stories confusing, his persistence annoying, and suspected his motives might be self-serving.

"I cannot give you my opinion, without seeing the situation with my own eyes," he said, hoping to end the matter. Shukla said, in that case, Mohandas must come to Bihar at once and see Champaran for himself. It was a summons that was repeated each time they met.

Kasturba first learned of Shukla's dogged persistence when he showed up at the Kochrab ashram one early spring day in 1917, asking her husband to fix a date, any date, for the visit to Champaran. This time Mohandas relented, probably out of sheer exasperation. He and Ba had been planning for some time to travel to Calcutta that April, he to attend a conference, and she to be with their pregnant daughter-in-law, Gulab when their new grandchild was born. He told Shukla that perhaps when the conference was over he might be able to take the train on up to Bihar for a few days.

When Ba and Bapu arrived in Calcutta early in April, Rajkumar Shukla was waiting at the station. Ba recognised him, but took little notice — she was impatient to see Harilal and his family. A few days later, on April 7, Mohandas announced he was leaving with Shukla to go to Champaran, but Ba's attention was elsewhere. Their new grandchild was due any minute. Then, in the days after the baby did arrive — a girl who was given the name Manu — Ba was totally absorbed in caring for Gulab and the newborn infant, cooking and taking care of the other children. And all this time (she could not deny it) she was also worrying about her troubled oldest son. Kasturba knew Harilal was still deeply in love with Gulab; she knew he was as devoted to his family as ever. But she sensed that he felt overwhelmed by the financial burden of providing for them.

Thus preoccupied, Ba was not aware that Bapu, still in Champaran, was now involved in his first full-scale campaign on Indian soil. Nor did she have any intimation that she herself would soon be summoned to Champaran.

My grandfather may have been a leader in search of a cause in that spring of 1917, but the cause of the tenant farmers in Champaran, even more so, was in need of a leader. Arriving on the scene with his volunteer guide Rajkumar Shukla, Mohandas quickly revised his sceptical opinion of "this ignorant, unsophisticated, but resolute agriculturist", who, in his words, had "captured" him. He learned that the farmers' woes were far more deep-rooted and widespread than even the persevering Shukla had pictured them.

For more than half a century, most of the arable land in this remote, inhospitable region had been owned by English planters who imposed, at their pleasure, an almost feudal regime. Champaran's peasants, often entire families, worked in the planters' indigo fields for infinitesimal wages. They raised their own subsistence crops on small plots rented from the landowners under a legally established procedure (similar to the sharecropping system once common in the southern United States) which required the farmers to plant fifteen per cent of their holdings in indigo and turn over the harvest to the plantation owners. Revenues collected by this capricious (and illegal) form of private taxation were used by landlords to cover expenses for a hunting party, pay for a trip to England, or buy a new elephant.

From the beginning, this system of land tenure had proved enormously profitable for the English landowners and immensely oppressive to Bihari farmers. What was probably India's first massive non-violent demonstration against British abuse of power had taken place back in the 1860s when a new colonial governor made a river boat tour of the Champaran region. Tens of thousands of peasants, men, women, and children, left work in the indigo fields and lined up for miles along the river bank, standing in silent protest as the British official's boat went by. Impressed and sympathetic, the governor recommended reforms; he was soon recalled to England.

Conditions, bad to begin with, had only grown worse following the development of cheap synthetic dyes by German chemists in the early

1900s. The world market for indigo collapsed. Unaware of this, Champaran's hard-pressed tenant farmers had accepted in good faith their landlords' seemingly generous offers to relinquish claims on their indigo harvest in exchange for increased rents. Only when the farmers tried to sell their worthless indigo crop did they learn they had been duped. A few of the bolder or more prosperous — Rajkumar Shukla among them — had tried to win refunds and cancellation of the rent increases by legal action. But their lawyers charged huge fees, their cases dragged on and on, and their cause got nowhere. The final blow came with the outbreak of World War I, when synthetic dyes from Germany became unavailable. Indigo prices again soared. Whereupon, Champaran's landlords not only reinstated the old sharecropping system, but also further increased rents. Farmers who refused to sign the new contracts were beaten up or arrested on false charges; their houses were looted, their crops confiscated.

That was where matters stood when Gandhi the observer arrived. Less than a week later, Gandhi the organiser was hard at work. A campaign on behalf of the farmers was taking shape in a pattern familiar to any who knew of Bapu's work in South Africa.

First, came the collection of facts — verified accounts of the farmers' grievances — to document demands for reform in a report to be submitted to the provincial governor. Calling together the lawyers who had been representing the tenants, he told them the time for court cases was over, and asked for their help in taking depositions, thousands of them. He also persuaded the lawyers (much to their own surprise) that this was public work which must be done for no fee, and warned them they must be prepared to go to jail if arrested for their efforts. Startled at first by the audacity of his suggestions, then intrigued by the novelty of the strategy, half a dozen lawyers not only pledged their support but also enlisted others to help in the campaign.

The next step was public announcements. Mohandas notified the newspapers of his concern about the problems of Champaran's tenant farmers; he also tried to inform the landowners and the district authorities. At the offices of the British Planters Association he was turned away by a secretary; the local British commissioner told him it was none of his business. Instead, he set off on a tour of Champaran, travelling by train, by elephant, or most often on foot, to conduct a personal investigation of conditions in the countryside. Though few people in the remote villages of northern Bihar had ever before heard of Gandhi, crowds of poor farmers gathered round him at every stop. The word had gone out: a Mahatma had come to help them, to save them from the landlords. Planters were outraged, the district commissioner was irate.

Mohandas didn't get far. He was arrested on April 16 — hauled down from the elephant he was riding; taken before a magistrate in Motihari, one of the district's principal towns, and charged with endangering the public peace. When ordered to leave "by the first available train", he courteously explained that "out of a sense of public responsibility" he could not do so. Trial was set for next day. Anticipating imprisonment, Bapu spent the night writing instructions to Maganlal at the ashram and a letter to the viceroy in Bombay.

Next morning the sun rose on an amazing sight. Overnight, news of the arrest of "their Mahatma" had spread, and streets around the Motihari courthouse were filled with hundreds upon hundreds of poor farmers, come to cheer their champion. The magistrate, needing time to ponder his next move (and to get in touch with higher authorities) set bail. Mohandas refused to pay, saying he preferred to go to jail. But it never came to that. The flustered magistrate released him on his own recognisance. A few days later all charges against Mohandas were dropped. The Lieutenant Governor of Bihar had sent word (presumably after consultation with the viceroy), that the district officials should cooperate with Mr. Gandhi in his inquiries. Thus, the preparation of a report to the governor on agricultural conditions in Champaran district became official. The farmers were jubilant, the lawyers were amazed, and Mohandas was calm. "What I did was simple," he later wrote. "I declared that the British could not order me around in my own country."

Mohandas rented a house in Motihari, and work on the report began in earnest; the lawyers gathered there each day to take statements from an endless stream of men — farmers coming in to town, often walking great distances, to tell their stories. But Bapu, with his tour of the villages still fresh in his mind, kept remembering the faces of all the other people he had seen — women and children living in appalling poverty, ignorance, and filth; old people dying from needless sickness and hunger; toddlers no older than three or four roaming about unattended, or toiling long hours in the fields beside their exhausted parents. How much could one lone report do to improve the lives of all these people? Mohandas was learning that, in India, battles would have to be fought on numerous fronts.

Poor people, he knew were impoverished in many ways; they had many needs. Above all else, the poor people of Champaran needed education. Not just reading, writing, and arithmetic, but practical education, too — instruction in proper health and sanitation practices, information about infant and childcare, training in self-reliance. In Champaran — in all of India, for that matter — the people most clearly in need of such knowledge, the ones who could benefit from it most, were poor women in remote villages. He was certain that the best way, perhaps the only way, to reach these women would be through other women. Who, then, was better fitted by temperament, talent, and experience to do that than his own wife?

Kasturba had no sooner returned from Calcutta than a letter from Bapu arrived at the ashram, describing his work in Champaran. He said he was recruiting volunteer teachers from far and near for a campaign of village education, and asked everyone who could be spared from work at the ashram to join him. What he wanted most of all, he wrote, was for Ba to come work with the farmers' wives and daughters. Devadas, he added, almost as an afterthought, should come, too; at seventeen, Devadas could help teach the children.

It was a call to action that Bapu's devoted wife, his proud youngest son, and his dedicated friends across India, could not refuse.

Throughout the long summer months, while Mohandas and the lawyers were busy with Champaran's legal and political issues, Kasturba, Devadas, and other volunteers took up the district's social and health problems. Several seasoned Phoenix Settlement veterans whose presence was a special comfort to Kasturba joined the effort; these included Chaganlal Gandhi's oldest son, Prabhudas, and even Henry Polak who spent several weeks in Champaran. On a visit from South Africa to report on the status of reforms there, Polak could not miss the chance to take part in Mohandas' first campaign in India.

Initially there were language difficulties, but they were soon overcome. A small clinic was opened in the district by a doctor from Poona who volunteered his services for six months. A number of simple thatched-roof schools were constructed by the villagers themselves, working with the volunteers. Children began attending classes taught by volunteer teachers, including Devadas and Prabhudas. Grown men who had always appended their thumb impressions on documents took pride in learning to sign their names.

Kasturba worked on a district-wide sanitation campaign — a massive job requiring massive re-education. For years, the men, women, and children, ignorant of the consequences, had been spitting, urinating, and even defecating, wherever it was convenient, and they had never known anything resembling regular rubbish collection. Moving about the district with a team of helpers, spending enough time in each village to reach and teach the people, Ba found this was something she knew how to do — easily, naturally and well.

She would usually begin by organising groups of women and children to clean the whole village. They were taught first how to make brooms; each woman was then given a broom and swept her own home; then the women and children all joined in sweeping the village's courtyards and lanes. Meanwhile, the men were learning how to clean wells and build drainage systems. Women and men, in separate classes, were learning about personal hygiene.

As the campaign progressed, opposition from landlords grew vengeful. Local newspapers printed bitter editorials about trouble stirred up by outsiders; peasants giving statements to the lawyers were threatened and harassed. Mohandas found detectives monitoring his every move, but his friendliness soon won them over to his (and the peasants') cause. The grass and bamboo schoolhouse in one of the villages where Kasturba was staying was burned down by arsonists, but local farmers, working with a few volunteers, soon replaced it with a durable brick school building. And so the work went on.

One day Mohandas came out from town to attend a village meeting. Asked to speak, he held forth at great length on the need for everyone to bathe and change clothes daily. He had told Kasturba he wanted to talk about this because he had noticed that the people always wore filthy clothes, and that the village, like many others, had no provisions for baths. The villagers listened patiently. They held him in such awe that no one dared speak up, but his criticisms rankled. Afterwards, some of the women cornered Kasturba, alone.

"Mahatmaji spoke to us about having a bath every day, and washing our clothes," they said. "But tell us how can we do that? These clothes we are wearing are all the clothes we have." To prove the point, one of the women insisted that Ba come into her hut and see for herself how bare of all personal belongings it was.

Ba was shocked. She had been working in villages like this for weeks but neither she nor the other volunteers had realised how desperately poor these people really were. Having no immediate answer for the women, she asked them to give her some time to think.

"We will find a way," she assured them.

That evening when she described the encounter to Bapu, he was equally surprised and dismayed. They discussed the women's plight, but agreed that getting donations of clothing for them would solve only the immediate problem. Exploitation of farm families by landlords was the root problem, Bapu said, and must be attacked with renewed vigour. He vowed he would not leave Champaran until basic reforms were won.

It was a vow he would keep. Before the year was out, as a direct result of his report on agricultural abuses, which went to the governor accompanied by some twenty thousand sworn depositions, an agrarian reform law was passed in Bihar province. It abolished the sharecropping system, prohibited further rent increases by the planters, refunded a portion of the increases the farmers had been forced to pay, and ultimately led to the departure from Bihar of most of the English planters. But all that would come later.

Early the next day, Bapu returned to Motihari, taking a number of men from the village with him to give affidavits to the lawyers. But Ba had to answer to the women who were waiting for her reply.

She was ready with a plan. Around noontime, she collected the women and the young children and led them to the river to bathe — all together. It was a hot, sultry day; most of the men who hadn't gone to town were working in distant fields. Ba was thankful for this, knowing how modest the women were.

She had decided to make a game of it. First, she asked the mothers to undress their children. Then she divided the women into two groups, and asked the first group to gather up the children's clothes, take them downstream, and launder them. Meanwhile, she and the other women took the children by the hand and waded into the shallow water, where each child, splashing and laughing, was given a bath. In the warm mid-day sun, the clothes were dried very soon. The children were dressed, groomed, and urged to go play in the village.

"And see that you don't dirty yourselves again," Ba called after them as they ran off. Then she turned back to the women. "It's our turn, now," she said with a smile.

Again, they were divided into two teams. Following Kasturba's lead, the first group of women entered the water and waded out to where it was neck-deep. There they took off their clothes and washed them, bathing themselves in the process. Then they made their way quickly back to the river bank where the other group of women linked arms to form a screen around the bathers while they dried themselves and got dressed. Then the groups changed roles.

"You see what a little cooperation can do?" Kasturba said, as they started walking back to the village. The women, all clean and tidy, with skin glowing and hair glistening in the sun, were laughing and chattering. They were happier than Ba had ever seen them.

She realised then that she was happy, too — and more hopeful than she had been in months. Since returning from South Africa, she had travelled great distances back and forth across India, really seeing her own country for the first time, becoming aware of its vastness, learning of its manifold dilemmas. The experience had left Ba depressed. So much misery and despair, so many people living in sumptuous luxury, so many others ground down by poverty. She, like Bapu, wanted to help the people. But what could she do, what could anyone do to help? India was too large. Its problems were too great. There was no place to start solving them. Champaran had now taught her that all was not lost. Champaran had proved to her that India's problems could be solved, after all — one district, one village, one afternoon, at a time.

# 21

The monsoons had been exceptionally heavy in Gujarat that summer of 1917, bringing in their wake floods and a virulent outbreak of plague. By July, the epidemic had spread inland to Ahmadabad, and municipal health authorities were soon overwhelmed by problems of polluted water, rats, fleas, lack of proper sanitation. Plague deaths began to occur in nearby villages like Kochrab, on the city's outskirts.

When the news reached Champaran, Mohandas hurried back to the Kochrab ashram to assess the danger. He decided the settlement must be moved to a safer location at once. After a brief search, he found a suitable site on the opposite bank of the Sabarmati River, some four miles north of Ahmadabad — a treeless, roadless, 150-acre tract of land, large enough to accommodate his growing colony of followers for some time to come. This location, as Bapu wryly noted in his autobiography, particularly appealed to him because the Sabarmati Central Jail was less than a mile away, and "jail-going was understood to be the normal lot of a Satyagrahi." He also knew that jails usually had clean surroundings.

The purchase of the land was completed in a week. A tin shed to serve as a kitchen was the first building erected on the site. While permanent houses were being built, tents were pitched to shelter the ashram's forty residents. That number, in due course, would grow to some two hundred and thirty. By mid-August the move was well underway, and Mohandas delegated responsibility for the continuing development of the new Sabarmati ashram (as it would be known) to his trusted lieutenant Maganlal Gandhi. But as Bapu was preparing to return to Champaran, he had a confrontation with his son Manilal — one that neither of them had sought or expected even though it had been long in the making. It was a dispute, which would be fateful in its consequences for my father, Manilal.

A few weeks earlier, Manilal had received an urgent letter from his older brother Harilal in Calcutta, asking him for money, whatever amount he could send. Harilal had by now become an alcoholic and Grandfather had urged everyone not to give him money which he used to buy drinks. For conscientious Manilal, this posed a dilemma. He worried about the toll his brother's financial struggles were taking on Gulab and the children. If Harilal was now making such a piteous plea, he must be in truly desperate straits. Yet Manilal's brotherly concern was tempered by his awareness that money matters had become a central focus of the long-standing conflict between Harilal and his father.

In truth, this was not the first time my father had yielded to an impulse (humane, but nonetheless proscribed by Bapu) to try to help his hard-pressed older brother. On a trip to Calcutta to visit Harilal and Gulab soon after they settled there, he had noticed how poorly furnished their home was, and had quietly gone out and bought pots and pans for Gulab to cook with. Conscientious as always, and mindful of Bapu's standing injunctions (not just against giving any money to Harilal, but also against the private use of any donations collected for public service), Manilal had scrupulously paid for the purchases with his own money, a small fund of savings retained from wages he had earned in South Africa between imprisonment. Thus, his surreptitious generosity had gone undetected.

Not this time, however. When he dispatched the money order to Calcutta, it had never occurred to Manilal that the postal authorities would send him a receipt, signed by Harilal. It arrived at the ashram with the general mail, and attracted the attention of the man sorting the letters. Instead of delivering the receipt to Manilal, he showed it to Bapu at the first opportunity, taking pains to point out the obvious: "Someone has been contravening your instructions, Bapu."

Mohandas glanced at the signed receipt, thanked the man briskly, and dismissed him promptly. Then he sent for Manilal.

"What is this?" he asked, showing him the receipt. "Have you sent money to your brother?"

Manilal was startled. With guilt written all over his face, he confessed: 'Yes, Bapu, I did."

"You know I have requested, for Harilal's own good, that no one at the ashram give or lend money to him?"

"Yes, I know." Manilal was still looking at the floor.

"Don't you realise how irresponsible your brother has become?" Bapu asked wearily. "Don't you know that the ashram money you gave him will only be wasted, or spent foolishly, or gambled away?"

No, Manilal wanted to say, he did not know that. He also wanted to explain that it was not ashram money he had sent to Harilal. Yet, given his father's insistence on poverty vows for all ashram members, he realised disclosure of the existence of his own tiny store of saved wages would only complicate matters further. What Manilal did say, in a quiet murmur, was that he had been moved by his brother's letter, and that ten rupees, after all, was not much money.

"It is not the amount that is important," Bapu replied, "it is the thoughtless action. How have you helped Harilal, if the money you send him only allows him to indulge in bad habits?"

Manilal said he believed Harilal was worried about his family. He said he even thought Harilal might be hungry.

"He might be," Mohandas said. "But he can always come here and repent for what he has been doing, and he will never be hungry again."

That was true. Manilal had no further explanations to offer.

"You realise that your indiscretion cannot go unpunished," Mohandas said. Manilal nodded. He waited in suspense for his father's next pronouncement. It was not long in coming: to atone for Manilal's wrongdoing, Bapu said, he intended to fast for one week.

For the next several hours, Manilal pleaded with his father, arguing that this was no time for Bapu to fast, not with the ashram in the throes of moving, and the reform program in Champaran still in progress. He insisted that he was responsible for his own misdeeds, and he, not his father, should do penance. To his great relief, Bapu at last agreed to reconsider — at least overnight.

Next morning, Mohandas announced his decision. There would be no fast, he said; his son must make his own atonement. And with that, he handed Manilal a railway ticket to Madras.

"You are to go to Madras and live there for one year on whatever wages you can earn as a labourer," Bapu said. "You will take no money from here. And you will not disclose your identity to anyone."

My father left for Madras determined to serve his time in exile without complaint, suffering if necessary, learning if possible. For the duration of the penance father slept on the sands of the Marina Beach, ate only grains and nuts, worked at any kind of job he could find, and told no one he was the son of Mohandas Gandhi.

As Manilal Gandhi's son, I am always amazed when I contemplate my father's undeviating loyalty to his righteous but exacting father. Time and again that loyalty was tested; Manilal often questioned and sometimes took bitter issue with Bapu's arbitrary decisions, especially on family matters. But he never let any disagreement with his father become a challenge to principle or a contest of wills. In the face of countless trials, Manilal's love for his parents, his respect for their ideals, remained intact, as did his own dignity and integrity. I doubt if a truer example of the concept of steadfast filial devotion could be found.

Yet in this instance, at least, I believe the unbending father, returning to Champaran, had to face an even more difficult trial than did the compliant son, shipped off to an anonymous future in Madras: Bapu had to explain to Ba why Manilal had been sent away in disgrace, simply for trying to help Harilal.

No one knew better than Kasturba that Mohandas' pursuit of perfection could sometimes become hurtful to those whom he hoped to perfect. But my sensible grandmother also knew by long experience how difficult it was in such cases to find words that would convince her stubborn husband he was being unwise or unjust. So Ba used her own behaviour, a quiet form of persuasion by Satyagraha, to bring about a change in Bapu's attitude. Indeed, it was she who first instructed him in these techniques. "I learned the lesson of non-violence from my wife," Mohandas once confided to an English friend, John Hoyland. "Her determined resistance to my will on the one hand, and her quiet submission to the suffering my stupidity involved on the other hand, ultimately made me ashamed of myself and cured me of my stupidity."

As evidence of his desire to make amends, Mohandas sent a letter, a few weeks later, to a well-known Madras publisher, recommending his second son Manilal Gandhi for employment; Manilal was soon hired to work at the printing plant. Then, several months later, when Albert West announced he was growing restive in South Africa and wanted to return to England, Bapu immediately dispatched Manilal to Phoenix Settlement to become West's successor and assume full responsibility for the continued publication of Indian Opinion and the nonviolent struggle against discrimination.

Kasturba, still in Champaran, received news of Manilal's departure for South Africa with mixed emotions. She tried not to worry about how far away he was going, or when she might see him again. Instead, she told herself that Mohandas was expressing his renewed faith in Manilal by entrusting him with this responsibility, and she rejoiced that their dutiful son, at the age of 26, was again in his father's good graces.

Kasturba left Champaran in the spring of 1918, proud of her

accomplishments there, content that her work with the women had brought real changes. Village streets were clean, the smells of rubbish and filth were gone, flies and mosquitoes had vanished, the people were cleaner in their habits, and there was hope these changes would endure. Yet, unaccountably, when she arrived at the new ashram and saw the little community taking shape on the banks of the Sabarmati River, her sureness of purpose, her sense of confidence, faded away.

She felt like an aimless visitor in a strange city. Everything was happening at once. Fruit trees and gardens were being planted, brick walks laid out; there was a cluster of plain whitewashed buildings, most still under construction — a school, a library, a weaving shed, cottages for residents. A flight of stone steps led down to the river; nearby was a grassy field where sunrise and sunset prayer services were held. The Sabarmati ashram would one day be Ba's haven.

The women, Ba found, had become wholly absorbed in spinning. Mohandas had long hoped that his ashram could help start a renewal of India's self-sufficient village economy by reviving an age-old cottage industry, the spinning and weaving of the cloth known as khadi. But spinning by hand had virtually become a lost art, so weavers at Kochrab ashram always used machine-spun yarn bought from a local textile mill. Recently, however, the Sabarmati ashram had unearthed an antique spinning wheel or charkha. Using it as a model, the ever resourceful Maganlal Gandhi had made other charkhas, improving the design in the process. Now, all the ashram residents, beginning with Mohandas himself, spent at least one hour a day at their spinning wheels. Ba quickly concluded that her first task at hand was to learn how to spin. She did. My grandmother became one of the ashram's most skilled spinners.

Of all the changes taking place at the fast-growing settlement, the one Ba was least prepared for was the presence of so many new faces — new people drawn by her husband's mounting fame. Visitors constantly came and went at Sabarmati, many stayed on as residents, and the place seemed always filled with strangers. For Mohandas, the whole world was his family — Kasturba had come to accept that as an essential part of his dharma, his truth.

For months Kasturba had been hearing the rumours about Harilal — he had been changing jobs and professions ever more frequently; he had lost the money he had borrowed to start a business; he had written an insulting letter to one of his former employers. She worried about how Gulab and the five children were faring. She longed to see them again, but had been unable to arrange a visit.

Thus, when Gulab and the children arrived at the ashram unexpectedly in late June of 1918, Kasturba was as surprised as she was pleased. She insisted they move into her new hut. She wanted her grandchildren close by so she could get to know them all again — from her oldest granddaughter, Rami, now ten, through the three little boys, Kanti, Rasik, and Shanti, to the year-old baby girl, Manu. Ba also wanted to spend some time alone with her daughter-in-law. She was distressed by the changes she saw in Gulab. This sad, careworn 26-year-old mother bore little resemblance to the exuberant sixteen-year-old bride she had once welcomed to Phoenix.

But the bond between them was strong as ever.

Gulab was soon pouring out her heart to her mother-in-law, confirming what Kasturba had been told by others but had not allowed herself to believe. Gulab spoke of how Harilal had been growing ever more disillusioned with life and with himself — bitter because he felt his father was unfair to him, ashamed because he had no money to buy essentials for his children. Fighting back tears, she told how her husband had become friendly with undesirable people, had acquired bad habits, and had now been dismissed from his latest job. There were even some rumours (which he denied) that he had been gambling with the firm's money. Gulab was weeping openly as she finished her story: some of their friends in Calcutta, aware of the privations she and the children were suffering, had paid for their train fares so they could visit the Sabarmati ashram and then go on to Rajkot to stay with her family.

Kasturba's first reaction was great anger at Harilal. But that emotion was alien to her — and futile, too. Her anger soon turned to sorrow, then sorrow gave way to a tender concern for Gulab, the children, and yes, Harilal, too. They all needed her love and attention.

Ba spent endless hours with her grandchildren over the next few weeks. She bathed them, told them stories, taught them songs; she washed and combed her granddaughters' hair; she made sweets for her grandsons. She took the children for long walks. She had more long talks with Gulab. Seeing the return of her grandchildren's smiles, hearing the sound of their laughter, watching Gulab's spirits begin to rise, Ba gave thanks their reunion was bringing solace to those she loved. When the time came for them to leave, Gulab still looked frail, but she was her optimistic self — predicting she and the children would stay only briefly with her widowed mother in Rajkot, confident they would soon be able to rejoin Harilal in Calcutta.

Kasturba saw them off at the railway station with a cheerful goodbye. But afterwards, trying to settle back into the ashram routine, she was restless and lonely. Her daughter-in-law and grandchildren had filled a void in her life; their departure left her feeling empty. She sent word to Mohandas that she wanted to join him in his travels.

Bapu's response gave Ba much to think about. Written from Nadiad, the headquarters for his recruiting campaign in the Kheda district, it was dated July 27, 1918:

Beloved Kastur,

I know you are longing to be with me. But we must continue doing our work. It is therefore best that you remain where you are. If you consider all children in the ashram as your own you will not miss yours. As you learn to love others and serve them with the same affection, you will experience joy welling up in your heart ...

Two days later, Bapu made another feeble attempt at consoling her:

Beloved Kastur,

Your unhappiness makes me unhappy. If it were possible to take ladies along I certainly would have taken you ... Haven't we learned to find happiness in separation? We will meet again if God wills so ...

More than one Gandhi biographer has written disparagingly of Kasturba, saying she "merged her personality with her husband's" or "lost her identity in his". This may be so. But it is equally true, in my view, that Mohandas merged his personality with his wife's, and found his identity (an important aspect of it, at least) through her. And I am convinced that it was in his mind, more than in Kasturba's, that the two of them were one.

The understanding that existed between my grandparents was, for the most part, unspoken. Written impressions of their personal relationship were recorded only by Mohandas, not by Kasturba. Yet, my grandfather's own writings yield implicit evidence of his dependence on his wife and intimations of his identification with her. He repeatedly testified, for example, that his basic philosophy of non-violence was simply a reflection of the basic qualities of Kasturba's character — "an extension of the rule of Satyagraha she practiced in her own person."

And I have become intrigued by a revealing pattern in my

grandfather's correspondence — a pattern I feel sure my intuitive grandmother, so intimately familiar with his moods and foibles, would have noticed: in some of the letters Mohandas wrote to Kasturba, particularly during periods of great stress in his life, he seemed almost to be addressing himself.

To Kasturba, those two brief (some would say unfeeling) letters from Nadiad, written in quick succession by her husband in response to her request to join him, were a cry from the heart. She had too many times watched Mohandas agonising over moral dilemmas, not to recognise the signs of emotional crisis. She had too often seen him assailed by self-doubts, tortured by feelings of guilt or shame, not to know that any misery he brought to her was a mere shadow of his own misery. What perturbed Ba most about Bapu's letters was not the words he had written, but the meaning she knew was embedded in those words. If her husband began a letter to his "Beloved Kastur" with the statement "I know you are longing to see me," she immediately realised that those words also meant, "I am longing to see you." If he admonished her ("As you learn to love others and serve them ... you will experience joy welling up in your heart"), she knew he was also admonishing himself. She sensed that the plaintive question ("Haven't we learned to find happiness in separation?") was one he himself was painfully pondering. And his words of comfort ("We will meet again if God wills so ...") told Kasturba that her husband must be suffering a despair at least as great as her own in that summer of 1918. She understood that Mohandas was himself in need of comfort.

The truth had become undeniable: his recruiting campaign was a disaster. Mohandas could not ignore, nor could he any longer endure, the moral, political, even physical repercussions of that campaign.

He had been persuaded to conduct his enlistment drive at the request of the viceroy, but only after convincing himself of two things. First, that if India proved her willingness to fight for the British during the war, the British would grant Home Rule to India more quickly after the war — an argument ridiculed as self-deluding by militant nationalists such as Tilak and Annie Besant; and second, that he was advancing the cause of nonviolence and Satyagraha by asking Indians to take up arms — a position condemned as self-contradictory by all but a few of his friends and co-workers.

When Mohandas arrived at the Sabarmati ashram on a mid-August morning for one of his periodic visits, Kasturba was horrified. She had worried about him, she had known instinctively that he was depressed, but she had never expected to see this gaunt, half-starved, wraith-like figure. Just a mild case of dysentery, Bapu said; he had been fasting to cure himself. Ba had a better prescription. For his mid-day meal she prepared a bowl full of lentils and some sweetened wheat porridge, two of his favourite foods. Bapu ate with relish and asked for second helpings. Ba was much relieved. She urged him to stay on at Sabarmati a few days, so she could fatten him up. He said he was expected back at recruitment headquarters. The work must go on. Mohandas returned to Nadiad that night — only to collapse, stricken by what would be the longest and most serious illness of his life. His dysentery became acute, he was feverish. Sometimes delirious, other times unable to move and scarcely able to speak, he was convinced that he was dying.

Doctors later said Mohandas had suffered a "nervous breakdown" brought on by exhaustion, a common diagnosis in those days. But my grandfather, who generally distrusted doctors, clung to his own explanation of the onset of his illness — overeating. Recalling the incident in his autobiography more than a decade later, he recorded how his wife had served him his favourite foods during his visit to Sabarmati. He had intended to "eat just enough to please Kasturba," he wrote, but instead, "I had my fill of the meal. This was sufficient invitation to the angel of death." Bapu's summation was simple: "She tempted me, and I succumbed." He obviously believed that self-condemnation for his over-indulgence (if it was such) should be equally shared by his wife.

Kasturba was frantic as the reports came in from Nadiad. Mohandas had refused all medicines, he was taking almost no nourishment, and he was growing weaker each day. She feared there was no one in Kheda who could care for him properly; she wanted him to be brought home, but he was far too ill to travel by train. Ambalal Sarabhai and his wife solved the problem by driving to Nadiad in their touring car and bringing Mohandas to Ahmadabad to be nursed back to health in the serene privacy of their home — life at the busy ashram, all agreed, would be too strenuous for him. The Sarabhais insisted on providing Bapu with the best medical care available. Ba visited him daily, encouraging him to take food and accept treatment.

Slowly, painfully, Bapu began to improve. When he insisted on returning to Sabarmati, it seemed a hopeful sign, though his stated reason (he wanted to die in his own ashram) was a gloomy one.

The move had barely taken place when tragedy struck the Gandhi family — and an awesome catastrophe was visited upon the world.

Statistics regarding the 1918 influenza epidemic are mind numbing. It was, in truth, a pandemic, an epidemic that reached every continent on earth. No other single calamity — no famine, no war, no pestilence, no destruction — has ever killed so many human beings in so short a period as did the global outbreak of so-called "Spanish influenza" during the final months of World War I. The number of deaths worldwide is usually given as more than twenty million. That is, at best, an educated guess. Harried doctors and overwhelmed officials were not concentrating on collecting statistics in the midst of the crisis; records are therefore incomplete, inaccurate, or non-existent.

But the mortality estimates from just one country provide a measure of the enormity of the loss of life: during the ten months the epidemic raged in the United States, some 550,000 people died of influenza. This far exceeds all deaths in combat among U.S. Armed Forces personnel in World War I, World War II, and the Korean and Vietnamese conflicts — a combined total of 423,000.

Nowhere was the pandemic's death rate more staggering than in India. The British Ministry of Health, in its official report on the disaster issued in 1920, stated bluntly that the total number of influenza deaths in India in the month of October 1918 was "without parallel in the history of disease." More recently, population studies of Pakistan and India by demographer Kingsley Davis have indicated that, on the subcontinent alone, the pandemic killed as many as twenty million — a strong indication that total world mortality has been grossly underestimated. But in India, as throughout the world, the true cost in human suffering and sorrow was counted, not in mass numbers, but in single losses, death by death.

Kasturba received the fearful news the second week in October. Her little grandson, three-year-old Shanti Gandhi, the fourth child and youngest son of Harilal and Gulab, had died of the influenza that was sweeping the country. Harilal was on his way to Rajkot from Calcutta; he and Gulab wanted Ba there for the funeral, too. Ba left the next day, but before she reached Rajkot, influenza had found another victim. Her beloved daughter-in-law had come down with the illness. Weak from years of malnourishment and a decade of successive pregnancies, Gulab could not fight off the disease. On October 18, 1918, only a day or two after becoming ill, she died.

This terrible blow, coming so soon after the first, was doubly devastating for surviving family members. All in their own way — a distraught Harilal and his uncomprehending children, Gulab's bereaved mother and sisters, a grieving Kasturba — attempted at first to deny the undeniable. But it was true: Gulab and Shanti were gone. In the days that followed, they all clung together, performing the sacred rituals, observing the hallowed traditions. They were joined by friends and relatives who defied the spreading contagion to offer consolation. Those who could not attend the funerals and cremations wrote letters or wired condolences.

While Harilal was still trying to find his bearings in a world turned upside down, he was surprised to receive a letter from his sick father. It was written in the neat handwriting of Mahadev Desai, to whom it had been dictated, and Harilal shared its message with his mother. Aware of the true affection and admiration Bapu had for his daughter-in-law (he sometimes said Gulab was a better person than he was) Ba was appalled at the clumsy, desperate attempt Mohandas had made to express his sorrow and extend sympathy to his estranged son. She realised that, to Harilal, this offering of bleak advice and cruel consolation must seem almost intentionally brutal:

> The only thing that pleases me is to be ever occupied with activity of the utmost purity ... One will find true happiness in the measure that one understand this and lives accordingly. If this calamity puts you in a frame of mind in which such happiness will be yours, we may even regard it as welcome.

But the depths of Mohandas' own grief, the extent of his remorse over the chasm of human misunderstanding that had come between his oldest son and himself, became apparent to Kasturba in his next letter to Harilal. It was an implied invitation to reconciliation, and a revelation of his own yearning for that reconciliation:

> One cannot pray to God for help in a spirit of pride but only if one confesses oneself as helpless ... As I lie in bed, I am filled with shame by the unworthiness of my mind. I fall into despair because of the attention my body craves and wish that it should perish. From my condition, I can very well judge that of others. I shall give you the full benefit of my experience .. I shall be a true friend to you. What would it matter if there should be any difference of opinion between us about any scheme of yours? We shall have a quiet talk ...

Once again, Ba heard the cry for help. A choice had to be made. When the thirteen days and nights of mourning period were over, she told Harilal that she wanted to help him make the hard decisions that had to be made about the children's future and his own. She said she was ready to care for her four grandchildren and provide a home for them for as long as he wished her to do so — it was clear he could not do it alone, and the burden was too great for Gulab's widowed mother and sisters. But right now, she said, she could not stay on in Rajkot. She had to hurry back to Sabarmati. Bapu needed her, and she needed to be with him.

Kasturba's instincts had again served her well. Back at the ashram, she found Mohandas more despondent than ever. He was still bedridden, still without appetite. To add to his miseries, Ba was told, he was suffering excruciating pain from a fistula caused by his protracted bout with dysentery, and had been submitting himself to radical treatments prescribed by new doctors. One had ordered ice packs for his entire body, another had prescribed injections of arsenic and strychnine — which the patient had rejected. Mohandas would later describe these practitioners as "cranks like myself". Finding no relief, Bapu had abandoned hope. At one point, he had gathered his ashram friends around him and delivered his own self-condemnatory requiem. All his life, he said, he had taken up things, only to leave them half-done; now, he was about to pass away, but if that was the will of God it had to be. His friends seemed more than happy to relinquish care of the invalid to Kasturba.

About a week after Ba's return, Vallabhbhai Patel came to Sabarmati bringing wonderful news. Germany had surrendered, an armistice had been signed! The war in Europe was over! Closer to home, the British had announced that recruiting in India was no longer necessary. Kasturba rejoiced, hopeful that the war's end might end some of the guilt and frustration that had been plaguing Mohandas, and speed his recovery. But he greeted this news, that once would have been of utmost concern to him, with listless indifference.

Bapu's friends had hoped that Ba's tender ministrations would ease his pain, and free him from broodings about death. But Mohandas, in his extremity, had come to resent his wife's concern, even her presence. While Ba was worrying about him, Bapu was confiding his thoughts about her to Mahadev Desai, who kept careful notes on all that was said. Bapu began one particularly shocking outburst by complaining that "I simply cannot bear to look at Ba's face." He went on to compare the wordless pain he saw there to the expression often seen on the face of a "meek cow", and to proclaim that "there is selfishness in this suffering of hers." But then, bringing himself up short, he admitted that "even so, her gentleness overpowers me and I feel inclined to relax in all matters."

I do not know if Ba was ever aware of what Bapu said about her at this lowest point in his depression. But I doubt if she would have altered her ways, even if he had said it to her face to face. She was losing patience with him. To her mind, his refusal to take proper food, his reluctance to accept remedies other than ones he prescribed for himself, and his diagnosis, discounted by every doctor who had been consulted, that he was at death's door, amounted to nothing less than an assault on himself. This man who could change people's hearts with his message of non-violence, was inflicting violence on his own body and mind. He even seemed ready to die, to choose death. It had to stop. Ba had just returned from a house full of real death, uninvited death. She knew she could not choose anything less than life, if it was within her power to choose. She had to rescue her husband from himself by whatever means she could devise.

Bapu's pain worked in Ba's favour. He agreed to go with her to Bombay in mid-December, and consult an orthodox physician. Dr. Dalal was decisive. Only surgery, he told Mohandas, would bring relief from pain and full recovery from the malady causing it. He was also blunt. He could not perform surgery until his patient was in better physical condition. Mohandas must immediately begin building up his strength by taking milk at frequent intervals.

Ba was standing by Bapu's bed when the diagnosis was made. She listened quietly to her husband's protests that he could not take milk. The doctor asked why. Mohandas explained. He had taken a vow against drinking milk years ago, as a matter of principle, because of the cruel methods used by some Indian farmers to milk cattle, and nothing could induce him to break that vow. It was clear to her that Bapu, sick as he was, remained as stubborn as ever.

Ba's mind was working furiously. After a moment's pause she spoke, softly but firmly. "Surely, then, you could not have any objection to goat's milk?"

Dr. Dalal seized upon Kasturba's modest proposal. "Goat's milk would be fine," he said.

Mohandas was momentarily nonplussed. But as he began to sort out his thoughts, he found that his wife had again "overpowered" him with her gentleness; he felt "inclined to relax in all matters." A vow was a vow, but perhaps Ba was right. He had been thinking of cows when he swore never to drink milk; goats had not crossed his mind. Perhaps it was true. Perhaps he could drink goat's milk and keep his vow, too — and thus find strength to renew his Satyagraha struggles.

That afternoon, Mohandas took his first glass of goat's milk.

"The will to live proved stronger than the devotion to truth," is the way he would later describe this decision, which he always regarded as a kind of compromise with his own conscience. But from that day on, goat's milk became a mainstay of his diet.

Thanks to Kasturba, Mohandas had made peace with himself — and signed an armistice with the realities of life.

# 22

The long weeks of Mohandas' recovery from surgery took place under Kasturba's watchful eye at Mani Bhavan, a spacious residence on Bombay's tree-shaded Laburnum Road. This comfortable home, given over to them by a generous relative of Dr. P. J. Mehta who, 30 years earlier, had welcomed young law student Mohandas to London, would serve for the next decade or so as my grandfather's unofficial headquarters whenever he was in Bombay. Today, it is preserved as a Gandhi museum, open to visitors.

During those early days of 1919, Mani Bhavan was a house of healing and laughter. Bapu was so relieved to be regaining his health that he sometimes reminded Ba of the irrepressible young Mohan she had known so many years earlier. When they acquired a goat to supply his daily sixteen ounces of milk, Bapu named the animal "Mother Goat" and made her a virtual pet in the household. Though he was still physically weak, Ba had a hard time keeping him in bed; if she sternly insisted he must rest, he playfully chided her about her "snappy temper," claiming she had reverted to her old bossy self.

"Yes, if it concerns your health I will show you I mean business," Kasturba said. "I will not have you walking about."

Smiling at her fondly, Mohandas declared "You are a greater tyrant than the British."

For Kasturba, proof positive that her husband was becoming well again in both body and spirit came in late January when Harilal, who had returned to Calcutta, sent his children to Mani Bhavan to be in Ba's care. Here were four subdued and sober youngsters suffering the after

223

effects of their recent loss, as great a bereavement as children can know. Rami, the oldest, was feeling most sharply the grief of Gulab's and Shanti's deaths, and it was soon apparent she needed her grandmother's constant comfort and concern. Bapu, therefore, paid tender attention to the younger children and, much to Ba's satisfaction, revelled in it. A week or so later, Mahadev Desai, who had joined them in Bombay to help Mohandas attend to any needed correspondence, shared with Kasturba something her husband had just dictated — an uncommonly affectionate letter to his estranged son Harilal. In this lengthy report, Bapu declared that plump little Manu's "radiance is ever growing brighter", described how the two boys, Kanti and Rasik, were playing on and around his bed, and concluded with the happy observation that "the scene reminds me of your childhood." Pondering Bapu's words, Ba marvelled that, in the aftermath of sorrow, a blessed harmony was returning to her family.

Mohandas took special delight in lighthearted dialogues with bright, six-year-old Rasik, Harilal's second son. He even wrote a nonsense poem for the boy — a fanciful account of Rasik's adventures at Mani Bhavan that began with a proud recital of the family tree:

> Rasiklal Harilal Mohandas Karamchand Gandhi
> Had a goat in his keeping;
> The goat would not be milked
> And Gandhi would not stop weeping

This brief idyll of convalescence came to an abrupt end one February morning when Mohandas read a newspaper account of the Rowlatt Bill — a piece of legislation being readied for passage by the Imperial Legislative Council in Delhi. He suddenly realised how alarmingly the political situation had deteriorated during his illness.

India, in fact, had been seething with unrest ever since the armistice. The lingering horrors of the catastrophic 1918 influenza epidemic had combined with India's postwar economic turmoil — skyrocketing prices, unchecked profiteering, spreading strikes, and widespread unemployment among demobilised Indian troops home from Europe — to push the Indian people to desperation. An uneasy colonial government, fearful of terrorist plots, had established a committee of inquiry headed by Sir Sidney Rowlatt, an English jurist, to assess the danger of revolutionary uprisings. The Rowlatt Bill embodied that committee's main recommendation — that the government, despite the return of peace, should not only retain but also actually extend the severe wartime emergency powers under which militant Indian Home Rule crusaders and Muslim nationalists had been summarily interned.

To Mohandas, the proposal of such wholesale suppression of basic democratic rights was a betrayal of his hopes for Indian self-government once the war was over. More fundamentally, the bill's provisions seemed to mock his abiding faith in British justice. Once the Rowlatt Bill was enacted into law, any Indian accused of "sedition" could be secretly tried without a jury, and condemned without right of appeal; dissidents would be denied the right to speak in public; mere possession of printed material deemed "seditious" could bring imprisonment for up to two years.

Though he had not yet fully recovered, Mohandas instantly decided to fight the Rowlatt Bill. From Mani Bhavan, he sent a telegram to the viceroy denouncing the legislation as "unjust, and subversive of the principle of liberty", and symptomatic of a "deep-seated disease in the ruling class." Then, with Kasturba and the grandchildren and his full complement of attendants (including "Mother Goat") in tow, he returned to Sabarmati ashram. There, on February 24, 1919, he convened a meeting of his co-workers to plan Satyagraha protest against passage of the bill. The tested first step of any Gandhian campaign, of course, was vow-taking, and that day a score of his most faithful adherents signed pledges vowing peaceful defiance of the Rowlatt Bill if it became law. Mohandas then set out to hold similar meetings elsewhere.

It was on March 18, while Mohandas was campaigning in Madras, that the bad news came from Delhi: the Imperial Legislative Council, disregarding the unanimous objections of its Indian members, had just passed the Rowlatt Act. Further protest seemed futile. Nevertheless, Mohandas spent the rest of the day conferring with colleagues at Rajaji's home, hoping at least to devise some strategy to delay or forestall immediate enforcement of the law's harsh provisions.

They went to bed without a solution. But in the middle of the night Mohandas roused himself from a half-sleep, certain an answer had just come to him — in a dream. It was as if that "inner voice" which was ever his trusted guide to righteousness had spoken directly to him and revealed a plan of action as ambitious as it was unique.

Next morning at breakfast, he announced that he intended to ask all the people of India to participate in a peaceful protest against the Rowlatt Act — a one-day hartal, or general strike. But this hartal, he explained, must be more than a mere work stoppage. It must be a solemn day of national mourning — a day of consecration and self-purification when, in preparation for the humiliations about to be

225

imposed upon them, Indians of every faith, caste, and region would abandon all other pursuits and spend twenty-four hours fasting and praying. Mohandas had no idea whether or not the entire country would heed his call; thus far, his protest campaigns in India had all been local or regional. Yet if the hartal were observed in only a few cities like Bombay and Madras, and perhaps in a few scattered regions like Gujarat and Bihar, he felt its meaning would be clear to the British.

The idea was accepted. The word went out; plans got underway.

As it turned out, Mohandas had badly underestimated the impact his appeal would have on Indians everywhere. For that matter, he had misjudged the probable reaction of colonial officials, as well. Millions upon millions of his countrymen were galvanised by the prospect of the Mahatma's hartal, sensing that here was something new in politics — the powerless joining together to confront their oppressors without violence or recrimination, but also without compromise or capitulation.

On the date chosen for the protest, April 6, 1919, all India came to a standstill "like a body whose heart has ceased to beat", according to Gandhi biographer Ranjee Shahani. No farmers were in the fields, no bullocks were yoked to ploughs, no carts moved through the countryside. In countless towns and villages, shops closed, schools and government offices were deserted, and streets were silent as people stayed home to pray and fast. In cities, there were mass meetings and processions marked by unprecedented fraternisation between Hindus and Muslims — in some places Hindus and Muslims even drank out of the same cups to affirm their alliance.

Bombay's hartal was led by the Mahatma himself. Early in the morning a multitude of men, women, and children, clad in white as a sign of mourning, gathered on the sands of Chowpati Beach near Mani Bhavan for prayers and ceremonial bathing in the waters of the bay. The crowd then marched silently through the streets, growing larger as it went, and stopping occasionally for more prayers and speeches. A tradition-shattering event took place in one mosque where Muslims not only invited the Hindu Mahatma to come in and address them, but also listened attentively to remarks delivered by Mrs. Sarojini Naidu — a Hindu and a woman! That evening, these two old friends drove slowly through the city in an open touring car, heading a procession of Satyagrahis who did a brisk business selling proscribed literature — including copies of M. K. Gandhis' *Hind Swaraj*, reprinted especially for the occasion. Though both buyers and sellers were acting in violation of the Rowlatt Act, Bombay police judiciously avoided making arrests. The day ended peacefully.

A different hartal story was being played out elsewhere. British officials, astonished by this show of Indian unity and strength of purpose, all at once perceived a grave new threat to the Empire. In Delhi, a mammoth procession was halted by apprehensive police who fired into the crowd, killing five Hindus and four Muslims.

What was the worst expression of British brutality took place in April 1919, in Amritsar, the capital city of the northern State of Punjab. The British administration imposed martial law in Punjab to curb "Indian intransigence". Severe restrictions on civil liberties restricted people from assembling for any purpose. However, in spite of these restrictions more than 10,000 men, women and children assembled in the Jullianwala Bagh, a garden that was enclosed by an 8-foot stone wall.

General Dyer, the British military Governor of Punjab, took this as defiance of his law and wanted to "teach the Indians a lesson". He ordered his troops to block off the only exit and fire into the crowd. Within one hour 386 men, women and children lay dead and 1,605 men, women and children were seriously injured. He forbade anyone from ministering to the injured for the next 72 hours.

The Mahatma kept the initiative and demonstrated his ability first to mobilise and then to call a halt to a national movement of unprecedented grandeur. In contrast, the government, displaying nervous as well as naked force, lost face in an irretrievable way and helped to precipitate the eventual fate of colonialism in India.

Kasturba knew it had happened again: her husband had changed. Mohandas had become a man with a single mission — freedom for India. He was pushing himself as never before, travelling constantly, spending ever more time writing and editing his new journals, *Young India* and *Navajivan*, and able to devote less and less attention to the Sabarmati ashram. Clearly, someone else would have to step in and keep things running smoothly.

By the summer of 1920, Kasturba, working in cooperation with her husband's loyal lieutenant Maganlal Gandhi, was overseeing all day-to-day operations at Sabarmati, solving problems as they arose and looking after the needs of visitors. Ba even made sure all residents woke up early enough to attend morning prayers. Expert at soothing ruffled feelings and reconciling misunderstandings, she was a natural mediator of occasional (yet somehow unavoidable) "family arguments" occurring among ashram members. And all this occurred at a time when her own family obligations were more demanding than ever.

At the age of 50, Ba was mothering her four grandchildren, Harilal's daughters and sons. At about the same time, Bapu had invited his

**227**

widowed sister Raliatben (for whom he, as her only surviving brother, felt ongoing familial responsibility) to come live at Sabarmati. "You will then find not one but many brothers," he wrote, "and be a mother to many children." It may not have occurred to Bapu that, given Raliatben's intractable orthodoxy on matters of caste, her ashram residency might pose problems to challenge even Ba's superb talent for tactful diplomacy.

My grandmother, at this time, was nearing the end of a long process of personal transformation. Over the years, her attitude toward her husband's ideas and ideals had slowly progressed (in the concise summary of Gandhi biographer B. R. Nanda) through successive stages of "bewilderment, opposition, acceptance, conversion, and championship". Aware now of the growing urgency of his efforts to convince all of India that Satyagraha was the best, perhaps the only way an unarmed people could combat oppression, Ba found her commitment to my grandfather's cause increasing with each passing month. To a remarkable degree, her experience was being shared by hundreds of thousands of others during this crucial period of 1920 and 1921. For this was a time of awakening in India — a season of hope when it seemed that the country's long-deferred dreams of independence could soon become reality. And Mohandas Gandhi, whose newly stated goal for India was "Swaraj in a year" had become the very embodiment of those dreams.

Gandhi's meteoric rise to pre-eminence at this point was based in part on the eclipse of India's better-known political luminaries — the unexpected death in July, 1920 of old-time radical B. G. Tilak, the declining influence of an increasingly irresolute Annie Besant. But the main forces propelling Gandhi's surge to leadership was his own unique personality, his tireless energy, his creative pragmatism.

Mohandas was eventually forced to accept his fate, albeit ruefully. "The woes of Mahatmas," he wrote, "are known only to Mahatmas." Kasturba, on the other hand, was aghast, and sometimes indignant at what Mohandas had to endure at the hands of Mahatma worshippers.

She saw the evidence each time he returned to the ashram from one of his cross-country tours. Instead of performing the simple welcoming ritual of massaging her husband's feet with oil, Ba had to apply medicinal ointments to heal deep cuts and scratches on his feet, ankles, and shins — wounds inflicted by those who threw themselves in Bapu's path and tried to touch his feet. A true devotee, in Kasturba's view, should try to follow in Gandhi's footsteps, not kiss his feet. Yet she marvelled, as never before, at her husband's surprising stamina, and the unexpected power of his message.

Kasturba's ashram duties prevented her from travelling with Mohandas as much as she wished during this period. But she was occasionally able to join him on trips to nearby towns or villages. Like everyone else at Sabarmati, Ba spent at least an hour each day spinning or weaving, and she took her charkha with her on these trips. The interest and excitement it aroused among the village women intrigued her; as they gathered around her asking questions, their shy curiosity reminded her of the poor women she had worked with in the Champaran region. It was then that Ba became one of the first to comprehend a simple truth. If the women of India learned how to spin and weave, they could play a vital role, as quiet "revolutionaries" in their own homes, in their country's struggle for freedom. Ba had no grandiose notions of her own importance, she had always supported Bapu's work as a wifely duty. Yet, remembering what she had been able to accomplish with the women of Champaran, she knew she must support his khadi campaign for a larger purpose — as her duty to India itself.

Kasturba began seeking out ways to reach the women of India with her message. Photographs of Mrs. Gandhi at work spinning or weaving appeared in Indian newspapers with increasing frequency, and demand for the charkha being distributed by Gandhi's followers increased all over the country. When Ba travelled with her husband, she would sit by his side at meetings, silently spinning. Soon, women who had never ventured out in public began attending the Mahatma's meetings — often bringing offerings of homespun yarn for the cause. When Gandhi inaugurated a nation-wide boycott of foreign-made goods by staging a series of public bonfires of clothing made from foreign cloth, Kasturba insisted (though not without a pang) on relinquishing her favourite sari to be burned. It was reported that the Mahatma gazed sadly at his wife's beautiful silk sari — a treasured gift from their old friend Gokhale, before consigning it to the flames. From then on, khadi-clad women showed up at the protest bonfires in force, bringing their own prized items of clothing to be burned.

Some revealing glimpses of a firm-willed Kasturba, slowly emerging from the shadows of her husband's eminence during this period, have been provided by Satyagrahis who worked with her at the grassroots level. One such was a young man named Vithal Laxman Phadke, who had been a resident at the Kochrab ashram before being sent by Gandhi to live and work with Untouchables in a village near Baroda. In recollections recorded years later, Phadke recalled Ba's visits to that area, and how she would question him minutely about conditions among the

Harijans. And then go with him to the location and visit each home, offering advice and instruction to the women.

He also remembered Kasturba's participation in local strategy sessions — in particular, a meeting presided over by Mohandas one hot summer day that lasted from early morning to late afternoon. Afterwards, during the evening prayer service held on an open playground, Ba noticed how tired her husband was. She insisted he go inside and retire.

"But it's too hot inside," Gandhiji protested.

Kasturba relented. "Very well, I will have a mat spread out under the tree and you can lie down on that while you talk to your colleagues." She also asked that a thin sheet be brought to cover Mohandas. Then she sat nearby, quietly spinning, listening to the informal discussion, and occasionally expressing her own views. Everyone forgot the passage of time and darkness enveloped them.

"Don't panic and don't be afraid," Mohandas was speaking in a soft voice to two men nearest him. Without moving, he explained that he felt something crawling at his side. I want you to lift the sheet covering me from both ends," he said, "and take it beyond the fence."

The men kept calm, did as he had asked, then rejoined the group.

When they reported they had just released, on the other side of the fence, a deadly six-foot long cobra, Kasturba uttered a silent prayer of thanksgiving. Without further ado, she then ordered everyone, Bapu included, to move indoors.

At 10.30pm on Friday, March 10, 1922, a police car drove up to Gandhi's hut in the Sabarmati ashram. Ahmadabad's superintendent of police went to the door, politely informed the Mahatma he was under arrest, then waited in the car while his prisoner collected a few belongings — a spare loincloth, two blankets, seven books. Roused from sleep, Kasturba and a dozen or so other ashram residents gathered to pray and sing a hymn as her husband was driven off to the Sabarmati Central Jail, less than a mile away. Next morning, she sent him some goats milk, some grapes, and more clean clothes.

Gandhi's arrest surprised no one — not after the tumultuous events and tense confrontations of recent months.

But the British, who had once scoffed at the Mahatma's "non-cooperation" movement, were now anything but complacent. Invoking the long-dormant Rowlatt Act, they reacted with a vengeance, banning all public meetings, muzzling the press, conducting midnight raids on Congress offices, and rounding up thousands of "dissidents" all over India.

The trial that followed, held on March 18,1922 in a small, crowded courtroom in Ahmadabad, has become legend. It is generally referred to by Gandhi biographers as "The Great Trial" because of the force and eloquence of the arguments my grandfather made in court that day. Charged with sedition, he accepted full responsibility for the "diabolical crimes" committed by his followers in Bombay and Chauri Chaura. "I knew I was playing with fire," he said. But he then proceeded to deliver a carefully reasoned, deeply personal explanation of "what is raging within my breast", one of the most damning indictments ever made of colonialism in general and colonialism in India in particular. Declaring he had no choice but to oppose such an evil system, he proclaimed his ongoing faith in nonviolent non-cooperation as the only practicable remedy for his country's woes, and asked the judge to impose the maximum penalty. Justice C. N. Broomfield, a barrister with a lifetime career in the Indian Civil Service and a genuine liking for the Indian people, responded. He acknowledged that Gandhi was, in the eyes of millions of his countrymen, "a great patriot, a great leader" who was looked upon even by those who differed from him in politics as "a man of high ideals and of noble, even saintly life." He described his own task, as perhaps the "most difficult a judge in this country could have to face" — and then proceeded to sentence the prisoner to six years.

Kasturba, who had been sitting in the courtroom throughout the trial, watched spectators crowd around her husband to pay homage to a hero — some offered gifts, many knelt to touch his feet. She accompanied him as officers led him out of the courthouse, past crowds shouting "Mahatma Gandhi ki jai", to a waiting police van, and rode with him as he was returned to Sabarmati jail.

The world has long remembered the power of my grandfather's "Great Trial" statement, but few are aware of the simple dignity and strength of an appeal dictated by my grandmother at the ashram that night, and published in the next issue of *Young India*, March 23, 1922:

My Dear Countrymen and Countrywomen,

My dear husband has been sentenced today to six years simple imprisonment. While I cannot deny that this heavy sentence has to some extent told upon me, I could have consoled myself with the thought that it is not beyond our powers to reduce that sentence and release him by our own exertions long before his term of imprisonment is over. I have no doubt that, if India wakes up and seriously undertakes to carry out the constructive programme of the Congress, we shall succeed not only in releasing him, but also in solving to our satisfaction the issues for which we have been fighting and suffering ...

The remedy, therefore, lies with us. If we fail, the fault will be ours. I, therefore, appeal to all men and women who feel for me and have regard for my husband wholeheartedly to concentrate on the constructive programme and make it a success ... Our success will not only solve the economic problem of India in relation to the masses, but also free us from our political bondage. India's first answer, then, to Mr. Gandhi's conviction should be that:

(a) All men and women give up their foreign cloth and adopt khadi and persuade others to do so.

(b) All women make it a religious duty to spin and produce yarn every day and persuade others to do so.

(c) All merchants cease trading in foreign piece goods.

Kasturba Gandhi

# 23

When I first began work on the story of my grandmother's life, I shared the standard assumptions that Mohandas and his non-violent movement were neutralised by the British during the 1920s. Then, in 1988, after the death in South Africa of my widowed mother Sushila Gandhi, I came into possession of a packet of family correspondence, handwritten in Gujarati, which she and my father Manilal had received from Bapu over the decades. These letters yielded fresh insights, which have shaped my understanding of this story.

I saw how Bapu, far from being silenced, had patiently used the 1920s to spread his message of non-violence nationwide and create a stronger, bolder voice for his people. I also sensed this period had been a time of hidden tensions and painful conflict in the lives of my grandparents and their sons. There was ample evidence recorded here, of the pressures that Bapu's unyielding belief in the stern precepts of his truth exerted on the entire family. Yet, equally important to me, there were revealing indications of the way Ba's stubborn faith in the healing power of her truth helped relieve those pressures.

For Kasturba, back at the crowded ashram, there could be no exemption from the everyday demands of human existence. On her own, faced with another long separation from her husband, she carried a heavy burden of responsibility. While Bapu was enjoying a serene solitude at Yeravda Prison, Ba was presiding over the chaotic bustle of daily activities at Sabarmati. While he contemplated the destiny of their country, she worried about the fate of their family.

Ba's immediate and ongoing preoccupation was the future well-being of her four sons. One was going astray and three were to be married. In India, the parent-child relationship has never been so impersonal that grown sons or daughters can freely ignore their elders' wishes. Adult Indians seek formal blessings from their parents for all major decisions, especially their marriages. Ba worried that Bapu, preoccupied with political issues, would never devote much attention to personal family matters. She was convinced without dogged persistence on her part, there would be no betrothals.

Kasturba was worried about Manilal, my father. She longed to see him, to talk with him. By all reports, he was doing a fine job of running *Indian Opinion*, but was restless and miserable in his isolation. Manilal would soon be thirty. Still, to Ba's dismay (and exasperation), Bapu had made no plans as yet for his betrothal, let alone his marriage. She undoubtedly would have been further dismayed had she known of the letter Mohandas had sent off to Manilal from his Sabarmati Jail cell the day after his arrest, on March 11, 1922.

Bapu had begun with a brisk announcement: "Tomorrow I shall be sentenced and my desire to write will diminish." Next, he had issued a few peremptory business instructions: "You have not sent the statement of accounts from there. Do send it, if not done yet." Then he had turned his attention to Manilal's personal situation:

> Now something concerning you:
> Ramdas says that I should write to you about marriage, that deep down you are eager to get married, but feel you can do so only when I release you from your vow [of celibacy]. You have taken the vow on your own, therefore only you can release yourself.

(At the age of 18 Manilal was found embracing a woman who was a resident of Phoenix. They were about to kiss. This was considered a flagrant violation of the rules. Mohandas did penance for this by fasting for seven days and eating only one meal a day for the next four months. Manilal took a vow of celibacy for 12 years.)

> My candid opinion is that the peace you are now experiencing is because of that vow. You can be free of your past misdeeds as long as you keep away from thoughts of marriage ... I can vouch for that. I am happy Ba has accepted me as her friend. I would be committing a great sin if I exercised my sexual right on Ba as a husband now. My work would suffer. I would lose everything in a moment.

After reading all this I want you to come to your own conclusion. I have written as a friend, I am not ordering you as a father ... If you cannot live without getting married, by all means get married. Hope you will write to me about your innermost feelings.

Bapu's blessings

The thought of her lonely son Manilal reading such comfortless words of counsel would surely have grieved Kasturba. Yet I am certain she would have felt equal anguish for her husband. Realising that Bapu had penned this letter at the very hour he was facing the bleak uncertainty of his own future, Ba would have sensed what fierce internal struggles were being masked by his cool detachment.

Then, of course, there was Harilal. Despite her concerns for the welfare of her conscientious second son, Kasturba's greatest qualms, as always, were for her errant eldest son. At 34, Harilal seemed more aimless and confused than ever. True, he had voluntarily sought arrest during the recent civil disobedience campaign — though that, in Ba's private opinion, was less an act of personal conviction than a bid for his father's attention. Yet Harilal continued to scorn Bapu's standing invitation to come live at Sabarmati — mainly, Ba suspected, because he abhorred the asceticism of ashram life.

A virile and ardent man, Harilal missed the sexual intimacy he had known with Gulab. For the past several years, he had been eager to remarry. Dutifully seeking parental consent, he had first broached the subject soon after Gulab's death, during discussions about the care of his children. At that time, both his mother and father had been aghast at the idea, but for different reasons. Bapu thought it morally wrong for Harilal ever to marry again and said so. Ba, remembering the tender, romantic love her son and daughter-in-law had shared, said she could not bear to think of his taking another wife so soon. Harilal often dared to argue with his father, but he could not so easily oppose his mother. He had dropped the subject, at least for the time being.

Now, in June of 1922, soon after being released from his own six-month imprisonment, Harilal visited his father at Yeravda Jail and again brought up the matter of his remarriage. This time, after some argument, Mohandas relented — on one condition:

"If you find a widow who has as many children as you have," Bapu said, "and if you both agree to accept each others' children as your own, then I will reconsider the issue.

Marry a widow? Harilal was taken aback. Such defiance of Hindu custom had never occurred to him, nor could he bring himself to consider it now. There is no rational explanation for the remarriage of widows among Hindus except that Hindus believe a marriage is only dissolved in Heaven. The truth, however, is that Hindu men don't mind their own philandering but do not wish to marry a woman who has had sex with someone already.

Dejected, he returned to Calcutta alone. But a few months later, when Kasturba and Ramdas brought his four children to that city to visit him, Harilal once more spoke of his wish to remarry, and complained about his father's unreasonable stipulation. And once more, he was caught off guard — Ba thought Bapu's idea was laudable.

Sensing Harilal's discomfiture, Kasturba pointed out that she fully supported her husband's condemnation of the cruel hardships suffered by widows in India. She said she also appreciated how, in denouncing child marriage, Bapu always deplored the fate of tens of thousands of young girls who became child widows to be shunned for life. Besides, Ba asked, how could anyone dispute the injustice of encouraging remarriage for widowers while denying it for widows?

"So, if you should marry a widow," she told Harilal, "a widow with or without children, it would not bother me in the least."

But something else was bothering Ba. Though he was usually quite open to reasonable persuasion, she could see that Harilal still found the idea unthinkable. Why? Did he simply lack the courage to face the opprobrium his marriage to a widow would bring? No, Ba told herself, it had to be more than that. Suddenly, she understood. Harilal was appalled at the prospect of trying to support so large a family, with more children perhaps to come. What, then, should she feel for her firstborn son? Sympathy? Impatience? Or, pity?

Harilal seemed grateful when Ba changed the subject.

On January 13, 1924, a telegram, addressed to Mrs. M. K. Gandhi and signed by Colonel Maddock, the surgeon general at Sassoon Hospital in Poona, arrived at Sabarmati:

"Mr. Gandhi operated on for acute appendicitis last night, had a very fair night, condition this morning satisfactory."

Details were sketchy, but Kasturba soon learned that colonial officials, alarmed by Bapu's sudden illness, and fearing widespread unrest if the Mahatma died in prison, had ordered that he be rushed to the nearest hospital. For his part, Mohandas, aware his life was in danger, had put aside his bias against Western medicine and consented to emergency surgery — but only after signing a statement praising the hospital staff and warning against demonstrations should he die.

Ba wanted to go to her husband's bedside at once, but she could not leave her ashram duties on such short notice, so she sent her son Devadas to Poona instead. Three weeks later, Devadas was still at the hospital, helping the ever-faithful Mahadev Desai acknowledge all the letters, gifts, telegrams, flowers, even food offerings, pouring in from all over India — "torrents of love", Desai called them. But the patient's recovery progressed too slowly for the uneasy British authorities. On February 5, they made a startling announcement: Mr. Gandhi was being freed that day, immediately and unconditionally.

Ba was both relieved and overjoyed by news of his release; knowing Mohandas needed a restful place to continue recuperating, she was further relieved when he was invited to spend a few weeks on Juhu Beach near Bombay, at the secluded estate of one of his wealthy Parsi supporters. But seclusion for the Mahatma was elusive. This quiet seaside home was promptly besieged by throngs of visitors — Gandhi's friends and followers, rejoicing at his liberation.

As soon as he regained his strength, Mohandas returned to Sabarmati where he immediately involved himself in ashram affairs with an intensity (and lightheartedness) that reminded Kasturba of the early days at Phoenix Settlement or Tolstoy Farm.

Simplicity, frugality, self-reliance. These continued to be Bapu's watchwords. And those closest to him were expected always to be paragons of these virtues — as Ba was reminded one day when she discovered that a box of personal effects had been stolen from her hut, apparently by thieves from the surrounding neighbourhood. Mohandas, refusing to call the police, expressed disappointment that anyone in the vicinity would believe the ashram had any possessions worth stealing. As for Ba's missing box, he said he was surprised to learn that she even had such a thing. Ba explained that it held her grandchildren's clothes; Bapu said the grandchildren should take care of their own clothes. Residents noted that, from that day on, Kasturba's kit of belongings was the tiniest of any in the ashram.

Kasturba, of course, made no direct editorial contributions to her husband's publications — although reports of her activities often found their way into print, and sometimes into public discussion. No article ever provoked more heated debate, for example, than Bapu's account of his wife's pivotal role in resolving a crisis of conscience at Sabarmati when one of the ashram's heifers became grievously ill: Ba had flatly refused to agree to his decision to end the poor creature's life with a lethal injection until, that is, she tried to care for the calf personally, saw its suffering first hand, and gave her assent. Given the Hindu belief in cow protection as a sacred duty, the contentious reader reaction was no doubt inevitable.

Ba must, however, be credited with one indirect but invaluable contribution to Gandhian literature. For it was only because of her discerning intercession in another tense situation at the ashram that an idealistic and talented young man was able to pursue his dream of working for Gandhi's cause. That young man, Pyarelal Nayyar, went on to become one of my grandfather's trusted secretaries, and would be regarded in due course as one of his most authoritative biographers.

A Brahmin from an old Punjabi family, Pyarelal, had become intrigued by Gandhi when, as a youth, he first heard him speak in his native city of Lahore. Shortly after finishing his university studies, Pyarelal arrived at Sabarmati, eager to volunteer his services. Mohandas welcomed him (educated young men were always needed), but allowed him to stay on as a resident only after making sure he understood all the requirements of austerity and hard work.

A few weeks later, Bapu received an agitated letter from Pyarelal's widowed mother. She could not approve of her son's joining the ashram, she wrote. Now that he had completed his education, he was expected to join the Indian Civil Service, as was the family custom, and get a lucrative government job. Bapu responded at once, inviting her to come to Sabarmati so that all three concerned parties could meet and discuss the question. Mrs. Nayyar arrived on the appointed day all right, only to find that both Mohandas and her son were too busy to talk to her. She would have to wait.

Ba, with her customary gracious hospitality, took charge. After the midday meal, the two women settled down on her cool verandah for a chat. Ba spoke highly of Pyarelal, of how able and dedicated he was, how ready to take on any task. But Mrs. Nayyar, instead of beaming proudly at praise for her son, seemed angry, resentful. In a rush, she began pouring out to Mrs. Gandhi, her complaints intended for Gandhi himself. After her husband's death, this unhappy mother said, she and her young daughter had sacrificed many comforts and used most of the family's resources to give Pyarelal, her only son, a proper education. Now he had left them to join a movement which offered him no career, no future. His younger sister still had to be educated and married. How could she cope with all these problems on her own? Mr. Gandhi, she declared, asked too much of his followers, and of their families.

Kasturba, listening attentively, saw before her a stranger whom she seemed to know intimately — a woman, about her own age, whose worries and fears she understood almost instinctively. Once before, years ago in Johannesburg, on the day Mohandas sent young Manilal on that exhausting walk, five miles home and back, to retrieve his forgotten glasses, Ba had tried to explain the importance of her husband's ideals to someone who felt he demanded too much. Searching then for the best way to make her own son appreciate his father, Ba had chosen to do what she very rarely did — to speak of her experiences as Mohandas' wife.

Now, seeking a way to help Mrs. Nayyar understand her son, Ba's choice was the same. In a soft, calm voice, she began recounting some of her own early disappointments, her own struggles to accept Bapu's new way of life. She spoke of sacrifices she and her sons had made (and not always willingly) to support his work, to follow his dream. But mostly, Ba talked of how the world was changing, why people had to change with it, and how Pyarelal, like so many others inspired by Gandhi, hoped to bring about these needed changes without violence. The more this tiny woman spoke — talking freely and movingly of the simple certainties of her own hard-won faith — the more impressed her guest became.

By the time Mrs. Nayyar finally met with Pyarelal and Mohandas later that evening, she had experienced a change of heart. Instead of demanding that her son return to his family immediately, the no-longer-reluctant mother proposed a compromise.

"You may keep Pyarelal for the next four or five years," she told Mohandas, "but you must send him back to me after that. After all, he is my only son, the only person I can look to for help."

"If that is so," Mohandas said with a cheerful smile, "why don't you and your daughter come and live with us in the ashram? That way, all of you will be together."

Even Ba's soothing influence had not brought Mrs. Nayyar that far. She told Bapu his suggestion was unacceptable. She had already given up a son to the Gandhi movement. Now he wanted them all.

Yet this, too, would change. In future years, with Mrs. Nayyar's approval, both of her children — daughter as well as son — would be ever more closely involved in the work and the lives of Bapu and Ba.

In 1926 my father, Manilal, fell in love with a Muslim woman. Both families knew each other. The following letter, dated April 3, 1926, is written in my grandfather's hasty scrawl:

Dear Manilal,

I have read your letter to Ramdas. I have also read Fatima's letter ... You follow the Hindu religion and Fatima follows Islam.

Your desire [to marry] is against your religion. It would be like putting two swords in one scabbard. What religion will your children follow? Who will have more influence on them? If Fatima forsakes her religion just for the sake of marriage she will be committing a crime against religion itself ... or is it that both of you have given up your religious beliefs?

Your marriage will be a great jolt to Hindu-Muslim relations. That issue cannot be solved by intermarriage. You cannot forget that you are my son. Society will also not forget it. If you go through with this marriage you will not be able to serve your people. I also think that you will be unfit to continue working for *Indian Opinion*.

I cannot seek Ba's consent, she will not give it, her whole life will be embittered ... I have no courage to tell her about this matter. May God show you the right path.

Bapu's blessings

Until I read this letter, I did not know that my father had once wanted to marry a Muslim. The Fatima referred to is someone I remember fondly from childhood, a close family friend, on best of terms with both my parents, whom I called Aunt Timmy. I can still only guess how Manilal reacted to Bapu's unyielding disapproval of the betrothal he had hoped to arrange for himself. And no one can ever know whether Bapu was right in assuming that such a marriage would have "embittered" Ba's whole life, but it seems unlikely, considering her generous, outgoing nature.

What I do know is that my grandmother, by the mid-1920s, was growing ever more restive, wondering what would become of her sons.

There was little Ba could do about Harilal at the moment. His way of living, according to news from Calcutta, was increasingly dissolute. And Bapu himself, in the pages of *Young India*, had fiercely denounced Harilal's latest financial disaster, a murky business venture in which money he had solicited from investors on the strength of his father's name was lost — or squandered, the rumours said, on wine, women and gambling. But Manilal's case was another matter. Having urged Bapu for so many years with so few results to arrange a marriage for Manilal, Ba was ready to take action herself.

She had already concluded privately that any one of three attractive sisters in a prosperous family of onetime cotton merchants would be a good wife for Manilal. The Mushruwalas, Nanabhai and his wife

Vijayalaxmi, were early converts to the Gandhi cause who had renounced the material life to devote their wealth and their lives to public service. Their home in Akola, some two hundred miles northeast of Bombay, was always open to ashram travellers, and Kasturba, on stopover visits, had taken notice of their bright and congenial daughters. The daughters had noticed her, too. I know this because the Mushruwalas were my maternal grandparents, and one of those daughters, Sushila, was my mother. Years later, when I was growing up in South Africa, she liked to recall the story of Ba's very first visit to Akola.

Sushila, at that time, was a teenager with romantic ideas and a vivid imagination. One day her mother announced that Mrs. Kasturba Gandhi, wife of the Mahatma, was coming to spend the night at their house. Sushila and her sisters (one a bit older, one a bit younger) and her cousins were all jubilant. Such an important person coming to their home — nothing this grand had ever happened to them! Though the girls all knew of Mrs. Gandhi, they had never seen her.

Kasturba visited Akola several times during the next few years. But, for Sushila, the most memorable Gandhi visit occurred one day in early January, 1927, when both the Mahatma and his wife came to call on her parents — and, as she soon learned, to ask them if one of their daughters would be interested in marrying their son, Manilal.

Sushila, a pretty twenty-year-old, with smooth skin, sleek dark hair, and gentle wide-set eyes, was with her sisters in the adjoining room, listening, but trying to stay out of sight.

"This is Manilal." Mohandas was showing her parents a picture. Manilal's wife, he explained, would have to take a vow of poverty; she would go to South Africa and live in the ashram there; she would be able to return to India only every three or four years. More and more curious, Sushila edged closer to the door. Ba was watching. And by the time the Gandhis left Akola (leaving Manilal's photo behind), there was no doubt in Ba's mind which sister should become Manilal's bride. Within days, a photo of Sushila was on its way to South Africa.

Things moved swiftly then. Some two months later, on March 6, 1927, Manilal Gandhi and Sushila Mushruwala were married in Akola at noon after a morning of fasting. After the ceremony, the bride, the groom, and the groom's family and friends boarded a second-class railway coach for the train trip back to Sabarmati. This once, in honour of the occasion, Mohandas did not insist on travelling third class. The newlyweds, looking nervous, carefully observed the proprieties and took their places in separate seats at opposite ends of the coach. But

Kasturba, seated beside her husband, felt bold, triumphant, even a bit giddy. She was at last welcoming a second daughter-in-law into her family; more than that, she was revelling in her role as mother of the groom, a moment of glory denied her twenty years earlier when Harilal and Gulab had married. This, Ba decided, was no time to be a slave to decorum.

First, she surprised everyone by asking her shy, new daughter-in-law to come sit in the seat facing her and help prepare an orange for Mohandas. Since the Mahatma was (in Sushila's words) "quite a perfectionist", this proved to be a painstaking operation. The orange had to be peeled with great care, all membrane had to be meticulously removed, and each section had to remain unbroken. But once the job was properly done, they all began to relax. Then, in another unexpected gesture, Ba invited her son Manilal to come and join them, too. He came.

So there they were bride and groom, sitting side by side in public, in defiance of all convention. Manilal did not say a word. Neither did Sushila. It was Kasturba who finally broke the silence — and at that moment, all of Sushila's apprehensions faded away.

"Why are you two sitting there dumb?" her new mother-in-law asked. "Don't you have anything to say to each other?"

# 24

Sabarmati, a centre of world attention on this day, had been in a ferment of anticipation for weeks, with friends, relatives, newcomers, and march volunteers appearing daily. Ba had been overjoyed when Manilal, Sushila, and their year-old toddler Sita, arrived from South Africa in December. Three years had passed since she last saw her son and daughter-in-law, and she had hoped to spend many happy hours getting acquainted with her new granddaughter. Ba had found almost no time to be with them. Like everyone at Sabarmati, she had been busy preparing for the start of Bapu's new civil disobedience campaign — the now famous Salt March.

Kasturba awoke early on March 12, 1930, long before her usual 4.00am rising time. She realised at once that the swarm of reporters and news photographers who had camped overnight in the fields around Sabarmati had already gathered outside the ashram gates. They were, of course, awaiting the departure of the marchers. Ba bathed and dressed quickly; she had much to do.

Seventy-nine Satyagrahis, led by Mohandas, would be setting out from the ashram at dawn, bound for the seacoast village of Dandi on the Gulf of Cambay, some two hundred and forty miles to the south. Their goal — to make and sell salt — might seem trivial, but their purpose was deadly serious. They were going to defy British rule, symbolically and conspicuously, by publicly violating the much-hated Salt Act — an ordinance which not only established a government monopoly on the manufacture of salt, but also levied a tax on the sale of salt, and even prohibited the extracting of salt from sea water.

Ba felt strangely elated that morning, making the rounds of the ashram in pre-dawn darkness to wake everyone for early prayers, and overseeing preparation of food for the marchers to carry with them. To think that collecting a pinch of salt from the sea could help free India! But if Bapu was right (and he generally was in such matters), this simple act would reach deep into the consciousness of the Indian nation and, hopefully, stir the conscience of its British rulers.

Yet Ba also felt a shiver of apprehension. Three generations of Gandhis would be marching to Dandi — her husband Mohandas, her son Manilal, and her oldest grandson Kanti, now nineteen, whom she had loved and cared for since he was a small child. No one knew what dangers they might face.

"You must be prepared to die," he told the marchers. "The British may use guns against us, but you must not fight back. If you surrender out of fear, it would be a disgraceful act. I would rather such people not come with me."

Ba had tried to reassure the women and girls staying behind, but on this morning, she was trying to reassure herself. During prayer service the previous evening, Mohandas had surprised her, along with everyone else, by taking a solemn vow — swearing not to return to Sabarmati until India won its freedom.

The sun had risen now, prayers had been chanted, the hour had come. Khadi-clad marchers, tense but eager, were in their places, exchanging farewells with the women and children.

One of those women was my mother, Sushila, and years later, she could still recall the scene in vivid detail. She was trying to say goodbye to my father Manilal with a brave face, but Bapu's words kept ringing in her ears: "You must be prepared to die ..." Trembling with emotion, Sushila broke away, ran over to Ba, and hid her tear-stained face in her mother-in-law's shoulder.

"Do you want your husband to carry with him the image of a weeping wife?" Kasturba asked, stroking Mother's head. Ba directed Sushila's attention to the other women. "Look," she said, "all of them are parting from sons or husbands. They are not crying, so why should you?" But the truth was clear to them both. Nearly every woman was now in tears.

Ba stepped forward then and addressed them all — a tiny, erect figure, speaking with a fierce dignity Sushila could never forget.

"Our men are warriors," Ba declared, "We are warriors' wives. We must give the men courage. If we are brave, they will be brave."

She turned and walked to the head of the procession where Bapu, wearing stout sandals and carrying a long bamboo walking staff, was about to lead the column of marchers through the gates. Ba stood looking into her husband's eyes for a long wordless moment. In her left hand was a small brass plate, filled with a waxy mixture of ghee and vermilion powder which she had prepared earlier that morning. Slowly, solemnly, she dipped the middle finger of her right hand into the bowl, then lightly touched Bapu's forehead, imprinting on his brow the familiar red kumkum dot. The gesture had deep meaning for all who watched. It was an invocation of good fortune for the departing traveller, and a prayer for his safe return.

But Ba had not finished. She began moving down the column of marchers, carefully anointing every brow with a kumkum dot. As she passed, each man's face revealed what a priceless farewell gift he had just received: the blessing of Kasturba's own confident serenity. Sushila stood transfixed, as though she, too, had been blessed.

"It was a different Ba that I saw at that moment," she would later recall. "All the human suffering she had witnessed through the years had left her face etched with deep lines of sadness. But, with all that, there was now radiance on that sweet old face — and an expression of fearless determination. The loving mother was now a soldier of Satyagraha, engaged in a grim battle. But she had not the shadow of a doubt about the justness of the cause or its ultimate victory. The fact that Bapu was leading the fight was enough for Ba."

At first, their fears seemed unwarranted. From the moment the marchers left the ashram and made their way through the festooned streets of Ahmadabad cheered on by the greatest throng of well wishers the city had ever seen, the Salt March became a triumphal parade across the Indian countryside. For the next three and a half weeks, the whole world charted the progress of Mahatma Gandhi and his pilgrims. Newsreels showed a gaunt old man in shawl and dhoti striding along on matchstick legs at a pace that tested the stamina of his most youthful followers. News photos pictured him addressing huge crowds of onlookers who knelt beside the road, or perched on walls and rooftops, even in treetops, in each village the marchers passed through.

Back at Sabarmati, Kasturba and the others followed news of the march with bated breath, each day expecting reports of a police crackdown. But the days passed, the marchers reached Dandi on schedule, and there was still no reaction from the government. Perhaps Viceroy Irwin had ordered police forbearance, believing the enthusiasm would spend itself. Mohandas, meanwhile, had not only written frequent reports on the march for his own newspapers, but had also found time to keep everyone at the ashram informed.

Manilal's unlimited courage was soon to be tested to the full. At sunrise on April 6, 1930, after praying for most of the night on Dandi beach, Mahatma Gandhi and his marchers waded into the sea for a purifying bath, then returned to shore. Before a battery of news cameras and a hushed multitude — some seventy-five thousand souls, Gandhi stooped to pick up a lump of salt-encrusted sand. Police were not present. There were no arrests. But the signal for the start of civil disobedience had been given. It was, as Jawarharlal Nehru wrote, "like releasing a spring".

Suddenly, all India was obsessed by the collecting, making, buying, and selling of salt. Beaches were lined with squatting villagers scooping up illegal salt from the sand; old women and young girls waded into the sea to collect contraband seawater in cooking pots. Pamphlets on salt making were hawked illicitly on Calcutta streets, and sophisticated city dwellers boiled sea water in kettles to make forbidden salt. Even Congress members, who had once dismissed the salt commotion, were auctioning off unlawful salt at the party's Bombay headquarters.

At his camp near Dandi, Mohandas continued to direct the movement, certain that exposing the repression was as important as publicising the movement itself. "I want world sympathy in this battle of right against might," he told foreign press correspondents. But his followers had welcomed imprisonment so peacefully and in such numbers that the salt campaign, by now, was no longer news.

Gandhi sent a brisk note to the viceroy announcing plans to lead a nonviolent counter-demonstration — the nonviolent occupation of the Government Salt Factory at Dharasana. For the British, this was too much. Gandhi had to be arrested, whatever the risks. In the early hours of May 5, they hauled him off to Poona to be held in Yeravda Jail "at the pleasure of the government". A public trial was a risk the government did not intend to take.

Just before the police lorry sped off into the night, one of Gandhi's followers, a young woman, asked if he had a message for Ba.

Mohandas smiled. "Tell her she is a brave girl," he said.

Ba summoned all of her courage to face the uncertainties that followed. News that Bapu had arranged, in case of his arrest, for their son Manilal to take over as leader of the promised raid on the salt works filled her with trepidation. With a husband and two sons in prison, and another in imminent danger, Kasturba felt as if she were reliving the worst days in South Africa, wondering which loved one to worry about first.

The answer soon came. On the uncommonly hot morning of May 21, 1930, twenty-five hundred unarmed "Gandhi raiders", all wearing white homespun shirts, dhotis and the familiar white "Gandhi caps", arrived at the Dharasana salt works, halted several hundred yards from the great salt pans, knelt in prayer, then, with Manilal in the lead, a small column of volunteers — 25 men, marching in ranks of four — began a slow advance across the open field. Ahead was a water-filled ditch; beyond that, a barbed wire stockade surrounding the salt pans, guarded by four hundred turbaned Indian policemen with steel-tipped lathis. Ignoring an order to disperse, marchers, in complete silence, moved on toward the stockade.

What happened next became an indelible image of the truth and force of Mahatma Gandhi's Satyagraha for all the world to remember — thanks largely to American reporter Webb Miller's graphic eyewitness story which was cabled round the globe by United Press:

... Suddenly, at a word of command, scores of native police rushed upon the advancing marchers and rained blows on their heads. ... Not one of the marchers even raised an arm to fend off the blows. They went down like tenpins. From where I stood I heard the sickening whacks of the clubs on unprotected skulls. The waiting crowd of watchers groaned and sucked in their breaths in sympathetic pain at every blow ... In two or three minutes the ground was quilted with bodies. Great patches of blood widened on their white clothes. The survivors without breaking ranks silently and doggedly marched on until every one of the first column had been knocked down. Stretcher-bearers rushed up unmolested by the police and carried off the injured ...

Then another column formed ... I could detect no signs of wavering or fear. They marched steadily, heads up, without the encouragement of music or cheering ... The police rushed out and beat down the second column. There was no fight, no struggle. The spectacle of unresisting men being methodically bashed into a bloody pulp sickened me so much that I had to turn away ...

Group after group walked forward ... Hour after hour stretcher-bearers carried back a stream of inert, bleeding bodies. I went to see Mrs. Naidu, who was directing the leaders in keeping the crowds from charging the police. While we were talking, one of the British officials approached her, touched her on the arm and said: "Sarojini Naidu, you are under arrest." She haughtily shook off his hand and said: "I'll come but don't touch me." The crowd cheered frantically ...

By eleven the heat reached 116° in the shade, and activities of the Gandhi volunteers subsided. I went back to the temporary hospital to examine the wounded ... They lay in rows on the bare ground in the shade of the palm-thatched shed. I counted 320 injured, many still insensible with fractured skulls. Scores of the injured had received no treatment for hours, and two had died ...

In 18 years of reporting in twenty-two countries I have never witnessed such harrowing scenes.

Manilal was "lost" — no one knew what had become of him. One of the first to be carried off the field at Dharasana, he had simply disappeared. Kasturba and Sushila, awaiting news at the ashram were in an agony of suspense. How badly had he been hurt? Had he been arrested? Had he died? Days passed, and still no word.

At last, a message came from Surat, a town some fifty miles from the scene of the raid. Manilal was in a prison hospital. His skull had been fractured, his recovery would be slow, but he would eventually be sent to the Sabarmati Jail to serve out his six-month sentence. The family's relief was so great, it seemed like joy.

On the day, some weeks later, that Manilal was brought to the jail, Sushila went with her mother-in-law to meet him. Ramdas and other Satyagrahis were there also, but even though Sabarmati Jail was almost next door, no one at the ashram had been allowed to see them since their arrests. Sushila had never been inside a jail before, and she felt as if she were suffocating. But Kasturba sat patiently in the head jailer's office waiting for her sons to be brought in. The interview, the police said, would have to take place in their presence.

When Manilal and Ramdas finally appeared, Sushila struggled to choke back her tears. Stark evidence of prison's hardships could be seen in their drawn faces — especially Manilal's. He had lost a great deal of weight (40 pounds, she learned later), and she couldn't bear to look at the ugly scars left by his recent head wounds. As she tried to regain her composure, Sushila became aware that Ba was speaking to Manilal and Ramdas with perfect calm — not commiserating with them, but inquiring about other Satyagrahis at the jail, getting news for families who were not permitted visits.

My mother was just one of many women who overcame doubt and fear during this bleak time of repression by following my grandmother's example. With more men being arrested every day, Ba believed it was up to the women, particularly the ashram women, to carry on the civil disobedience campaign. Bapu himself had said as much, in a letter sent to them from his prison cell at Yeravda. "I have put all my hopes in you women," he wrote. "I strongly feel that the ultimate victory of non-violence depends wholly on women."

Kasturba took on that challenge with a will. She now left the running of the ashram to others and resumed her travels, going from town to town, urging women to take part in the newest phase of civil disobedience — the picketing of government-owned liquor stores. Ba explained, that women were better qualified than men to spearhead this campaign, since Indian policemen would hesitate to arrest women, and Indian men, the store's main customers, would be reluctant to cross a women's picket line. Ba's pleas were persuasive and liquor sales fell precipitously.

"Ba, it seems, is doing some good running about" This was Mohandas' gleeful reaction, recorded in a letter dated October 12, 1930. Soon after, he would ask that yarn he had spun in Yeravda Jail be woven into a sari for Ba as a token of his esteem. Ba's work, he wrote, proved his long-held theory: "I believe the strength which women possess is given them by God. Hence they are bound to succeed in whatever they undertake."

Kasturba always considered herself a quiet person who wanted to do her duty without fuss or adulation. By this time, though, admiration for Ba was so commonplace that adulation was inevitable.

Several months after her reunion with Manilal and Ramdas in Sabarmati Jail, Kasturba travelled to the Punjab to visit the prison in Gujarat town where her youngest son Devadas was being held. Somehow, word of her arrival preceded her. When her train pulled into the railway station, several thousand people were waiting.

Ba turned to one of the leaders of the group with a question. "Who is coming? Why are there so many people here?"

"We have come here to welcome you," he said.

"Me?" she blurted out. The idea seemed to distress her.

"Yes, yes," the young man said. He explained that they planned to carry her in a procession through the town. Ba was distressed but there was nothing she could do.

Kasturba soon accompanied Grandfather to high level discussions with the Viceroy in Simla. Kasturba was equally tart when Lady Willingdon received her the next day. It was the first time a Vicerine had ever invited the wife of the Indian leader, causing eyebrows to be raised among the British officials and their wives.

When Lady Willingdon said she would like to obtain some of the coarse homespun khadi Gandhi had popularised to make India self-sufficient Kasturba replied she would be happy to send her some.

"I want to get in closer touch with the Indian people that way," said Lady Willingdon. "Could you send me something in mauve?"

"Certainly. I'll send you lots of mauve," said Kasturba. "And by the way, I like your idea of getting in closer touch with the Indian people by sampling our homespun materials. You would also know them better if you lived down in the plains, where they dwell, instead of up here on these mountain heights."

As a result of the Simla talks Mohandas had to lead a delegation to the Round Table Conference in London. Ba declined to go saying, "I have a lot to do here." The ship had no sooner cleared the harbour than Ba was on her way back to Ahmadabad to work among the poor, and to attend to her latest concern, helping former prisoners readjust to family life. A few weeks later, seven trunks filled with clothing, and personal belongings arrived without warning at Sabarmati ashram. They came from Mohandas and were directed to Kasturba. Several days passed before anyone found out why. Bapu, it turned out, had been shocked to see the mountains of luggage his companions were taking with them to London. This, he declared, was not the simplicity they strived for. He asked them to reconsider and repack. Then, when the *Rajputana* put in at Aden, its first port of call, he shipped the excess baggage back to his wife, confident that no one could put it to better use than she. For, as Bapu well knew, Ba's ability to reach and teach people had grown each year, and her influence, particularly among the women of India, was now unmatched.

The most recent demonstration of that influence had occurred only a few months earlier, when Indian women in South Africa donated funds directly to Kasturba, unsolicited, to support her work. Ba had acknowledged their generosity in a brief letter that my father Manilal printed in *Indian Opinion*. That thankyou letter, so simple in its sincerity, so modest and appealing in its directness, may provide an indication of why and how my grandmother was becoming a power to be reckoned with at home and abroad:

Dear Sisters,

I am in receipt of £25 collected by you. I am touched by your concern about India from such a distance, and am grateful for the same. I hope you are not using foreign clothes. Wherever we may be we cannot forget we should not use foreign goods. I hope your life and attitudes are reflections of Indian heritage and culture.

Kasturba Gandhi's Greetings

# 25

The news of the breakdown of the Round Table Conference in 1931 sparked spontaneous protests in India. Attempts to organise a new civil disobedience campaign were quickly snuffed out. The government was taking ever more drastic steps to crush Congress and curtail activities of any group which supported it, and to end Gandhi's hold on the Indian people — at least insofar as possible. The party's buildings were searched and occupied, its books seized, its funds frozen or confiscated. Censorship was invoked again, journalists were prosecuted, newspapers were fined for printing criticism of the government. It even became a crime in some provinces to publish photographs of Gandhi or his co-workers.

Civil liberties ceased to exist — any police officer could arrest anyone. In its clean sweep of "undesirable elements," the government jailed 15,000 Indians in January, another 18,000 in February. This time, a surprising number of those imprisoned were women.

Kasturba was one of the first to be arrested. After witnessing her husband's arrest in Bombay, Ba had returned to the ashram where she and several other women were immediately picked up and transported to the Sabarmati jail nearby. At the same time, some of the ashram's movable property was confiscated and carried away. Though Ba had been jailed in South Africa, this was her first incarceration in her own country. It would not be the last. During the next two years, she would be hauled off to jail five more times.

Like most of the women arrested during this massive new wave of repression, Ba received a relatively short sentence, just six weeks. Yet the treatment of all women political prisoners was, by directive, "rigorous" rather than "simple" and seemed calculated to intimidate or humiliate.

Kasturba, however, (perhaps because she was such a familiar and respected figure at Sabarmati Jail), was accorded some privileges not granted to the younger women. She made the most of them.

As soon as she was released from jail, Kasturba wanted to go and see her husband at Yeravda in Poona. But she learned, to her chagrin, that Bapu was refusing to receive visitors, a decision he had explained in a letter to Devadas, also in jail. One must accept the fact, Bapu wrote, that "imprisonment means absence of rights." Since he was having many problems sending and receiving mail, he felt it only "proper" to forgo having visitors also. Even so, he had some misgivings:

"... Ba will feel the shock the most. But she is born to endure shocks. All those who form or keep connections with me must pay a heavy price. It can be said that Ba has to pay the heaviest."

By mid-summer, Mohandas had relented and was seeing visitors again. But Kasturba was not among them. Rearrested and given a six-month sentence this time, she was again locked up in Sabarmati Jail.

Finally, in mid-September, a brief letter from Mohandas did arrive — sent to the ashram from Yeravda, with instructions that it be delivered to Kasturba by hand. It contained startling news:

"...You have probably heard about my fast. Do not get frightened in the slightest degree, and do not let the other women get frightened ... I think after having lived with me for 40 years, you will be able clearly to understand."

On September 20, 1932, Mahatma Gandhi had begun, a "fast unto death" to protest the new Indian constitution just proposed in London — one that not only granted separate electorates (which he still opposed) to Hindus, Muslims, Sikhs, and so forth, but established, in addition, a separate electorate for "Depressed Classes", i.e. the Untouchables. This idea had originated with Dr. B. R. Ambedkar, a stubborn and aggressive Untouchable leader, educated at Columbia University in New York, who mistrusted all caste Hindus, including the Mahatma.

Dr. Ambedkar argued that voting rights for the so-called Depressed Classes were more attainable under British rule than in some future Hindu-dominated, independent India. But to Gandhi, the proposal was anathema. Its acceptance by Hindus would write caste discrimination into India's constitution, delay reforms already under way, and further threaten the unity he believed was a basic prerequisite for Indian independence. He was fasting, in his words, "to sting the Hindu conscience into right religious action."

Mohandas was certain that Ba, undistracted by talk of electorates and politics, would discern without explanation, that he was fasting to uphold the simple religious truth of the oneness of all humanity. And he had faith that Ba, who had long ago and with great soul-searching made that truth her own, would agree without question that it was a truth worth living for — even dying for.

As soon as Kasturba arrived at Yeravda Jail, she was taken to an inner courtyard where she found Bapu lying on a white iron cot in the shade of a mango tree, motionless and silent under the watchful eyes of prison guards. It was her first glimpse of her husband in almost nine months, and she saw at once that he was sinking fast, his life was indeed at risk.

Pyarelal, in his book, *The Epic Fast* (as it later came to be known), gave this account of Ba's bedside reunion with Bapu:

> She was superb. Calm and collected as ever, she did not betray the slightest trace of agitation or grief.
>
> "Again, the same old story," she remarked as she greeted him. Forced banter, however, could hardly conceal what must have been to her a terrible ordeal of the soul.
>
> She promptly took charge of Gandhiji's little improvised nursing establishment ...

On the morning of September 26, 1932, Gandhi's strength was ebbing away fast. His blood pressure had reached alarming heights; his weight, normally about one hundred and ten pounds, had dropped below ninety-five; he was passing in and out of consciousness. Shortly after noon, panicky negotiators finally reached agreement on a complex formula which, in lieu of a separate electorate, guaranteed special primaries and reserved legislative seats to Untouchables. The Yeravda Pact, as it was called, also included an unprecedented declaration: "Henceforth, no one is to be regarded as Untouchable."

Gandhi's "magic" had won a signal victory for human rights. After this, there could be no turning back, no matter who ruled India.

Then, the moment came. It was time for the Mahatma to break his fast. Ba, who was standing beside Bapu's cot, helped him raise himself to his elbow, and held a glass of orange juice to his lips. As he took his first sip, the entire world seemed to heave a sigh of relief.

Few of those present knew that Kasturba's role had been specified by the Inspector General of Prisons for India, Colonel E. E. Doyle, who believed it was her presence, more than anything else, that had kept the Mahatma alive until the Yeravda Pact was signed.

"One more thing," the thankful colonel had said earlier that afternoon, when he personally delivered the approved document into Gandhi's hand, "the fruit juice must be handed to you by Mrs. Gandhi."

Kasturba served the final weeks of her sentence in the women's section at Yeravda Prison, visiting Mohandas daily, and preparing food for him on a small Primus stove made available for the purpose. Bapu soon regained his strength, and Ba regained the weight she had lost — as always, she had cut her own intake of food to a bare minimum while her husband was fasting.

At times, Ba almost felt like giving thanks for Bapu's fast. Harrowing as it was, it had brought the blessing of a family reunion of sorts. Ramdas, too, was moved to Yeravda to complete his jail sentence. There were frequent visits from Devadas, who was free again; even Manilal appeared one day, bearing apples from South Africa and oranges from Zanzibar. Though Bapu's letters had insisted it was a needless waste of funds, Manilal, Sushila and four-year-old Sita, had just arrived in India for a hurried visit. "On hearing of my fast," Bapu reported to a friend, "they could not restrain themselves."

When Ba suggested that she "resume her duties" as soon as she was free, Bapu readily agreed. Thus, on December 3, 1932, Kasturba represented her husband at the opening of an anti-Untouchability conference in Madras. From there, accompanied by several other women, she went on a tour of the region to plead for Harijan rights. She took time off only for a brief stopover at Sabarmati ashram to assure herself that, in her continued absence, all was still going well, and a visit to Yeravda Jail to check on Bapu, who, after another brief fast of only two days, had won reversal of the prison policy that prohibited Satyagrahi inmates from doing menial work deemed appropriate only for Untouchables.

By the year's end, a backlash was in full swing among orthodox Hindus, and Kasturba Gandhi's advocacy of the Harijan cause came in for bitter criticism. "The resentment, even against Ba, was bound to come," was Bapu's rueful reaction. Worse still, in February 1933, Ba was sent back to jail — presumably for disregarding a government warning to "refrain from civil disobedience." The *New York Times* reported simply that Mrs. Gandhi was "arrested on a secret charge."

For my grandparents, the year 1933 became a cycle of arrests, jailings, fasts, releases, and re-arrests, repeated with monotonous regularity. In May, Mohandas began a twenty-one-day fast, not against the government, but for "self-purification" and to urge greater efforts on behalf of the Harijans. Kasturba was shocked that he should undertake so long a fast so soon after surviving his "fast unto death".

British officials, even more shocked than Kasturba, and more fearful than ever that Mahatma Gandhi might die in their custody, released him from Yeravda Jail. They also released Ba from Sabarmati Jail.

Soon Kasturba was arrested again — the sixth time in just two years — and given another six-month sentence to be served in Sabarmati Jail. Apparently the British now regarded Mrs. Gandhi, due to her own unique ability to involve women in the independence movement, as even more of a threat to law and order than Gandhi himself.

This time, in Sabarmati Jail, Ba was separated from other inmates, permitted no visitors, and allowed to correspond only with her husband — just one letter, sent or received, each week. Knowing he was her only link to the outside world, Bapu wrote Ba long, newsy, encouraging letters, copies of which were preserved by his diligent secretaries. But no one knows how many Ba received, or whether her messages reached him, since his travels were taking him to remote areas where postal service was poor or nonexistent.

Kasturba, who at the age of 64 had spent almost all her waking hours in the company of others, was now truly alone for the first time. Yet, paradoxically — and somewhat to her surprise — she was not uneasy nor even particularly lonely in her solitude.

But Ba, being Ba, found that recounting the activities of women from high-ranking families as she sat in her jail cell in 1933, was not nearly so heartening as recalling the actions of ordinary women from ordinary Indian families. She had seen them in countless numbers, picketing in the streets, taking lathi blows from the police without flinching, and going to jail without complaint. Yet their physical courage and material sacrifices were rarely acknowledged.

Ba had highest hopes, perhaps, for Pyarelal Nayyar's younger sister Sushila Nayyar who, at fifteen, had spent a summer at Sabarmati ashram at her own request. It was only because Mrs. Nayyar knew and trusted Kasturba, that she had permitted her eager but gently reared daughter to join the ashram on a temporary basis. Mrs. Nayyar's instincts were sound. Under Ba's kindly and discreet tutelage, the bewildered young girl, who had never before drawn well water or laundered her own clothing, was spared the indignity of exposing her ignorance to others at the ashram. Sushila had returned to Sabarmati every summer since, even after she began studying medicine — an ambition Ba had carefully nurtured, arguing it was more vital to India's future for a young woman as capable as Sushila Nayyar to become "Dr. Nayyar" than to get arrested and go to prison.

There was another wedding — one that had been postponed even longer — that Kasturba recalled with special satisfaction. She was still thankful to have been present, on June 16, 1933, when Devadas Gandhi, at age 33, had become the last of her four sons to claim a wife. The wedding, a simple one, had been arranged at once.

Memories could not sustain an imprisoned Kasturba forever. One of the last women arrested during two years of repression, she was, by early 1934, one of the few still in jail. She was due to be released in May, but time was passing ever more slowly, and Ba was growing restive. Then, at the end of April, as if in celebration of her forthcoming liberation, Ba received joyous news: she had become a grandmother again three times over, in a single week!

On April 14, 1934, in South Africa, Manilal's and Sushila's second child was born — a boy named Arun. In India, Ramdas' and Nirmala's third child, a girl named Usha was born on April 18, while Devadas and Lakshmi's firstborn, a girl named Tara, arrived on April 22. I cannot say when I first learned that Ba was in prison at the time I was born. Perhaps it is something I always knew. But I now realise that my determination to learn more about my grandmother and her life has always been rooted in that knowledge.

Kasturba Gandhi was free at last — but her life was in danger.

Though Ba had known that Bapu's work for Untouchables was rousing bitter animosity among radical Hindus, it was only while travelling with her husband, just days after her release, that she learned how deep that hatred had become. In June of 1934, Kasturba, Mohandas, and several others were riding in an automobile in the city of Poona, en route to the Municipal Hall where an overflow audience was waiting to hear Gandhi speak. Suddenly, a homemade bomb was hurled at their car. The unknown bomb thrower, as it turned out, aimed poorly; the bomb hit the car following theirs, injuring seven people, though none seriously. Bapu, after a brief prayer of thanks to God that no one was fatally injured, insisted that the meeting proceed. But as they left the hall that night, Ba couldn't help thinking how much more secure and predictable life had seemed behind bars.

Kasturba Gandhi was free — but she was also homeless.

Ba had known for some time that Bapu intended to disband the Sabarmati ashram. The property's fate, uncertain ever since the Salt March, had been decided when its seizure became likely during a wave of punitive expropriations accompanying the governmental crackdown.

Mohandas had forestalled this in the autumn of 1933, just before he began his ten-month Harijan tour, by deeding the ashram to a newly formed society, the Order for the Service of Harijans to be used for the welfare and advancement of India's Untouchables. Most of the Satyagrahis who were still in residence at Sabarmati had left to work on village projects elsewhere, or to live in other ashrams.

Though Kasturba had been aware of these changes while in prison, she had not reckoned that, without Sabarmati ashram to go to upon her release, she would have no place to call home. Mohandas was in Central India, living in a tiny mud hut in the village of Sevagram near Wardha, not far from the ashram founded by his disciple Vinoba Bhave. But when Ba joined him, she recognised all the signs; her husband was in desperate need of solitude and meditation.

Such prolonged soul-searching was not for Kasturba. She had proven to herself many times over that indecision was a disorder for which activity was the cure. If Mohandas, at the moment was not demanding all of her attention, then she had sons to visit, new grandchildren to meet, friends and relatives to help in time of need.

And so it was. For more than two years, Ba lived her own life. A purposeful pilgrim hurrying on and off trains, crisscrossing the country on missions of mercy, journeying to far-flung towns and villages to encourage rural improvement, spending weeks at a time getting reacquainted with her sons and their families, occasionally travelling with Bapu on his tours, or staying with him at Wardha if he needed her. A random record of Kasturba's itinerary can be found in Mohandas' ongoing correspondence with friends and relatives, which included casual but frequent mentions of his wife's travels.

Ba was constantly on the move — to Benares with Bapu, where he spoke to a large gathering of Untouchables; to Ahmadabad with her ailing son Ramdas for a series of treatments from a nature doctor; to Bombay with her granddaughter Sumitra, Ramdas' oldest child, who needed eye treatments; to Delhi, where Devadas had settled in a well-paying job, to visit his family and rest a bit herself; to Deolali, to attend a rural exhibition. Back to Delhi, to help care for her baby granddaughter Tara, who was ill; to Bombay again, where Ramdas had moved his family and was joining a printing business; to Borsad with Bapu and Mahadev Desai, to help conduct hygiene and sanitation campaigns in nearby villages. To Delhi to visit Devadas and his family again, this time with her granddaughter Manu, Harilal's youngest child; to Simla with Devadas, while he recovered from a fever. And, in April of 1936, Ba travelled to Nagpur with Bapu, to attend an All India Literary

Conference. There, they met briefly, unexpectedly, and unhappily with the wayward Harilal, who announced — half-jokingly, perhaps, but with an edge in his voice — that several of his friends of various faiths were seeking to convert him to their religions.

That encounter was an echo of times past, and a harbinger of things to come. Kasturba was still trying to forget the last time she had seen Harilal. It had happened on another of her tours with Bapu.

Their train had halted briefly at the small town of Katni where a crowd of darshan-seekers was on the station platform, hoping for a glimpse of Mohandas. The usual shouts of "Mahatma Gandhi ki jai!" filled the air. Then, Ba heard a voice raised above all the others: "Mata Kasturba ki jai!" ("Victory to Mother Kasturba!") Peering through the open train window, she was startled to see her son Harilal standing on the platform dressed in rags, looking old and ill. He pushed his way through the crowd and handed her an orange, saying, "This is for you, Ba, a token of my love." And to Mohandas he had said, "If you are so great, you owe it all to Ba." Before there was time to say anything else, the train began to move. As it gathered speed, pulling out of the station, Ba had heard the voice again: "Mata Kasturba ki jai!"

Ba had always defended Harilal, found excuses for him, but she had felt at times that the conflict between her husband and her son was taking place in her own heart — and her heartache was for them both. Now, after seeing Harilal again in Nagpur, she realised that his bitterness, his frequent bouts with alcoholism (for that is what it was), his perpetual borrowing of money (even from his own grown children), were making it ever harder for her to understand him, let alone defend him. Most painful of all were Harilal's letters deriding his father which had been appearing in many newspapers of late, often alongside reports of his latest brush with the law. Ba was fighting the certainty in her own heart that her firstborn son was lost forever.

Her worst fears were soon confirmed. Only a month later, in May of 1936, the news was broadcast across India: Harilal Gandhi, son of the Mahatma, had converted to Islam in a public ceremony in one of Bombay's biggest mosques, taking Abdullah Gandhi as his new name. He did this, he said, "to improve himself", but it was rumoured that his "improvement" was mostly financial. His new-found Muslim friends were addressing him as Maulvi ("Great Teacher"), and he had been making public preachments about his conversion. Some weeks after that, while Ba was in Delhi visiting Devadas, there was more news — widely published reports of "Abdullah's" latest misconduct.

Ba called Devadas to her side and dictated the following letter:

My dear son Harilal,

I have read that recently in Madras policemen found you in a state of drunkenness at midnight in an open street and took you in custody. Next day, you went before a magistrate who fined you one rupee. He must have been a very kindhearted man to have treated you so leniently ...

I do not know what to say to you. I have been pleading with you all these long years to hold yourself in check ... Think of the misery you are causing your aged parents in the evening of their lives ... Though born as our son, you are indeed behaving like our enemy.

I am told that in your recent wanderings you have been criticising and ridiculing your great father. You are only disgracing yourself by speaking ill of your father. He has nothing but love in his heart for you. He has offered to keep you with him, to feed and clothe you, and even to nurse you. But you have never paid any heed to his advice. He has so many other responsibilities in this world, he cannot do more for you. He can only lament his fate [and] quietly suffer all the disgrace.

But I am unable to stand the mental anguish you are causing ... Every morning I rise with a shudder at the thought of what fresh news the newspapers will bring. I sometimes wonder where you are, where you sleep, what you eat. Perhaps you take forbidden food ... I often feel like meeting you. But I do not know where to find you. You are my eldest son and nearly 50 years old, [yet] I am afraid of approaching you, lest you humiliate me.

I do not know why you changed your ancestral religion. That is your affair ... [I did not like it] but when I saw your statement that you had decided to improve yourself I felt secretly glad, even about your conversion, hoping that you would now start leading a sober life. But that hope also was dashed to pieces. I hear that you go about asking innocent and ignorant people to follow your example. What do you know of religion? What judgement can you exercise in your mental condition? People are liable to be led astray by the fact that you are your father's son. In time to come, if you go on like this, you will be shunned by everyone. I beseech you to turn back from your folly ... Your father always pardons you, but God will not tolerate your conduct ...

Kasturba was not yet finished. She dictated another letter — to be sent to newspapers throughout India. She was writing, she said, in hopes "the feeble voice of a wounded mother" would "awaken the conscience" of the Muslims instrumental in her son's conversion:

... I fail to understand your action. I know, and I am glad, that a large number of thinking Muslims and all of our lifelong Muslim friends condemn outright this entire episode... Instead of redeeming my son, I find his so-called change of faith has actually made matters worse. You ought to reprimand him for this and try to wean him from these bad habits, [but] some have even gone so far as to give the title "Maulvi" to my boy. Does your religion permit such persons as my son to be called Maulvis? What pleasure do you find in lionising him like this?

If you truly consider him your brother you will not do as you are doing, [it] is not at all in his interest. But if your desire is merely to hold us up to ridicule I have nothing more to say to you. You may do your worst. But I feel it my duty to repeat what I have told my son. Namely, that you are not doing the right thing in the eyes of God.

# 26

apu's eye had fallen, not wholly by chance, on Segaon, a tiny, primitive village located only a few miles from Wardha, but lacking even such bare amenities as roads, shops, or post office. Bapu had learned that his wealthy friend and disciple, Jamnalal Bajal, owned a large parcel of arid land in Segaon. In due course Bajal had offered it to Gandhi as the site for a small-scale, model experiment in rural development. By March of 1936, when Bapu wrote a long memo entitled "My Idea of Living in a Village" and sent it off to Bajal, the two men had apparently already discussed the work to be done in Segaon. The memo, reflecting Bapu's mood during this period, was concerned mostly with personal living arrangements:

> If Ba desires, then with her, otherwise, I would live alone in a hut in Segaon ... As little expense as possible should be incurred in building the hut and in no case should it exceed 100 rupees. Whatever help I might need [in the construction work], I should obtain from Segaon ... I will continue my outside activities, but people from outside should not come to see me at Segaon. They may see me at [Wardha] on days fixed for my going there ...

Mohandas obviously did not intend to found another ashram. He planned to live in the wilderness as a semi-recluse. From the moment work got underway at Segaon, however, it became clear that another ashram had found him. By July, just weeks after construction of Bapu's humble one-room mud hut was completed, it was being shared by seven other people.

Later that summer, Ba and her granddaughter Manu, were the first family members to get a look at Bapu's latest home. After trudging the five hot, dusty miles from Wardha to Segaon on foot, Ba and Manu arrived at the forbidding, snake-infested site, only to find they must accommodate themselves as best they could in one corner of Bapu's crowded hut.

No wonder, then, that Ba chose to resume her visits to the homes of friends and relatives until her own little cottage was ready for occupancy in December of 1936.

Kasturba's hut, like her husband's, was a one-room affair with plastered mud walls and floor, and a thatched roof covered with earthen tiles. But it was graced by a spacious verandah, and had what Bapu described as a "somewhat city appearance." It had also cost somewhat more to build than Bapu's hundred-rupee (then about £6) limit for his own quarters. To Ba, settling down in her own home again after almost three years of wandering, it must have seemed like a small palace.

Now, other followers gathered and, inevitably, the familiar work of building a new Gandhian community began. A small colony of mud and bamboo houses rose from the barren ground surrounding the two original buildings. Roads were cut through the wilderness, gardens were planted, wells were dug, a community kitchen was built. A school was started for children from nearby villages, and the headquarters of the All-India Village Industries was moved to Segaon. Old comrades — among them Henry Polak and Herman Kallenbach — came to visit and relive past endeavours. New converts arrived.

By the fall of 1937, the Mahatma's would-be hermitage looked like a small village in itself. So much so that Mohandas, who still found it hard to believe he had unwittingly started another ashram, decided he should choose a name for his latest venture in communal living. He called it Sevagram, meaning "Service Village".

My earliest memories of Ba and Bapu date back to the spring of 1938, when my parents took me on my first ocean voyage, from South Africa to India. In fact, during this, my first visit to their homeland, I was introduced to all four of my grandparents. I remember a scene, one that took place at the Sevagram ashram that spring, vividly.

I was sick, with a very high fever — the exact nature of the illness I do not recall. I do remember the cure prescribed by my grandfather — a six-day fast, with nothing but water for sustenance.

By the third day, my fever had come down to normal. I was hungry and demanding food. My mother appealed to Bapu: since I was so much better, wouldn't it be all right for me to break the fast? Bapu said no. At that point, I was later told, I began to wail — piteously, vociferously.

Suddenly, a soft presence was at my side, soothing hands raised my head, a glass of orange juice was held to my lips. As I took my first thirsty swallow, I heard Ba's voice, calm and resolute: "I am not going to let this child starve."

How happy I was at my grandmother's welcome intervention. But my most indelible memory of that moment is my grandfather's reaction — his quizzical smile and small sigh of resignation, as he quietly turned away. Even at that tender age, I think I realised I had just witnessed a struggle of wills in which Bapu had been bested, and I sensed it was not the first time Ba had overruled one of his edicts.

Accounts of similar incidents recur in the recollections of relatives and ashram dwellers who knew my grandparents through the years. Some stories picture Ba as the only person Bapu ever feared. An example is the tale of how Motilal Nehru and several other notables once dropped in for a visit at the ashram and Bapu furtively prepared a meal for them himself because Ba was sleeping and he dared not disturb her (she was annoyed anyway, when she found out).

In most stories of ashram life, however, Ba emerges as the presiding adjudicator to whom everyone took their complaints when Bapu's demands seemed too oppressive. In his book, *The Torchbearers of the Gandhi Family*, Kakasaheb Kalelkar, a Gandhian philosopher and sometime ashram resident, described the situation this way:

> The ashram was really an academy of principles according to Bapu — principles to be observed with firm discipline. In this exacting atmosphere, Kasturba was everybody's mother, the main source of love and kindness, and, in comforting others, she often went against the rules. Bapu, in the end, had to accept defeat and declare that Ba was exempted from the regulations of the ashram.

Clearly, Ba was charting her own course more and more now, dispelling any notion that she blindly obeyed her husband's every command. Equally as strong-minded as Mohandas, she inspired equally fierce devotion among co-workers. Over the years she had learned to read a little. She was slow, but she could read the newspapers and letters. She had picked this up on her own with the help of her friends. She had, however, always resisted Mohandas' attempts to give her formal tuition.

One young man, Amritlal Nanavati, later recalled his experiences as a teacher at the Sevagram ashram. His book, entitled *In the Service of Ba and Bapu*, offered affectionate and revealing glimpses of the mature Kasturba he knew of these years:

Along with duties in the community kitchen, I was teaching the residents classical Indian vocal music. One day I was explaining a new rhythm to one young woman, who found it difficult to follow, though I repeated it several times. But Ba, listening from a distance, repeated it perfectly ... Even at her age she was a quick learner.

Kasturba also enrolled in one of Amritlal Nanavati's reading classes, and was a diligent, even a demanding student:

Class started at 8.00am. Ba was always present on the veranda a few minutes early, waiting eagerly. Exactly at eight, she would look at her watch and tell me, "It's time to start our work."

She would then light the oil lamp and read the Twelfth Chapter of the *Gita*, which she was trying to learn by heart. After that came hymns and, if time allowed, she also read a few pages of Bapu's autobiography in Gujarati. At the end of the study period, she would once again look at her watch and tell me that class time was over.

Not all of Ba's "disciples" understood and appreciated her in the way Amritlal did, and some could not fathom her relationship with Bapu. One modern young woman took it upon herself, after her first few weeks under Ba's tutelage at Sevagram, to write to Mohandas and accuse him of taking advantage of his compliant wife. She said she had seen Kasturba endure unnecessary hardships daily, trying to observe his harsh ashram restrictions. This new resident may have heard that Ba once described Bapu's way of life as "a path full of thorns" — if so, she had failed to note Ba's explanation of why she chose to follow that path, "The whole world looks to him for guidance," Ba declared, "and I must stand by him."

When Kasturba learned of the "letter", she called the young woman in and delivered a few sharp words on misguided loyalty.

"Whatever Bapu has decided to do here is for my welfare," she announced sternly. "I am convinced of that. I may be uneducated, but I need no protection from you."

While Bapu was extremely stern about rules and regulations, especially when it entailed the use of public funds, Kasturba was more lenient and loving. Once a group of young women from the nearby Mahila (women's) ashram came to visit.

Located some six miles from Sevagram, the Mahila ashram was run on Gandhian concepts; young and destitute girls were trained in vocations that enabled them to care for themselves and prepared them to work for village improvements as well. After the Mahatma became their neighbour in 1936, it had become a ritual for a group of these young women honour him each year on his birthday, October 2, by making the long trek over to Sevagram to spend the day.

Before one such birthday, they wrote to Gandhi to remind him they would come as usual. He wrote back saying they were welcome, but they should bring their own food and drink, since water from the well was the only hospitality the ashram could offer them. This was typical of Bapu's disapproval of wasteful expenditures — to him, it seemed extravagant to entertain twenty or thirty women who were coming to the ashram solely to celebrate his birthday.

Undisturbed and undeterred, the young women rose very early on the appointed day. They each packed a lunch, then left Mahila ashram — on foot, and arrived at Sevagram in time for prayers at 5am.

Afterwards, while Sevagram residents got busy with routine chores, the visitors from Mahila ashram were left to fend for themselves. Almost famished by mid-morning, the young women went to the well and washed, then sat down under a tree and began to eat their lunches.

Kasturba was startled to find them there a bit later.

"What are you girls doing here?" she demanded. "Why aren't you eating with the rest of the ashram community?"

When they told her of Bapu's conditions for their visit, Ba was exasperated. "What nonsense!" she said. "You come along with me."

She led them to her little hut, got them comfortably settled on the shady verandah, and offered them some of the sweets she always kept on hand there. Then she had Sevagram's pantry opened, brought out all the molasses, peanuts, and buttermilk she could find, and began distributing this bounty among the visitors.

At about this moment Mohandas came on to the scene.

"What is going on here?" he asked.

Ba chided him. "Don't tell me your ashram has become so bankrupt that it cannot feed a handful of guests."

"But there is no need for all this," he protested. "I explained conditions to the girls before they came here."

"You may explain what you like," Ba said good-humouredly. "But right now these young women are sitting on my veranda. They are my guests, I am their hostess, and no guest of mine goes away hungry." Bapu smiled and went his way.

This was when Bapu was having problems with fluctuating blood pressure. As part of his home remedy and also because the dry hot weather made sleeping indoors stuffy and uncomfortable Bapu would sleep outside in the open. In winter months it could be bitterly cold in Segaon, and there came a day when a doctor, called in for consultation, told Gandhi that if he wanted his health to improve, he must sleep indoors, at least in winter. That was easier said than done. Not only was the patient reluctant but there was a question of where he could be properly accommodated. To solve this problem, Mirabehn, without consulting Bapu, vacated her cottage for him — a move which irritated him no end. He refused, Bapu said, to disturb anyone. But that evening, after prayer services, Kasturba took charge.

"From now on, Mohandas sleeps in my cottage," she announced.

The matter, according to Sushila Nayyar, was "settled then and there". Bapu's bed was moved into his wife's room; she and their small grandson Kahandas (Ramdas' boy, who was sharing Ba's hut while visiting the ashram), moved their beds on to her veranda.

Mohandas had a restful night. Next morning, when his daily stream of visitors began to arrive, he was in a reminiscent mood.

"Poor Ba," he exclaimed, partly to himself, partly to his guests. "This little cottage was specially built for her. I supervised the construction myself so she could have some comfort and privacy in her old age. But now I have taken possession of it, and my coming here means she has to give it up altogether. Wherever I go, the place becomes like a dormitory." He sighed. "It hurts me, but I must admit Ba never complains. I can impose on her, make her do anything I like."

As he was completing his last sentence, Kasturba walked into the room. With a sidelong glance and a mischievous smile, Bapu went on talking. "But that's as it should be," he said. "If a husband says one thing and the wife another, life would become miserable. Here, the husband has only to say something and the wife is ever ready to do it."

At that, Ba's cheerful smile turned into spontaneous laughter — laughter so contagious that everyone else joined in, and the little hut resounded with sounds of mirth.

By this stage in their lives, however, husband and wife truly did seem in accord on all things; except on rare occasions, they were acting as one. One of the very last times Ba strayed from Bapu's "path full of thorns" occurred during our family's 1938 sojourn in India. My mother Sushila, who was with Ba at the time, believed the incident stemmed from a gross miscalculation on her mother-in-law's part — Kasturba's "Himalayan blunder", she called it.

Unless Mohandas was in poor health, Kasturba often chose not to accompany him on his travels in those days, preferring to devote herself to her own work. But on learning, one spring day, that he was scheduled to attend a political meeting in the remote town of Delang in Orissa province, south and east of Calcutta, Ba announced that she was eager to go along. My mother and several other women, including Mahadev Desai's wife Durgabehn, decided to join the party as well, and it became a pilgrimage of sorts.

The great attraction in Delang was the Jagannath Puri temple, regarded by all Hindus as one of the four most important and sacred temples in all of India. Neither Kasturba nor the other women had ever visited this famous shrine, and they longed to do so, even though it was reported that Harijans were not permitted to worship in the Puri temple. Bapu's demand that self-respecting Hindus shun any temple refusing entry to Untouchables was, of course, well-known to all of them — and especially to Ba, who, after all, had taken part in the national campaign to open the temples to all worshippers. But surely, they told each other, just looking at the great temple from outside for a few minutes would do no harm to anyone.

Once the party arrived at Delang, Mohandas was completely immersed, as usual, in his political work. On the morning his wife, his daughter-in-law Sushila, and the other women set out for Puri, he raised no objection. Like everyone else, Bapu assumed it was a sight-seeing tour, and concluded that their visit would even be a form of Satyagraha if they stood outside the temple, just where Harijans were allowed to stand, and refused in protest to go any farther.

What happened when the group arrived at Puri temple says a great deal about how torn Kasturba must have been, even at this late date, between loyalty to the old traditions of her Hindu upbringing, and commitment in the new spiritual insights her husband was giving to the world. After standing outside in silent reverence for a few minutes, Ba found the religious attraction of the great temple irresistible. She started forward toward the entrance, and Mahadev Desai's wife Durgabehn joined her. The others were surprised.

"Ba, you mustn't go inside," Sushila blurted out, embarrassed to be speaking to her mother-in-law so boldly. "Bapu is against it."

"I know," Ba replied. "But we are here for the first time, we may never come back. I cannot leave without going into the temple."

That evening the news reached Mohandas. He was hurt, he was angry as never before. Seeing this, Ba was suddenly contrite. She confessed her error, asked forgiveness. But Ba was not the target of Bapu's ire — as he made clear at a public prayer meeting that night.

"I must be held responsible," Mohandas proclaimed, "I neglected my wife's education." Then, in the very next breath, he was taking Mahadev Desai to task for neglecting his wife's education. If Mahadev hadn't been so remiss, Bapu declared, Durgabehn would have convinced Ba to stay outside, instead of going into Puri temple with her.

Mahadev, devastated by such criticism, wrote a letter next day, trying to resign his post as secretary. This pained Bapu all the more:

"If you are like my son, can I not rebuke you for a misdeed?"

Mahadev and Mohandas eventually healed their rift and purged their souls by fasting for several days (a penance in which they were joined by everyone involved, including my mother). Then, in articles written for *Harijan Weekly*, each man lamented the unhappy incident and listed his own shameful transgressions. Mahadev, for example, confessed he had been so upset by Bapu's unexpected reproof that, at one point, he had loudly bemoaned his fate with a familiar epigram:

To live with the saints in heaven
is a bliss and a glory.
But to live with a saint on earth
is a different story.

In 1938, spontaneous uprisings against arbitrary rule by local princes began erupting across India. Gandhi, Nehru, and other leaders feared mass violence if the movement spread unchecked. More than that, they worried that the unity and stability of a future free India would be endangered, if people in the princely states had no training in democracy, no preparation for self-rule. So Congress gave guidance and moral support to campaigns for civil and political rights in the states of Mysore, Travancore, Jaipur, and Hyderabad. But not until protests broke out in Rajkot did the crisis reach its climax.

At the outset, prospects seemed promising for settlement of the Rajkot people's long-standing grievances. Vallabahbhai Patel, Gandhi's trusted friend and organiser, had taken a hand in negotiations with the Thakore (the local ruler), and in December of 1938, they reached an agreement on formation of a political reform committee, and amnesty for all jailed protesters. But the Thakore, almost immediately, backed out of the agreement; he refused to appoint the reform committee as promised, and resumed the arrest of dissidents.

Mohandas, remembering that his father had faithfully served as dewan to a generous Thakore of Rajkot who happened to be the current ruler's grandfather, was initially inclined to absolve the prince of blame. He assumed this "cold-blooded breach of a solemn covenant" was being engineered by the British political agent in Rajkot, and he approved Patel's decision to renew the protest campaign — symbolically, on Independence Day, January 26, 1939.

By this time, though, it was abundantly clear that the present day Thakore was a despot who was perfectly capable, with no prompting from anyone, of causing untold misery for the people of Rajkot — and particularly for the women of Rajkot. There had been persistent rumours about the Thakore's sexual abuse of some of his young women subjects. It was the prince's habit, according to these reports, to kidnap beautiful young girls, take them to his royal "fun house" (a summer bungalow near the village of Tramba, a few miles outside the city), molest them, then set them free.

The rumours, which were eventually confirmed, had outraged the women of Rajkot — so much so, that a number of them had enlisted in the campaign for political reform. They began offering Satyagraha — using nonviolent public protests to court arrest. The Thakore readily obliged them, and one of the first women demonstrators to be hauled off to the Rajkot jail was Vallabhbhai Patel's daughter Maniben.

News of these events was greeted with high indignation at Sevagram. Kasturba was especially disturbed, for Maniben was one of her favourites among younger women in the independence movement. What was happening in Rajkot, Ba declared, was no longer a matter of political rights, it was now a question of women's honour. And she intended to do something about it — as Mohandas disclosed in an editorial published in *Harijan* on January 31, 1939:

... My wife feels so much about the sufferings of the people that, though she is as old as I am and much less able than myself to brave such hardships as may be attendant upon jail life, she feels she must go to Rajkot. And before this is in print, she might have gone ...

Kasturba, in fact, had left for Rajkot — having hurriedly arranged for another dedicated young woman, Mridula Sarabhai, daughter of long-time Gandhi adherent Ambalal Sarabhai, to accompany her. Planning an early return, Ba had decided to leave her visiting grandson Kahandas in Bapu's care. But Kahandas missed his absent grandmother so much and cried so constantly, that Bapu was soon forced to admit defeat and send the child home to his parents.

Ba no sooner arrived in Rajkot, than she began speaking to groups of women, urging them to join the protest, to stand up for their rights and demand protection from abuse. The Thakore was well aware of her activities — after all, the mere presence of Kasturba Gandhi in the state of Rajkot was news. On February 3, 1939, she was summarily arrested, and (in what the Thakore may have intended as an ironic touch), was taken to Tramba to be confined in the royal summer residence — the very bungalow made notorious by all the rumours.

Though Bapu was notified of Ba's arrest (she had been detained, as a "state guest" is how he described it in telegrams to friends) he knew few details at first. But he paid tribute to his wife's courage in an article entitled "Why Kasturba Gandhi?" which was published in *Harijan* on February 6, 1939:

> I had not intended to say anything about my wife having joined the Rajkot struggle. It had never occurred to me that she would. But she is and has been for years absolutely free to do what she likes. When she heard of the arrest of Maniben [Patel], she could not restrain herself. She felt a personal call ...
>
> The reader must realise my ancestral connection with Rajkot, and know that Kasturba is a daughter of Rajkot. [It] is no doubt an insignificant place on the map of India, but it is not insignificant for my wife and me ... The Rajkot struggle will be a stage forward in the fight for freedom. And when it ends in success, as it must sooner or later, Kasturba's share [in it] will count ... Satyagraha is a struggle in which the oldest and the weakest in body may take part, if they have stout hearts.

For almost a week, Ba was kept in solitary confinement, locked away in a dark, closet-like room of the Tramba bungalow. Apparently, the Thakore believed if she were left alone in strange surroundings with no contact with other human beings, she would be overwhelmed by fear and have second thoughts about the agitation she was leading. But the prince did not know Ba. She never wavered, never complained.

In Rajkot, meantime, word of Kasturba Gandhi's arrest had intensified protest and spawned fresh clashes. The agitation was evidently threatening enough to cause the Thakore to have second thoughts about his treatment of so famous a prisoner. Ba was not only released from solitary confinement, but her companions, Maniben Patel and Mridula Sarabhai, detained separately in Rajkot jails, were brought to Tramba to share her captivity in the royal bungalow. Though kept under guard at all times, they were allowed brief strolls outside on the grounds. Also, their mail privileges were restored, and Ba received the letters Bapu had been writing to her each day.

Despite the many reassurances contained in these brief daily messages, they reveal how apprehensive Mohandas was about the state of his wife's health (she had recently suffered several fainting spells), and the circumstances of her imprisonment. "I read about your transfer [to Tramba] in the newspapers," he wrote early on. "Stay free of care wherever you are placed. God is with you wherever you go." Then, a day or so later: "You are being put to a severe test. You must let me know the difficulties you face." He sent ashram news and greetings: "We all feel your absence." He offered encouragement: "Be brave now ... Do not feel uneasy." But he also worried constantly about her health: "What medicine would you want sent from here?" And another question: "The doctor now visits you there?"

When Bapu learned belatedly, on February 13, that Ba had been held in solitary confinement (for the first time in her life), he sent her the serene assurances of a seasoned veteran: "You have now had good experience of staying alone also. But I forget. When were you alone? Rama has always been with you. And when He is there, it does not matter whether others are or not." Yet a truer measure of Bapu's deep concern about Ba may have been expressed in his note to Maniben and Mridula, after he learned they had been sent to Tramba: "It is God's grace that you both are there," he wrote. "Blessings from Bapu."

Although he had not intended to be drawn into the struggle, Gandhi was now determined to visit Rajkot and confer with the Thakore in person — and not just about the ruler's reneging on his promises of reform, or even about his imprisonment of Kasturba and the other women. Mohandas had received reports that prisoners arrested, as dissidents in Rajkot were being so badly mistreated that many, in protest, had gone on hunger strikes.

Gandhi arrived in Rajkot on February 27. Early next morning, he went to two state jails where talks with prisoners convinced him that they had suffered severe and indefensible punishment. He also visited the royal bungalow in Tramba for a brief reunion with Kasturba and her companions.

Without doubt, the prince and his ministers were evasive connivers who would never yield ground nor honour their solemn pledges unless further pressure was applied. But if pressure involved a resumption of Patel's civil disobedience campaign, even more misery and repression would be visited on the people of Rajkot. The only option that seemed open to him, therefore, was one he dreaded to use — a fast unto death unless the Thakore agreed to negotiate in good faith. Gandhi so notified the prince, requesting a response by noon of March 3. He also sent a message to Delhi informing the viceroy, Lord Linlithgow, of the situation.

Suddenly, what had started as a minor conflict in a remote corner of India was about to become a full-scale political crisis.

No reply having arrived from the Thakore by midday, Gandhi began his fast on March 3, at the home where he was staying in Rajkot. After one of his favourite hymns was sung, he dictated a statement to the press. Then he dispatched Dr. Sushila Nayyar to Tramba with a message for Kasturba. His decision had been sudden, and he wanted to get word of the fast to his wife personally, to protect her from the shock she would suffer if she learned of it from news reports.

Kasturba was more grieved than shocked when Sushila Nayyar delivered Bapu's message. "I could at least have been warned that a fast was imminent," she said.

"But no one knew about it," the young doctor explained. "Bapu broke the news to us early this morning." Sushila then handed Ba the note Bapu had dictated to be delivered, once Ba knew of his fast.

"I hope you are all calm and collected," Bapu had written. "But if you cannot remain at peace there, you can come to me."

Kasturba didn't understand. But Sushila Nayyar explained that Bapu was wondering if Ba wanted him to ask the state authorities to allow her to be with him during the fast? It was up to her.

Now Ba was shocked. Bapu, of all people, must realise that asking for her release so she could be with him would go against the very principles of Satyagraha — no matter what the dangers of a fast.

"By no means," she declared. "I shall be quite content here, if they let me have daily news of him. God has taken care of him during all his previous trials, and will pull him safely through this, too."

Kasturba was quiet for a moment. Then she allowed herself one faint murmur of misgiving: "But is it possible he will expose himself to risk once too often?"

That same question was being asked in government offices all over India. Telegrams were flying between the provincial ministers and the viceroy and between the viceroy and the Thakore. By the time Gandhi's fast was in its third day, the decision about whether to ask for permission to join her husband was no longer Kasturba's to make.

On March 5, the Thakore's deputies (acting on their own after firm hints from the Paramount Power) freed Kasturba Gandhi from her imprisonment in the royal bungalow in Tramba, and escorted her to her husband's bedside in Rajkot.

"How did you get here?" Mohandas asked bluntly.

"Why, the government has released me," Ba was puzzled. Once again, Mohandas had surprised her — first he wanted her to come, now he seemed unhappy she was here.

"Then where are Maniben and Mridula?" he asked.

Only then did Kasturba realise that, in her growing anxiety about Bapu's condition, and her eagerness to be at his side, she had abandoned another responsibility.

"They are still in jail at Tramba," she replied.

"You can't forsake your colleagues," Mohandas reminded her.

"Of course not."

"What will you do then?" Bapu asked.

"I will go back to Tramba this evening," Ba said firmly.

"And what will you do if they refuse to arrest you again?"

Bapu seemed to be enjoying the teasing and testing. Ba knew that was a good sign, and she was not to be outdone.

"I shall sit outside the palace all night if they don't allow me in."

They were relaxed now — two proud old veterans, happy with themselves and each other, enjoying the familiar banter.

Ba returned to Tramba that evening at her own request. The guards at the bungalow obliged by taking her in for the night, but next morning Kasturba, Maniben, and Mridula were all released.

On the following day, March 7 an agreement was reached. The Thakore gave amnesty to all prisoners arrested during the protests, and agreed to appoint a political reform committee, just as originally pledged. Mohandas then ended his fast, and he and Kasturba returned to Sevagram. But the final chapter was not written until years later. In 1956, with the help of the Gandhi National Memorial Trust, the Thakore of Rajkot's summer residence (the very bungalow where Ba was imprisoned for her role in the Rajkot Satyagraha campaign) was converted into a women's medical centre known as Kasturba Arogyadham or Health Clinic. Offering a variety of services, including a maternal and child health centre, a tuberculosis clinic, and mobile health units equipped to take medical and educational programs to surrounding villages, the Kasturba Arogyadham is still operating today — one of several active memorials to Kasturba Gandhi in existence around the world.

# 27

Kasturba's health had frequently been a matter of concern. But she had a remarkable capacity to respond to treatment and recuperate rapidly. Not so, however, after her return from Rajkot. In the succeeding weeks Ba fought coughs and colds, suffered malaria and was so frail and listless that Mohandas became truly worried. She obviously needed medical attention, yet he must first persuade her to accept it. Sushila Nayyar, in whom Ba had great faith, was now in Delhi completing post-graduate studies in medicine; Bapu knew that Ba wouldn't dream of asking her to interrupt her education again. However, there was a solution. Devadas and Lakshmi lived in Delhi, and Ba always enjoyed spending time with her little grandchildren.

Mohandas sent telegrams to Sushila and Devadas, explaining Ba's condition. When they met Ba's train, Sushila was appalled that Kasturba was travelling alone at her age and in her physical condition. How could Bapu do that, she asked. Kasturba explained:

"It was nothing," she said. "I was put on the train by Mahadev at the Wardha station and the other passengers agreed to help me if I needed any assistance. So why should I need an escort?" Ba's travel arrangements had clearly been her own idea.

In Delhi Ba stayed with her son and daughter-in-law, and Sushila dropped by two or three times a day to examine her. With rest and treatment Ba improved rapidly. Once she was feeling stronger, Ba began to miss the simplicity and community of the ashram and the morning and evening prayers, which were not sung at Devadas' home.

One day Ba asked Sushila Nayyar if she could stay with her in her dormitory for a few days so they could recite the prayers together, just as they did at Sevagram. Sushila agreed. It was summer, a hot, dry season in Delhi; the heat in Sushila's hostel room was so intense that Ba could not sleep. To cool the room, Sushila poured water on the cement floor and left the fan on all night at full speed. A few days later, Ba was struck by bronchial pneumonia. She was moved back to the comfort of Devadas' home, where, after many days of intensive care she began to recover.

Mohandas sent daily telegrams inquiring after Ba's health, and wrote long and loving letters to Ba herself. After they were read aloud to her, Kasturba kept the letters under her pillow. In moments of solitude she would take the most recent letter, put on her steel-rimmed glasses, and read the words over and over again. Everyone agreed it was Bapu's letters more than anything else that brought her back to health.

She was now impatient to return to Sevagram. However, this time Devadas insisted that he, Lakshmi, and their three children would go with her.

Kasturba quickly got back to her normal routine. Later that summer, she joined Mohandas on a short tour of the Northwest Frontier provinces to help strengthen Hindu-Muslim unity. She agreed to take Sushila along to monitor her health. By the time they returned to Sevagram, Ba seemed fully recovered, not only from her most recent illness, but also from the lingering aftermath of her Rajkot imprisonment. Bapu, for the first time in months, felt relieved.

The moment couldn't have been more opportune. The world and Mahatma Gandhi were caught in a cataclysm of violent change. World War II became inevitable.

Looking back, I realise that Bapu could muster little time to spend with us children. He was constantly meeting with visitors, writing or dictating to his assistants, or going away for a few days. But whenever Bapu was at Sevagram, I could count on one thing. After sundown, around 6:15, he took an evening walk, and Ba often went too. I always tagged along, staying as close to my grandparents as possible, for I had found this was a good time to ask questions. On his walks, Bapu had time to answer me patiently, but if I pestered him during the day when he was conducting serious business, my questions did not seem so welcome. He never lost his temper or asked me to leave, but he never ignored me either. Instead, he would quietly put his arm around my shoulder, place his palm over my mouth, and go on talking to his visitors.

There were no such problems getting Ba's attention. She spent hours with us sharing our afternoon naps, inviting us to help in the kitchen, and finding just the right task for every child. But the highlight of each day came when chores were done, and a group of children — as many of us as could crowd onto the verandah of Ba's hut — gathered to hear her tell stories.

The routine was always the same. First, Ba would offer us treats — soft, sweet, chewy balls of jaggery, a concoction made from molasses and ghee and crushed roasted peanuts, which she made for us everyday. Then, she would sit on a mat on the floor and we would jostle to crowd around her. Ba's voice was soft, very soothing, but her stories were magical and captivating. We did not want to miss one word.

All too soon, it was time for us to return to South Africa. Though I was too young to fathom the unspoken fears surrounding our wartime parting in early spring of 1941, I sensed how hard it was for the adults. Still, I remember no tears, no long faces. What I took home with me was a lasting memory of parents and grandparents who, even in times of stress, could be calm and loving and playful.

I confirmed that childhood impression recently, when I re-read the brief tribute Sushila Gandhi prepared in 1944, as a daughter-in-law's contribution to the Kasturba Gandhi Memorial Number of *Indian Opinion*. In one passage, my mother recalled the mood at Sevagram as we prepared to leave. While Ba was showering us with attention, going out of her way to express her love, my mother was being just as solicitous in turn, trying to anticipate Ba's every need:

A few days before our departure, Bapu jokingly began to chide Ba "Why not give up this ashram," he asked, "and settle in a big comfortable bungalow with our sons, their wives, and our grandchildren? Then you can rest, lord it over your daughters-in-law, and they will serve you." Then he turned to me. "And you, Sushila, I see you devoting most of your time to serving Ba. How has she bribed you for that?" I replied in the same mischievous spirit. "By serving you, Bapu, I would be fortunate to get a few strands of yarn spun by you, but I know Ba will reward me substantially." Bapu laughed heartily, and left us.

Later, as I was packing, Ba quietly brought me her farewell gift made just for me — a delicate white sari woven from cotton yarn hand spun by her. But Bapu, seeing my surprise, was not to be outdone. "Do you know," he asked with his most impish smile, "that I spun half that yarn?"

At the time America declared war on Japan, following the attack on Pearl Harbour on December 7, 1941, more than 20,000 political detainees were languishing in Indian jails. Many had been imprisoned for over a year for participating in a limited civil disobedience campaign Gandhi had launched the previous winter to demand immediate independence for India. Based on individual acts of Satyagraha, rather than mass demonstrations, the protest had been designed to increase pressure on an unresponsive British government.

After Japan entered the war and posed a threat to South Asia, Britain unilaterally committed India, and other countries of her Empire, to the war. The leaders and the people of India were not even nominally consulted. It created a great deal of dissatisfaction leading to the Congress Working Committee, meeting at Wardha, to pass a "Quit India" resolution. In order to become a willing partner in the British war effort, the resolution declared, all India must feel "the glow of freedom", and it warned that unless British rule ended immediately, Congress would "reluctantly be compelled to start a mass civil disobedience movement, under the leadership of Mahatma Gandhi." The final decision on this momentous issue would be left to the All-India Congress Committee, summoned to meet in Bombay in early August.

For the next three weeks, tensions built. Mohandas said: "Leave India to God ... Or to anarchy." That was his advice for the British. But Mohandas, optimist that he was, did not really believe that the end of British rule would plunge India into anarchy. Writing in *Harijan*, he predicted that India's leaders, when faced with real responsibility, would unite and form a provisional government to see their country through any emergency.

William E. Fisher, a correspondent of *Life* magazine, was invited to stay for the evening meal, and there he met Gandhi's wife for the first time. The *Life* reporter's description of an aging (and once again ailing) Kasturba is a moving one:

... She sat next to him [Gandhi], a tragic shrivelled-up little creature, eating some special tonic preparations. I was told she had been very ill, this being one of the first meals she had taken with the others for a long time. She had, I think, one of the most beautiful faces I ever saw, a face filled with devotion and kindness. Gentle and enduring spirit seemed to shine through her wrinkles.

When Mohandas and his entourage left for Bombay on August 2,

1942, Kasturba was well enough to go with them. She faced no great hardship, for the whole group stayed at a spacious mansion owned by industrialist G. D. Birla on Nepean Sea Road. Birla, a follower of the Mahatma for some twenty years, had made his residences in various cities available to the Gandhis, as needed.

For the next few days, the entire country waited nervously for the All-India Congress Committee's deliberations to begin. In Delhi, Dr. Sushila Nayyar had been reading reports, hearing rumours, and growing more and more apprehensive about the outcome. On August 4, she met a friend in Government employment who told her orders had been issued for the arrest of Mohandas and other Congress leaders.

Sushila panicked: concerned about Bapu, and even more about Ba, she asked the dean of the medical school for leave of absence and caught the first train to Bombay. When Sushila arrived at Birla House her brother Pyarelal and Mohandas were at a meeting. Everyone was surprised to see her.

"I heard everyone was going to be arrested," the young doctor explained, "and I didn't want to be left out."

Ba was impatient with her. "These battles are going to go on and on," she said, "you should not interrupt your studies because of rumours."

Mohandas, too, was unworried, confident he would not be arrested, even though some of his remarks at the opening session on Friday, August 7, came close to calling for open rebellion. At one point he to Congress members, "Here is a mantra, a short one, I give to you ... 'Do or Die.' We shall either free India or die in the attempt."

Back at Birla House next morning, Sunday, August 9, the whole party awoke at 4.00am for their routine morning prayers. Mahadev Desai complained he had not had time to sleep.

"Why, what was the matter?" Bapu asked.

"The telephones were ringing constantly," Mahadev replied. "Everyone wanted to know whether you had been arrested."

Mohandas laughed. "The government is not so foolish as to arrest the man who is their best friend in India today."

As soon as morning prayers were over, about 5.00am, a servant told Mahadev the police were waiting to talk with him. "So the rumours are true," he thought.

A few minutes later he hurried back to Bapu's room and announced, "They have come to take you."

"So?" Bapu seemed surprised. "How much time do we have?" "Half an hour," Mahadev replied.

"Are we all being taken?"

"No. They have warrants only for you, me, and Mirabehn."

"Good," Mohandas said. "Then we must get ready quickly." While those arrested collected a few belongings, everyone gathered to chant another round of prayers — Kasturba most fervently of all. Though apprehensive about being separated from Bapu again, Ba knew where her duty lay. She asked God to protect her husband and to give her strength to carry on his struggle.

Just before going down to present himself to the police, Mohandas called Pyarelal aside and dictated a message to the country:

> Let every non-violent soldier of freedom write out the slogan "Do or Die" on a piece of paper and pin it on his clothes, so that in case he died in the course of offering Satyagraha, he might be distinguished by that sign from others who do not subscribe to non-violence.

News of Mahatma Gandhi's arrest raced like wildfire through Bombay and across India. Hundreds of people thronged to the gardens of Birla House, spilling over into the streets. Kasturba, forgetting the weakness caused by her recent illness, kept busy all morning, talking to people, offering comfort, giving instructions. Though her face showed signs of strain — she had no idea where her husband and the others had been taken — her spirit was strong.

"Bapuji was to address a mass meeting at Shivaji Park this evening," someone reminded them. Another said, "I hear the place is already filled with people. With Bapu in jail, what can we do?"

To everyone's surprise, Kasturba was the first to speak up. "There is no need to despair," she said. "I will address the meeting."

The group was caught completely off guard. For as long as anyone could remember, Ba had acted quietly, doing her work without fuss, avoiding the limelight. But here she was, boldly offering to take her husband's place and speak out before hundreds of thousands of his aroused followers. Did she have the physical and mental stamina to undertake so demanding a task? And wouldn't she be arrested, too?

From those close to her came protests. "It is too dangerous," they argued. "Your health won't stand another imprisonment."

"Nonsense," Kasturba said. "Do you expect me to stay outside of prison when the whole nation is being locked up inside?"

It was decided that Ba should go to the mass meeting, accompanied by Dr. Sushila Nayyar. If they were arrested, they would go to jail together and Sushila could look after her.

Now it was Kasturba's turn to dictate a message. Speaking thoughtfully, using the simple, personal, unadorned language that had long since endeared her to the people of India, she had Sushila write down the words she intended to say that evening at the meeting:

Gandhiji poured out his heart to you for two hours at the All-India Congress meeting last night. What can I add to that? All that remains for us is to live up to his ideals. The women of India have to prove their mettle. They should all join in this struggle, regardless of caste or creed. Truth and nonviolence must be our watchwords.

At a quarter to five that Sunday evening, Kasturba descended the great staircase at Birla House, ready to be driven to Shivaji Park, about fifteen miles north of the city. At the foot of the stairs, one of her nephews, Kanu Gandhi, waited with some hurriedly made badges. He stepped forward to pin one on Ba's sari.

"What is this?" she asked.

"It is the 'Do or Die' badge that Bapu asked all volunteers to wear," Kanu explained.

Ba smiled at him. "But this mantra is imprinted on my heart," she said. "Why should I need a paper badge to remind me?"

Kasturba stepped out onto the portico, followed by Sushila Nayyar and several others. An Indian police officer was waiting.

"Mother," he said respectfully. "Please don't go. They will arrest you."

"How can any mother stay at home," she asked, "when her sons and daughters are being persecuted by the British?"

She turned — a tiny, dignified figure, holding herself very erect — and walked toward the car that was waiting to take her to Shivaji Park.

The police officer followed. He was instructed to arrest everyone leaving Birla House, but obviously had no heart to arrest Kasturba. He made one last plea.

"Mother, please don't go," he said and then let the car pass. He decided to let someone else do the dirty work. He loved Ba like his own mother and he was not about to arrest her and send her to prison.

Ba reached Shivaji Park where an estimated hundred thousand people waited patiently for someone to address them. When Ba walked up to the rostrum and delivered her moving address they went wild with emotions. There was thunderous applause.

The police quietly whisked her and Sushila away to prison. They were unprepared for Ba's arrest. They took Ba to the Arthur Road Prison in Bombay.

In the car Sushila saw that Kasturba was exhausted. She felt her pulse and forehead and decided Ba had a slight fever. Then she noticed that tears were gleaming in Ba's eyes, something she had seldom seen before.

"What is it, Ba?" Sushila asked.

For a long moment Ba remained silent. She was gazing out of the window of the police car, studying everything and everybody she saw with lingering tenderness. At last, turning to Sushila, she said, "I have a feeling I will not come out alive."

Sushila felt a chill down her spine. "Why do you say such things, Ba?"

"It's nothing," Ba replied, "just a feeling. But perhaps this British government wants all of us dead, anyway."

As she and Ba were being escorted into the Arthur Road Jail, Sushila saw busy pedestrians going about their daily tasks or hurrying home to an evening meal. No one even suspected that Ba would be brought to this jail.

Suddenly, in her despair, Sushila wanted to cry out at them.

"What's the matter with you people?" she wanted to shout. "Don't you see who this is? Don't you recognise Ba?"

# 28

When plans were being made for the internment of Mohandas Gandhi in 1942 the British were apprehensive about his frail health, a legacy of frequent fasts and lengthy incarcerations. They feared the 73-year-old Mahatma might not survive another imprisonment. Seeking a secluded place where he might be detained in comfort while a retinue of doctors and officials kept an eye on him, they concluded that the Aga Khan Palace was ideal. It was big, properly walled, and standing in resplendent solitude amid lush rice and vegetable fields, 12 miles outside the city of Poona. The wealthy old Aga Khan, potentate of the Ismaili Bohra sect of Islam, was living in Switzerland during the war years, and agreed without objection to the appropriation of his Poona property for the duration. Thus, Gandhi and his colleagues, after their arrest at Birla House, were taken directly to the Aga Khan Palace. Though this was called a Palace, it was a Palace only in size. The rooms were bare in keeping with prison regulations.

However, no such advance arrangements had been made for the imprisonment of the Mahatma's wife. In deed, the authorities had not intended to arrest Kasturba at all. Convinced that she was too old, tired and weak to pose a significant threat to the Empire, they were wholly unprepared for her spirited show of defiance. When she and Dr. Sushila Nayyar were picked up on the evening of August 9, the police had received no instruction to transport them to the Aga Khan Palace, nor had their arrival at Arthur Road Prison in central Bombay been anticipated. The two women were escorted to a dark, dank cell reserved for prostitutes or petty thieves. A stench that the young doctor identified as gas from leaking sewage pipes pervaded the cell. Soon, they were provided with iron cots, dirty mattresses made from coconut husks and even dirtier bed covers. Appalled, Sushila returned the sheets, but kept the mattresses and spread Ba's own small smooth mat over the one issued to her.

They spent a restless night. Kasturba, falling victim to a severe attack of diarrhoea, awoke several times and had to grope her way to the toilet. By morning, she was miserable. Sushila asked the prison doctor for medicine and some fruit to replace the coarse jail diet. Such amenities were not provided to prisoners, he said. Sushila then requested permission to telephone and ask a friend to bring the items Ba needed. The doctor said, "Our orders are that you are to have no direct contact with the outside world." Only after protracted discussion did he agree to send some medicine and fruit from the hospital. Two apples arrived late that evening — nothing else.

The following morning they were allowed to move their beds on to a veranda where Kasturba could rest more comfortably. Another prisoner, a young woman new to the movement, was arrested and brought to Arthur Road prison. She was overawed that her fellow-inmate was Kasturba. Then she was aghast when she learned that Ba was ailing for want of medicine; she gave the jailer all the money she had with her, asking that it be used to buy the required remedies. After that, Ba's condition began to improve.

Prison officials debated whether Kasturba Gandhi should be shifted to the Aga Khan Palace. The question remained undecided, since orders for any transfer of prisoners had to come from authorities in Delhi. Late the next evening Ba and Sushila were told they must be ready to leave Arthur Road Prison within two hours, but no one would tell them where they were going.

Shortly after midnight, the two women were loaded into a van, driven to a nearby railroad station, and hustled onto a train. When they disembarked a few hours later, they found themselves at the platform of Poona station, and assumed that the waiting police car would take them to the familiar Yeravda Jail. Kasturba's mood suddenly brightened. Mohandas was no doubt being held at Yeravda. But, much to her disappointment, the automobile headed out into the countryside.

Thirty minutes later they pulled up at the gates of a large two-storey brick building surrounded by high walls topped with barbed wire. Military guards admitted them into the handsomely landscaped grounds. Only then did they learn from the police inspector on duty that this was the Aga Khan Palace, now serving as a prison for Mohandas Gandhi and others arrested with him.

Ba's heart was racing with excitement as the car parked by the veranda where a servant was busy sweeping. Though weak and tired from the journey, Kasturba climbed out eagerly.

"Which is Bapu's room?" she asked the man sweeping the veranda.

The man recognising Kasturba bowed politely and said, "The one at the end."

Followed by Sushila, Ba entered the designated room, Mohandas and Mahadev Desai were seated on the floor engrossed in paperwork. Then Mahadev looked up and an instant smile of pleasure lighted his face. But Bapu, always a stickler for the rules, wanted to know:

"Did you ask the authorities to send you here?"

"Certainly not," Kasturba said indignantly. "I didn't even know where you were." Then, in a flash, she realised that his sharp question had been prompted by deep anxiety. Knowing nothing of what had happened after his arrest, Bapu obviously thought that she, in her determination to join him in prison, had not only disregarded the poor state of her own health (ever one of his prime concerns), but had also asked for special treatment, a violation of all Satyagraha principles.

"Don't worry," Ba said soothingly, "I made no requests."

"We were arrested," Sushila interjected. "We spent the last two days in Arthur Road jail."

"And the government brought us here of their own accord," Ba added.

Mohandas relaxed, then smiled. Soon, a guard appeared and led Kasturba and Sushila off to be officially registered as prisoners.

Infused with new energy, now that she knew Bapu was well, Ba insisted on carrying her own luggage, a small bag, to her assigned room next to Bapu's.

Very soon with regular medicine and healthy food, Ba's strength was restored. She was the first to rise for morning prayers and joined Bapu in his evening walks around the grounds.

Wanting to spend her time fruitfully Ba turned her attention to her husband's schedule. But Ba could do little to help with the work that kept Bapu busy most of the day. She would supervise the gardeners, sometimes go into the kitchen and teach the staff how to cook some of the dishes that Bapu liked. She was never at a loose end.

Then, on August 14, it was announced that Colonel M. G. Bhandari, Inspector General of Prisons, would visit the Aga Khan Palace next day. Ba joined in the flurry of preparations to spruce up the prison.

Sweepers were out early on the morning of August 15, racing against time to get the whole yard swept clean before the Inspector General arrived. Guards paced nervously up and down; prison officials seemed to be everywhere. Gardeners did last minute pruning, and Kasturba and Sarojini Naidu arranged bouquets of fresh-cut flowers for each room. Only Mohandas — who pointed out that Colonel Bhandari was coming to inspect prison arrangements, not prisoners — chose not to alter his routine. Bapu was in his room getting his morning massage when Mahadev, Ba, and the others hurried out onto the veranda to greet the arriving Colonel.

Mahadev, stepped forward and stretched out his hand to welcome the Colonel but collapsed to the floor. He clutched at his chest, gasped for breath and lost consciousness. Momentarily, everyone, including Colonel Bhandari, seemed immobilised by shock.

Kasturba was the first to act. She called out to Dr. Sushila Nayyar.

"Sushila! Come quickly! Mahadev is unconscious."

Sushila hurried out, not sure she had heard correctly. There was Mahadev, lying on the veranda floor. She searched for his pulse, but found none; his heartbeat was faint, his breathing spasmodic. She got her medicine bag and tried to revive him with an injection.

Mohandas arrived then, Kasturba at his side. He knelt by Mahadev's prostrate form, calling his name.

Ba cried out: "Mahadev, Mahadev — Bapu is calling you."

It was no use. The gentle man who for 25 years had been Gandhi's indispensable aide and trusted confidant, was dead.

A pall of gloom settled over the palace. The mourners could not hold back their tears. The flowers that had decorated the rooms were now decorating Mahadev's lifeless body. A few hours later he was cremated on the grounds of Aga Khan Palace.

Mohandas believed it was only fitting that his colleague, a prisoner in life, be a prisoner in death also — a symbol of his country's desire for freedom. The ceremony was an intimate one. There was no time to summon Mahadev's wife or his children; only those who were there at the palace attended.

As the last embers consumed the body, Sushila heard Ba murmuring to herself, repeating over and over an anguished question: "Why did you take Mahadev and not me?" Life changed, subtly yet disturbingly, for the detainees in Aga Khan Palace following Mahadev's death. The sudden loss of their comrade took a great toll on their spirits. And with each passing day they felt more isolated, more invisible.

They were not permitted newspapers at first, but that order was revoked in response to one of Bapu's letters of complaint. Only then did they learn that news of Gandhi's arrest had triggered widespread riots throughout India. They were allowed no visitors, and their correspondence was subject to rigid censorship. The prisoners could send letters only "to close relatives on domestic matters".

As their frustrations mounted, so, too, did their irritability and restlessness, apathy, and finally, despair. Bapu, with more jail time than the others, recognised the symptoms: they were experiencing paralysing despondency. The best cure for this malady was to be occupied every moment of the day. He worked out timetables for the entire group — activities that would keep them busy every minute of the day.

Mohandas and Kasturba, imprisoned together in their 61st year of married life, agreed to revive the long-abandoned educational project.

Over the years Ba had picked up a smattering knowledge of English, and had learned to read simple Gujarati, her native language. Now Bapu scheduled daily writing lessons. He introduced her to basic geography (using an orange as a globe), and read and discussed with her several books on the subject of history. One hour each day was reserved for study of the *Gita*, many sections of which Ba already knew by heart.

Kasturba enjoyed this regimen tremendously, anticipating her lessons more eagerly each day. But, at 73, memorising or remembering lessons was proving more difficult.

"The long bouts of illness have numbed my brain," she lamented.

One day Mohandas found a fourth-grade Gujarati reader filled with poetry. Knowing Ba's love of music, he improvised a way to help her memorise some of the poems, which could be sung to a beat. Every evening before prayers, the two of them would sit together on the veranda, singing poetry. It was a cheerful touching sight.

Then one day a careless statement made by Mohandas caused the lessons to come to an abrupt end. Though Kasturba had learned to write her writing was still immature. Mohandas felt this was a good time to get her to practice her writing skills. In the modified work schedule he included an hour of writing.

To conserve paper Kasturba plodded with her writing skills on a slate. One day she learned that a prisoner could requisition notebooks from the prison authorities.

"Can you get me a notebook," she asked Mohandas at an inopportune moment Bapu was unhappy with the way things were shaping up. Indian politicians were ignoring his advice, which meant the future of the country was not going to be moulded in the image he had in mind. To add to these tensions Ba had not done her lessons correctly.

"I'll get you a notebook when you learn to write properly. Until then you must use the slate," Mohandas said caustically.

This remark cut Kasturba to the bone. She quietly placed her slate on Mohandas' table, and said resolutely, "I am done with my lessons for life, thank you." She then walked out of the room. He tried to make amends but it was too late. A few days later Pyarelal tried to soothe her ruffled feelings by giving her a notebook as a gift. Ba knew where it came from. She took the notebook and placed it on Bapu's desk, saying, "What does an illiterate like me need a notebook for?"

That was the end of the educational programme. She never picked up her slate again, in spite of numerous apologies tendered by Mohandas. That notebook — a grim reminder of his indiscretion — remained in Grandfather's possession till the day he died.

One day as Mohandas worked, Ba appeared in his room and asked what he was writing. She seldom inquired about such matters.

"A letter to the viceroy," Mohandas explained. "The British have been spreading falsehoods about the 'Quit India' movement," he added.

"What kind of falsehoods?" Ba asked.

"They are telling people that the 'Quit India' movement was seeking a violent overthrow of the British Administration. They are trying to find sympathy for their repression at home and abroad," Mohandas explained. He was intrigued by Kastur's curiosity since she hardly ever showed interest in political affairs. He was patient and explained the details of British propaganda and its effects on the people around the world.

"As you know we were all arrested even before we could launch the struggle, so how do they conclude that we were planning violence?" he said.

"I hope this does not mean you will go on another fast," Ba's anxiety was unmistakable. "Remember, you are not getting younger and these fasts take a heavy toll on your health."

Bapu burst into laughter. "You worry unnecessarily. But how did you conclude that I will go on a fast?"

"After so many years, how could I not know?" she answered. "I think I know you better than you think."

Kasturba said no more. She knew Mohandas would do what he had to do. She had no doubt that he was in the right. As a dutiful, doting wife she expressed her genuine concern about his health, but if a fast were the only recourse against the British propaganda then she would support her husband to the hilt.

However, the others in the palace prison were alarmed to learn that Mohandas might embark on another fast. Later that day some of them tried to reason with him. Dr. Sushila Nayyar, the medical adviser to the ashram family, pointed out that the last time Mohandas had fasted, in 1939, his condition had become grave within five days. Since then he had grown older, the hardships of prison life had sapped his energy, making the possibility of his withstanding such an ordeal very doubtful.

Bapu rejected all her arguments. Dr. Nayyar tried a different approach; did Bapu think Ba, in her delicate state of health, could endure the strain of worrying about him if he undertook another long fast? He dismissed that idea, too.

"None of you know Ba as well as I do," Bapu said. "She has tremendous strength. She will bear the strain better than any of you."

In the end, however, Bapu agreed temporarily to put aside his letter to the viceroy. He would seek God's guidance, he said, and obey His call. For the next week, he sat quietly for half an hour each day, lost in meditation, while everyone anxiously awaited the outcome.

"It is good Bapu has agreed to listen to the command of God," Sarojini Naidu said one afternoon. "In his present state of health, even God will not ask him to fast."

"I agree," Ba replied. "But don't forget one thing — it is he who is going to translate God's command."

She was right. God's approval was never in doubt. But Mohandas wanted Kasturba's approval, too, and he got it. Just before he revealed his decision they were closeted together in his room for almost an hour. Then Ba emerged to dumbfound them all with the statement that she, too, was now convinced that fasting was the only way Bapu could protest the government's false accusations.

The three-week fast got underway on February 10, 1943. Kasturba and Mohandas began the day together with a morning walk to the spot where Mahadev Desai had been cremated; they said a short prayer, left a garland of flowers, then returned to the palace.

Kasturba had announced that she would honour Mohandas' fast, as she always did, by limiting her own diet to one meal of fruit and milk each day. Everyone protested, but it took Bapu himself to dissuade her. She agreed to take two meals of fruit and milk a day, insisting it was only to keep up her strength so she could minister to Mohandas.

During his first two days of fasting, Bapu was active and in good spirits. On the third day, he was much weaker. Dr. Manchershah Gilder, a government physician who had treated Gandhi for high blood pressure, was transferred to Aga Khan Palace to take care of Bapu. By day six, Mohandas' condition had further deteriorated.

Ba, seated beside his cot throughout the day, suggested adding a few drops of lemon juice to the water to make it more palatable.

"No, not now," Mohandas replied. The vigil continued.

As Gandhi's fast moved into the second week, news from the Aga Khan Palace could no longer be suppressed. All India was seized by intense anxiety. Crowds gathered daily outside the palace gates to keep watch. Three Indian members of the Viceroy's Council, appointed because of their pro-government, anti-Congress views, resigned after calling for the Mahatma's immediate release. The government was bombarded with similar demands from near and far. Playwright George Bernard Shaw was, predictably, both flippant and blunt: "The King should release Gandhi unconditionally, and apologise to him for the mental defectiveness of his cabinet." But authorities in Delhi and London, their attitudes hardening under duress, ignored all criticism and renewed their harsh rhetoric. Viceroy Linlithgow called Gandhi's fast "political blackmail with no moral justification", while Prime Minister Churchill, himself never one to mince words, was reported to have said, "Let him starve, if he insists."

Still, some concessions had to be made. Gandhi's sons, Ramdas and Devadas, recently released from prison themselves, were allowed a short visit. Then, in a surprise move, the government opened the palace gates to all. Hundreds of people poured into the grounds and silently passed by Mohandas' room. They saw their leader asleep on a cot, his breathing laboured, but they went away assured that his spirit was still unyielding. Kasturba greeted everyone who filed by. She was rewarded by the sight of many beloved faces, including those of several of her grandchildren.

By mid-morning on the 13th day, Mohandas was sinking rapidly. His heart action was feeble, his skin was clammy, his kidneys were failing. Attending doctors, in their daily communiqué, predicted his life would end before nightfall if the fast continued.

Instead of sitting by her husband's bedside as usual, Kasturba had been out on the veranda since early morning, in silent prayer before a sacred tulsi plant. Her eyes were closed, her expression serene, she was oblivious to people passing by. Sushila Nayyar and Mirabehn, watching from the doorway of the room where Mohandas lay near death, were moved almost to tears by the sight of Kasturba in such trustful communion with the Almighty in whom she had total faith. Sushila's medical training told her that the miracle Ba was praying for was the only thing that could save Bapu now.

On impulse, the young doctor moved to Mohandas' bed, bent down, and whispered, "Is it not time to add fruit juice to the water?"

His eyelids fluttered; almost imperceptibly, he nodded. Sushila raced to the kitchen. She ordered two ounces of orange juice, mixed it with four ounces of water, and hurried back to Bapu. Very slowly, she began offering him tiny sips of the liquid.

That was the sight that greeted Kasturba when, tranquil and assured, she walked into the room. Nobody had to tell Ba what Bapu was drinking. She had known he would not die.

From that day on, Gandhi's nausea disappeared. He became alert, almost cheerful; his condition, despite continuing exhaustion, remained stable. On March 2, his 20th day of fasting, palace gates were opened to the public for the last time. Prison officials announced that no outside observers, other than the Mahatma's sons, would be admitted next day when he broke his fast. To their surprise, Mohandas flatly rejected that concession, saying he and his wife had agreed that if the public could not witness the end of the fast, there was no need for their sons to be there, either.

And so, on the morning March 3, 1943, only detainees and prison attendants were present when Ba, performing the familiar ritual one more time, gave Bapu a glass of undiluted orange juice, and sat quietly at his side for the 20 minutes it took him to drink it.

Throughout the fast, Kasturba had somehow found energy to keep going all day, every day, often refusing to rest. But once the fast ended and Mohandas was on the mend, Ba's strength began to fade. On March 16, she had an attack of breathlessness and coughing that lasted for two hours. Another, a week later, lasted four hours. In the Aga Khan Palace, concern about Bapu's health gave way to new worries about Ba's health. There could be no doubt — she had a serious heart ailment, and prospects for her recovery were uncertain.

Thanks to Bapu's dogged persistence, the government (which had earlier taken pains to deny "a rumour circulating in some quarters that Mrs. Gandhi is dead") finally granted permission for Ba's sons to visit her regularly.

But it was Ba herself who arranged for a more distant relative, their 15-year-old grandniece Manu Gandhi, to join them at the palace. A great-granddaughter of Mohandas' beloved Uncle Tulsidas Gandhi,

Manu had been jailed during the "Quit India" demonstrations. But before that, she had lived at Sevagram ashram for three years following the death of her mother, and Ba had come to regard her as her own granddaughter. At Ba's urging, Sushila Nayyar and Dr. Gilder notified Colonel Bhandari that Kasturba required a full-time nurse-companion — someone like Manu Gandhi, "who can speak her language and is known to her personally."

Colonel Bhandari needed no further prompting; he had held Ba in high regard since their first meeting on the day of Mahadev Desai's death. Cutting through red tape, he had Manu Gandhi transferred from her prison in Nagpur to the Aga Khan Palace in the last spring of 1943. It was a timely move, arriving just as Kasturba was stricken with a mild attack of bronchial pneumonia; the girl proved to be an excellent nurse and a devoted companion. Sooner than anyone had expected, Ba was well enough to resume her daily rounds.

This was the first time anyone realised that Kasturba was keenly interested in games — she wanted to play them all. However, her first feeble attempts to hit a ping pong ball, let alone a badminton shuttlecock, across a net convinced her that these games were far too strenuous, so she sat on the veranda and watched others play. But Carrom was less demanding. Ba joined the group one day, and quickly became such a Carrom enthusiast that Mirabehn would find her practicing in advance for the daily games. Ba was a stickler for fair play, never taking her eyes off the board when the game was in progress. She was also surprisingly competitive. The others, to please her, sometimes tried to arrange for her to win, usually in the final round. But Ba quickly realised what was happening and put a stop to it. They weren't playing fair.

Despite visits from Devadas and Ramdas, Harilal, whom she hadn't seen for many months, was achingly present in her thoughts and prayers. So, too, was Manilal. Her letters to Phoenix Settlement, usually dictated to Manu, became more frequent. I was surprised to find, tucked away in the folder of Bapu's letters which my mother gave to me before her death in 1988, several notes Ba had written to my parents from Aga Khan Palace.

Each letter was full of reassurances: "I am well. Do not worry. We live as God keeps us." Or, "We have received your photograph. Do not know when we will meet, but seeing your picture was soothing." Or, "Sushila, Pyarelal, Mirabehn, etc., are well, and Bapuji is well, too." And, again, in a special message from her daughter-in-law Sushila: "Everybody at your mother's place [in Akola] is also well." The letters always contained a hurried roll call of family names with brief updates: "Devadas visits us often." "Ramdas [with his family in Nagpur] writes that everybody is well there." "Rami [Harilal's daughter] was here." "Lakshimi writes to me when I write to her." "Kashiben [wife of Chaganlal Gandhi] writes often." And in each letter, unfailingly, Ba begged for news of her grandchildren: "What is Ela doing?" "Happy to know Sita and Arun are busy studying." "Ela must have started running by now." "Do write about Arun's studies." "Does Sita know Gujarati? If she does, do make her write to me."

Kasturba was obviously well informed about events in South Africa. Several of her letters refer to some legal and political problems my father was having in that summer of 1943, troubles brought on, apparently, by his editorials in *Indian Opinion*: "We learned that Manilal's life was threatened recently. It worries me, but what more can I write? I know you are brave." In her next letter, Ba asked, "Have you decided not to mention the name of the person who has sued you in the newspaper? Let us know what happens."

I felt a gratifying sense of intimacy to find that Ba had made a brief allusion, in a letter dated August 2, 1943, to one of my most vivid childhood memories — our family's labours (just then underway) to build a new house at Phoenix Settlement. And I was especially interested to see that my grandmother had addressed this letter, like several others, to my mother alone, for it exemplifies the durable bonds of understanding that linked Kasturba to her daughters-in-law:

Dear Sushila

We have heard about the verdict ... Even if you have lost the case do not lose heart. Hope you are facing it with courage [and] others around you are giving all their support to Manilal. Bapuji says this is nothing new for a publisher.

Do write to me if Manilal is much hurt by this, because I am worried this adds to your expenses, which have increased because of the addition to the press building and construction of the new house. You must have suffered also, but you are understanding, and you must be a great help to Manilal ...

Bapuji's and Ba's blessings to all of you.

October 2, 1943 was to be Mohandas' second consecutive birthday in prison. To give themselves something to do, his fellow detainees at the Aga Khan Palace decided to decorate the dining room with lights and bunting, and have a celebration. Kasturba, seized by the excitement of the moment, was eager to participate.

As the date drew near, however, she became frantic about one thing. Somewhere at Sevagram, she had a red-bordered cotton sari made from yarn spun by Mohandas, which she had carefully put away with instructions that when she died, her body should be draped in it before cremation. Now, she wanted desperately to wear that treasured sari in honour of Bapu's birthday. Ba sent a note to the ashram asking that it be sent to her. But none of the residents still free and living at Sevagram could find it, and Kasturba, not trusting her memory, could not tell them where to look. The day was saved by Manu Gandhi, Ba's young grandniece, who recalled from her own stay at Sevagram exactly where the sari was kept. She wrote out instructions, sent them to the ashram, and the sari arrived, much to Ba's satisfaction, in time for her to wear it at Bapu's birthday party.

That celebration marked one of Kasturba's last carefree moments. Shortly afterwards, she suffered her first serious heart attack. And this time, she was slow to rally. My uncles Devadas and Ramdas had warned my parents, even before the arrival of a letter from Kasturba herself confirmed their diagnosis, that not only was Ba's heart failing, but also her resilient, self-sustaining optimism.

To Manilal and Sushila, this letter (the last my grandmother would ever send to them) seemed subtly different from earlier ones. The mood was sombre, and the usual words of comfort were few and far between.

In January of 1944, Kasturba suffered two more heart attacks. She was now confined to her bed much of the time. Even there, she found no respite from pain. Spells of breathlessness interfered with her sleep at night. Yearning for familiar ministrations, Ba asked to see an Ayurvedic doctor. After several delays (which Bapu felt were unconscionable), the government allowed a specialist in traditional Indian medicine to examine her and prescribe treatments. At first, she responded — recovering enough by the second week in February to sit on the verandah in a wheel chair for short periods, and chat with the gardeners who brought her freshly cut flowers. She predicted she would soon be enjoying walks with Mohandas again. Then came a relapse. The doctor said Ayurvedic medicine could do no more for her.

Bapu now began to spend many hours sitting beside her. She would doze off, her hand in his, her head resting on his chest; waking to find him still there, motionless, she would fondly chide him: "What are you doing here? Go away and take a walk."

One day Ba posed a question to Bapu that had nagged at her for some time. "Why do you demand that the British quit India?" she asked him. "Our country is vast, we can all live here. So let them stay if they like, but let them stay as brothers."

"I only want the British to quit as rulers," Bapu replied gently. "Once they cease to be our rulers, we have no quarrel with them."

Kasturba nodded, comforted to know that she and Mohandas were still in accord — as ever they should be. But Bapu was unable to answer Ba's next query. Though she had not spoken of it before, she now confessed that, above all else, she longed to embrace her firstborn son again before she died. Her question: where was Harilal?

At Mohandas' request, the police launched a search for Harilal, and eventually traced him to Poona. He had made his way there after hearing of his mother's illness, but had showed up at the gates of the Aga Khan Palace so drunk he was turned away. On the morning of February 17, Harilal came to the palace again, looking very thin and pale, but still slightly intoxicated. He was already showing signs of the tuberculosis, which would cause him to die a derelict in a Bombay hospital a few years later. This time, he was admitted.

The reunion was tender. But it was over almost before it began. Next day, on learning that Harilal had been given permission for only the one visit, she grew distraught.

She urged Mohandas to write to Colonel Bhandari and insist that Harilal, like Ramdas and Devadas, be allowed to come whenever he wished.

Bapu wrote, the permission was granted, but by then Harilal was nowhere to be found. He had disappeared once more, presumably on another drunken binge. Kasturba tried to put this devastating disappointment out of her mind.

To those who tried to bolster her sagging morale saying "You will get better soon," Ba would respond, "No, my time is up."

Bapu was sending that same message to South Africa, in reply to a cable that had arrived on February 20, from the son of the wealthy Parsi family who, long ago, had been among his earliest benefactors. Jalbhai Rustomji had just learned of the seriousness of Ba's illness, and wanted to arrange passage to India for Manilal and Sushila so they could be with her. Mohandas' cabled response was terse: "Thanks. Ba slowly going. Manilal and Sushila should continue their work. Love, Bapu."

On Monday afternoon, February 21, police again located Harilal.

They rushed him to the Aga Khan Palace just as he was — dirty, dishevelled, reeking of alcohol, and scarcely able to stand upright. Officials knew the urgency, they knew his mother was literally on her deathbed. Still, in retrospect, it seems they could have waited a few hours until he sobered up and cleaned up, and spared Ba a final agony.

When Harilal lurched into his mother's room, he was incapable of any emotion beyond anger at having been so rudely snatched from his dissolute rounds. But Kasturba, never having seen her oldest (some say dearest) son in this drunken condition, was overcome with despair. Moaning piteously, she beat her forehead with her hands. Harilal was hustled out of the room, out of the palace, out of her life.

Tuesday, February 22, 1944 dawned clear and bright. In the painstakingly manicured gardens of Aga Khan Palace, the daffodils, cannas and marigolds were in full bloom, radiant in the morning sunlight. One of the gardeners was squatting at the far edge of the verandah, head bowed, cheeks tear-streaked. His grief was the nation's grief. A government communiqué issued late Monday evening had stated that Mrs. Gandhi's condition, after deteriorating for many days, "is now very grave". Overnight, crowds had gathered outside the palace to keep watch; hundreds more would arrive during the day.

At last, the gardener saw Mohandas emerge from Kasturba's room. Palms joined in respectful greeting, he scrambled to his feet. "Tell me," he said, "how is my mother Ba?"

Bapu placed a comforting hand on the man's shoulders. "There is no change," he said, "and no hope." He asked the gardener to convey that news to the crowd waiting patiently outside the palace gates.

Kasturba had spent a fitful night, unable to sleep, and refusing all sustenance, even water. After conferring with the others at Aga Khan Palace earlier that morning, Bapu had made a wrenching decision: "I think all medicines should be stopped. We should leave everything in the hands of God." The doctors had agreed.

By this time, Ba was drifting in and out of consciousness. Once, when someone gently touched her brow she seemed startled. "Who is it?" she asked, raising her hand. She seemed greatly comforted to find it was Bapu.

Around 3.00pm, she became aware that Devadas, prepared to observe a sacred Hindu custom, had brought a container of holy water from the Ganges to her bedside. Ba opened her mouth gratefully to accept a drop. Afterwards, she seemed at peace, smiling weakly at Bapu and others assembled in her room. "There must be no weeping and mourning," Ba told them. "My death should be an occasion for rejoicing." Then, closing her eyes, she murmured a quiet prayer. "God, my refuge, Thy mercy I crave."

Yet even after this tranquil benediction, Kasturba continued to cling with remarkable tenacity to a slender thread of life — which inspired in Devadas one last desperate hope. Ever since reading a news report about a new wonder drug called penicillin, Devadas had been pestering the government to have a supply flown to Poona for his mother. Now, on this very day, the drug had arrived from Calcutta; it was waiting on the palace verandah, ready to be administered.

Shortly after seven that evening, Devadas took Mohandas and the doctors aside. In what he would later describe as "the sweetest of all wrangles I ever had with my father," he pleaded fiercely that Ba be given the life-saving medicine, even though the doctors told him her condition was beyond help. It was Mohandas, after learning that the penicillin had to be administered by injection every four to six hours, who finally persuaded his youngest son to give up the idea.

"Why do you want to prolong your mother's agonies after all the suffering she has been through?" Bapu asked. Then, with utmost compassion, he said, "You can't cure her now, no matter what miracle drug you may muster. But if you insist, I will not stand in your way."

Devadas bowed his head. He had no further pleadings to offer. The doctors looked relieved. And before anything more could be said, someone came running out of Kasturba's room, calling to Mohandas.

"Come quickly, Ba wants you. She seems to be in distress."

Indeed she was. Kasturba was sitting upright in bed, gasping for breath. Mohandas sat beside her and put his arms around her. "What is it? What is the matter?" he asked, speaking softly, as if to a frightened child.

"I do not know," she whispered.

She leaned her head on his shoulder. Almost at once, she seemed more comfortable. He tenderly stroked her hair. She smiled.

Moments later, at 7.35pm, Kasturba Gandhi stopped breathing. The sound of muffled sobs rose from the small circle of Ba's loved ones gathered round her bed. But soon, as if to give solace to each other, they began chanting one of her favourite prayers. Bapu, forcing back tears, joined in. Then he moved to a corner of the room where he sat, praying and keeping vigil all through the night.

In spite of the British Government's desire to control and censor news, people heard of Ba's failing health and hundreds assembled outside the tall prison gates to stand vigil for the woman they loved so dearly. People prayed, cried, stood silently, defied the heat of the day, hunger and thirst.

When a sombre prison guard walked up to the gate and whispered, "Ba is no more," an anguished and poignant wail rent the air. Even prison guards and officials could not hold back their tears.

Telegraphed news accounts of Kasturba's death were speeding around the world, even as preparations for cremation began. While Devadas, Pyarelal, and the younger mourners — Manu, Kanu, Rami — cleaned Kasturba's room and cleared it of all furniture, Sushila Nayyar and Mirabehn carefully bathed her body, washed and combed her hair, and dressed her in the red-bordered sari spun and woven for her by Mohandas. Sushila anointed her brow with the red kumkum mark. Mirabehn made a colourful garland of flowers from palace bouquets, and placed it around Ba's neck. She also tied smaller garlands around her wrists, entwining them with the five glass bangles symbolising love and devotion, that Kasturba had worn for most of her life — ever since they were placed on her arms on her wedding day. The body, peaceful in repose, was placed on a bier in the centre of the room. Then they all went out to the gardens and gathered more flowers, all they could find at that late hour, to be arranged like a fragrant blanket over Ba's recumbent form. Finally, an oil lamp was lighted and placed near her head. All was in readiness for the morrow.

The government, wary of public reaction to news that the beloved wife of Mahatma Gandhi had died in prison, sent an urgent emissary to the Aga Khan Palace late that Tuesday night to find out what funeral arrangements Mohandas wanted to make. Should Ba be cremated outside the prison so that the whole nation could participate, or should she be cremated within the prison courtyard where only the prisoners could pay their last homage? There was yet another dilemma. Traditional Hindu custom requires that a son — preferably the eldest — perform the last rites. In Ba's case it would mean that at least one, if not all of her four sons, be permitted to enter the prison for the funeral.

Indeed, the prison gates were open to the entire family during Ba's illness. Members of the family and close associates of the family were permitted to stay or visit. However, Ba's death changed the circumstances.

"Either the whole nation be allowed to participate in the funeral or no one." Bapu's injunction put the British in a bind. Should they release all the political prisoners and face the possibility of reinvigorating the non-violent freedom struggle, or suffer the ignominy of conducting the funeral of the "Mother of the Nation" in prison? The British chose the latter.

The eldest son, Harilal, had abandoned the family, and the second, Manilal, my father, was in South Africa and unable to travel to India in time for the funeral. Bapu told his two other grief-stricken sons, Ramdas and Devadas: "If the people of India are not allowed to pay their respects to Ba, you must suffer the same anguish. I cannot permit you to enjoy special privileges."

Word had come, meanwhile, that one of Gandhi's wealthy followers in Bombay wanted to buy sandalwood for the cremation. Mohandas said the offer was generous, but the luxury of a sandalwood cremation was not for the wife of a poor man like himself. A prison super-intendent, overhearing the conversation, interrupted. "Bapu, I have some sandalwood which can be used."

"Where did this come from?" Bapu asked.

The superintendent realised he must tell the truth. "The wood was bought for your funeral at the time of your twenty-one-day fast. The government did not want to be caught napping."

It was a poignant moment, but Mohandas, seeing the man's embarrassment, smiled wanly and said, "In that case, it must be mine and I want it to be used for Kasturba."

By ten o'clock on Wednesday morning, more than a hundred people, including several dignitaries from nearby Bombay, and a number of mourners from Sevagram ashram, were standing quietly on the palace grounds, waiting for Ba's funeral to begin. A great many more faithful souls, equally silent and sorrowful, had joined the crowds gathered outside the gates. Most of them had first learned of Kasturba's death by reading the editorial tributes in morning newspapers, such as that printed on page one of *The Times of India*:

Mrs. Gandhi ranks among the great women of India. The keynote of her life was a high steadfast devotion to her husband ... Unassuming, gentle, shy of public speaking, the role of a leader hardly suited her. But it was Kasturba's destiny that she should marry one who was to become the most prominent man in Indian public life. For 60 years she was his constant companion, following him through all the vicissitudes of a Mahatma's wife, courting imprisonment with him in the role of political agitator, picketer, and Satyagrahi ... Seldom have the wives of great men earned so much gratitude. She won for herself, perhaps without realising it, a unique place in the memory of the Indian people. A brave woman with a large and kind heart, she was known to India's worshipping millions simply as "Ba" — mother.

As Kasturba's flower-bedecked bier was carried along the path to the secluded site already hallowed by the cremation of Mahadev Desai, the assembled mourners followed with measured step — a kind of impromptu guard of honour.

Kasturba's body was lifted from the bier and placed on the waiting funeral pyre. For a moment — but only for a moment — her husband's composure seemed shaken. He quickly wiped away the tears with a corner of his shawl, and led the mourners in a brief memorial service, simple and all embracing. Passages from the *Bhagavad Gita*, the *Qur'an*, and the New Testament were read by Mohandas himself; Mirabehn read a Psalm from the Old Testament, Dr. Gilder recited sacred Zoroastrian scriptures, and a chorus of ashram singers chanted Hindu bhajans. Then, as Mohandas stood, staff in hand, the sandalwood was piled on the body, ghee was poured, and Devadas stepped forward with a burning torch to light the funeral pyre.

On this cool February morning Bapu stood near the burning pyre — praying and reflecting — as his companion of almost 65 years was consumed by fire. "The best half of me is dead," he said in a voice full of pathos. "What am I going to do now?"

It took a very long time for Kasturba's small body to be reduced to ashes. For a while, Mohandas stood beside Pyarelal and watched the burning pyre, shielded from the noonday sun under an umbrella held by Mirabehn. Later, after bidding farewell to friends who had come to share his grief, Bapu moved to a chair placed in the shade of a nearby tamarind tree, and continued watching, rejecting all pleas from his worried companions that he return to the palace and rest. As sunset approached, a few flames were still flickering and the embers still glowed. Bapu still refused to end his vigil.

"How can I leave her during her last moments on earth," he demanded. Then, striving for a lighter note, he said, "She would never forgive me if I did."

Darkness was descending when Bapu and his friends at last began their sad trek back to the palace. A photo someone took of that moment shows the little group moving slowly through the deepening twilight, silhouettes etched black against a cloud-filled sky above.

Devadas and Ramdas had been granted permission to stay with their father at the Aga Khan Palace until Friday, when they were to gather

Ba's ashes in a traditional Hindu Sinchana ceremony, as she would have wished, and carry them, as Mohandas wished, to Allahabad to be immersed in the sacred waters at the confluence of the Ganges and Jamna rivers. Surrounded by relatives and friends during those two days of waiting, Mohandas struggled to assess his loss.

"I cannot even imagine life without Ba," he said, at one point."She was an indivisible part of me, and her going has left a void which will never be filled." In his response to a letter of sympathy from Lord Wavell, the latest new Viceroy of India, he sounded the same theme: "I feel the loss more than I had thought I should ... Without my wishing it, she chose to lose herself in me, and the result was that she became truly my better half."

Meanwhile, all India was in mourning. The homage paid to Kasturba Gandhi at the time of her death may, in retrospect, seem like no more than a pale foreshadowing of the paroxysms of grief that would convulse independent India four years later, when Mahatma Gandhi, apostle of peace and religious harmony, was felled by a bullet fired by a vengeful Brahmin Hindu assassin, and himself became a victim of the very kind of factional fanaticism from which he had struggled to free his country and the world. But in February of 1944, the spontaneous outpourings of sorrow and love prompted by news of Ba's death were unparalleled. Condolence resolutions were passed by councils of state in the Punjab, Bengal, Orissa, and the Frontier Provinces. At Sevagram, a private memorial service was held in Ba's hut. In Rajkot, as in a number of other cities, hartals were observed. And in New Delhi, plans got underway to establish the Kasturba Gandhi National Memorial Fund, with proceeds to be spent for the welfare and education of women in India.

But for those who were with Bapu at the Aga Khan Palace in the days following Ba's death, no memorial to her, no tribute to her virtues, spoke more eloquently than a startling discovery made on Friday, February 25, 1944. On that day, Kasturba's sons went with earthen pots to the site of her cremation, to collect, with due ritual, the remains from the funeral pyre.

Lying there in the cold ashes, among what my uncle Devadas later described as "a literal handful of tiny motherly bones", they found five gleaming glass bangles. That these delicate symbols of Ba's fulfillment of her dharma, her devotion to her life's duty and destiny, had so miraculously survived the raging fires of the funeral pyre intact and unbroken, was recognised by all who had known her as a sign of eternal salvation — an intimation that Kastur Kapadia Gandhi had achieved a blissful reunion with the infinite.

It was another year before Bapu and other political leaders were let out of prison. Life was no longer the same. After Ba's death the zeal and vigour seemed to have gone out of Grandfather's life. The last years seem, in retrospect, to be anti-climatic. Grandfather was tormented by the thoughtless act of denying Ba the notebook. He knew this caused her mental anguish during the last weeks of her life. In that moment of thoughtless indiscretion Bapu had smashed Ba's dream. Now she was gone forever and the memory of the hurt look on Ba's face would haunt Bapu the remaining years of his life.

The years between February 1944, when Ba died, to January 1948, when Grandfather was assassinated, were tumultuous for Bapu. On the one hand he witnessed the victory of his philosophy of nonviolence while on the other he saw the shattering of his dream of a united country. He was betrayed by the leaders of the Congress Party, his erstwhile colleagues, who evidently used him to gain power. When freedom was inevitable the Congress decided they no longer needed Gandhi's leadership.

If Indian independence meant the dismantling of the British Empire, Sir Winston Churchill declared in the British Parliament, then we will ensure that India too is dismembered. The Conservatives in Britain were determined to exact a heavy price for India's freedom and the Hindu and Muslim leaders made it easy for them. If the only way the politicians could get power was by dividing the country into India for Hindus and Pakistan for Muslims, so be it. The consequences to the common man of this political decision did not matter. Partition eventually led an estimated 15 million to be uprooted from places they had considered their own for generations. The anger and frustration generated unimaginable violence that consumed the lives of an estimated one million people and left India and Pakistan in a never-ending spiral of violence.

Those who were close to Grandfather could see and sense his anguish and despondency. He no longer exuded the zest for life that he did not so long ago. In the interest of political unity, Grandfather maintained a cheerful façade and gave no indication to anyone of the pain and turmoil he felt.

I was with Grandfather during this tumultuous period. I was 13 then and was amazed at his capacity to be loving and grandfatherly one moment and a serious politician the next. He spent an hour with me every day and he told me stories and examined my lessons. Often while talking we would spin cotton on a little hand machine that he invented.

It required a good measure of patience and skill. Bapu was, of course, very good at it. In my youthful zeal I sometimes challenged grandfather to a competition to see who could spin the fastest and the thinnest yarn. I learned much later that he had written to my parents acknowledging my ability to spin a little better than him.

The horrifying violence between Hindus and Muslims that followed the partition of India once again catapulted Grandfather to the political centre stage. He felt compelled to go to Bengal where some of the worst massacres were occurring, to bring to the people some sanity and peace. With a handful of colleagues, both men and women, Grandfather walked from village to village pleading for peace and harmony. In a few weeks he was able to stop the people from fighting and killing.

On August 15, 1947, the day power was transferred to the Indian people, the Congress leadership invited Grandfather to New Delhi to participate in the joy of independence.

"What is there to rejoice," Bapu asked, "when thousands of my countrymen are slaughtering each other?"

While the rest of India rejoiced Grandfather continued to walk the backwoods of what is now Bangladesh.

Early in January 1948 Grandfather came to New Delhi only to find the government of free India pandering to populist demands that Pakistan be denied the cash assets due to them. The Hindu fundamentalists wanted these funds to be used to compensate Hindus who lost their lives and property in Pakistan. Grandfather considered this immoral. The violence was a direct consequence of partition. When politicians accepted the division they should have expected the violence. He reminded the people that Muslims too had suffered the loss of lives and property. If India was going to begin its independent life on immoral and unethical decisions grandfather wanted no part of it. He went on a fast unto death.

The government relented and paid Pakistan its dues. This generated a new crisis. Hindu fundamentalists saw this as pandering to Muslim demands. Both actions (fundamentalists and the Congress Party administration) realised they had one thing in common: the belief that a martyred Gandhi was better (for them) than a living Gandhi. They were convinced that he had to be assassinated. The fundamentalists engineered the assassination plot while the administration looked the other way.

Had Grandfather lived he would have demanded radical changes in politics and in the lifestyle of politicians and bureaucracy. The Brahmins and Kshatriyas, the two top castes, who dominated Indian administration and politics at the time of independence, wanted no part of this revolution. They coveted the pomp and pageantry of the British. They were determined to slip quietly into the oppressive Imperialist structure built by the British to dominate over the Indians. In other words a brown oppressor replaced the white oppressor.

When it was certain his life was in danger Grandfather refused to accept any kind of security. This suited the government's nefarious plans. He was tired; he felt he had done the best he could; he realised that others must carry on the work along the path he had chartered and, he believed in the protection of God more than the love and protection of mere mortals.

"If I am destined to live I will be protected by God," he said. "However, if God does not wish me to live no human can protect me."

He was martyred at 5.16pm on January 30, 1948. The assassin, Nathuram Vinayak Godse, a rabid Hindu fundamentalist, shot Grandfather three times at point-blank range. As Grandfather fell to the ground, his life ebbing out of the three gunshot wounds, he held his palms together in prayer and uttered the name of the Hindu Lord: "Ram, Ram," while his eyes, fixed on those of the assassin, appeared to say: "God bless you, my son."

# Index